Class, Politics, and Popular Religion in Mexico and Central America

Library of Congress Cataloging-in-Publication Data
Class, politics, and popular religion in Mexico and Central America /
   Lynn Stephen and James W. Dow, editors.
         p.   cm. — (SLAA publication series)
   Includes bibliographical references.
   ISBN 0-913167-40-1
   1. Mexico—Religious life and customs. 2. Central America—Reli-
gious life and customs. 3. Religion and sociology—Mexico. 4. Religion
and sociology—Central America. I. Stephen, Lynn. II. Dow, James.
III. Series.
BL2530.M4C42   1990
306.6'0972—dc20   90-41631
                                                                   CIP

Copies may be ordered from:

American Anthropological Association
1703 New Hampshire Avenue, N.W.
Washington, D.C. 20009

Class, Politics, and Popular Religion in Mexico and Central America

Edited by Lynn Stephen and James Dow

Contributors

> Leigh Binford
> Frank Cancian
> John K. Chance
> James Dow
> Duncan M. Earle
> James B. Greenberg
> Michael James Higgins
> James Howe
> Stephanie Kane
> Lynn Stephen

Foreword by Jeffrey David Ehrenreich

Volume 10
Society for Latin American Anthropology Publication Series
Jeffrey David Ehrenreich, General Editor

A publication of
The Society for Latin American Anthropology
and The American Anthropological Association

1990

CONTENTS

Foreword   vii
Jeffrey David Ehrenreich

Preface   ix
Lynn Stephen

1   Introduction: Popular Religion in Mexico
and Central America   1
Lynn Stephen & James Dow

Part I.   The Impact of State Politics and Economic Development on Religious Hierarchies

2   Changes in Twentieth-Century Mesoamerican *Cargo* Systems   27
John K. Chance

3   The Politics of Ritual: The Mexican State and
Zapotec Autonomy, 1926 to 1989   43
Lynn Stephen

Part II.   Peasant Economic Relations and Changes in Local Religious Systems

4   The Zinacantan *Cargo* Waiting Lists as a Reflection of Social, Political, and Economic
Changes, 1952 to 1987   63
Frank Cancian

5   The Political Economy of the *Velas* in the   77
Isthmus of Tehuantepec
Leigh Binford

Part III.   Political Conflict and Local Religion

6   Sanctity and Resistance in Closed Corporate
Indigenous Communities: Coffee Money,
Violence, and Ritual Organization in Chatino Communities in Oaxaca   95
James B. Greenberg

7   Appropriating the Enemy: Highland Maya
Religious Organization and Community
Survival   115
Duncan M. Earle

Part IV. Missionaries, Institutionalized Churches, and Popular Religion

8   Mission Rivalry and Conflict in San Blas, Panama   143
James Howe

9   Shamans Reconsidered: The Emberá (Chocó) in Darién, Panama   167
Stephanie Kane

10   Martyrs and Virgins: Popular Religion in Mexico and Nicaragua   187
Michael James Higgins

Part V. Conclusions

11   The Dynamics of Religion in Middle American Communities   207
James Dow & Lynn Stephen

Notes on Contributors   215

Cover Photo: Lynn Stephen
Cover Design: Ellen Herman

FOREWORD

It is a pleasure to present this volume to the members of the Society for Latin American Anthropology and other readers interested in the ethnology of Latin America. Its publication marks a significant step forward in the activities of the Society for Latin American Anthropology and for the *SLAA Publication Series,* which first began to publish edited volumes in 1976 under the auspices of the Latin American Anthropology Group (LAAG, SLAA's precursor group). A few years ago, as a result of the reorganization process through which a number of previously independent academic associations became official units or divisions of the American Anthropological Association, the Society for Latin American Anthropology became committed to producing its publications through the AAA's facilities in Washington, DC. This volume, *Class, Politics, and Popular Religion in Mexico and Central America,* edited by Lynn Stephen and James Dow, is the first book to be produced, from original inception to final product, through the newly established process.

The history of this volume began when Lynn Stephen and Duncan Earle organized a session for the 86th meeting of the American Anthropological Association in Chicago, 1987. The title of the symposium was "The Political Economy of Religion in Mexico and Central America," and it was sponsored by the Society for Latin American Anthropology. The book was later submitted to the Society for Latin American Anthropology to appear in its publication series. The distribution of this edited volume through the American Anthropological Association marks the completion of a cycle carried out in the manner that the reorganization plan had in fact ideally conceived–timely research presented in the scholarly program at the annual meetings of the AAA sponsored by and later made available through the publication programs of the unit groups. The SLAA aspires to produce future edited volumes in similar fashion.

And what of the book itself? The essays in this volume represent a broad spectrum of state-of-the-art ethnographic research conducted in peasant and indigenous communities of Mexico and Central America. The authors are among the most actively engaged scholars working in this region. Employing a variety of ethnographic research methodologies and styles, these case studies individually shed light on structures and processes of "popular" religious institutions, which, to some degree fall outside the realm of establishment religion. The role of popular religion is explored against the backdrop of politics and economics at the community and national level. Religious ideology is explored as it affects, and is affected by, political, social and

economic processes.   Through the skillful organization and commentaries of
the editors, the essays taken collectively emerge as a coherent and insightful
analysis of the broader implications of class, politics, and religion in Mexico
and Central America.   The result is that the whole of this book is truly larger
than the sum of its parts.   Students of Mexico and Central America, along
with scholars interested in the ethnology of Latin America will find the
descriptions and analyses in this book essential for a current understanding of
the religious and political processes that shape life in Latin American
communities.

Jeffrey David Ehrenreich
Mount Vernon, Iowa, September 1990

PREFACE

This book grew out of a panel which I organized with Duncan Earle, sponsored by the Society for Latin American Anthropology at the 1987 American Anthropological Association meeting held in Chicago, Illinois. Titled "The Political Economy of Religion in Mexico and Central America," the panel attempted to bring together scholars of Middle America who have done work in the 1980s in the area of religion. The panel sought to build on an earlier generation of scholarship which focused primarily on changes in civil-religious cargo systems in Mesoamerica, and to compare cargo systems scholarship with other work being done on missionization and liberation theology in Central America. The panel included both current and historical perspectives. The insightful concluding and comparative comments of James Dow and Stephen Gudeman suggested some general conclusions that could be worked into a comparative perspective on religion in contemporary Middle America.

All the panel members enthusiastically supported the idea of a publication and they worked with James Dow and myself to rework their papers into a dialogue that addressed the issues of (1) the relationship between popular religious forms, capitalist development, and class formation; (2) the role of the state in determining popular religious forms; and (3) the ways in which popular religious activities can serve as a basis for social movements and grassroots political participation. Critical to this effort has been an openness on the part of each author to take on the complexity of popular religion in contemporary Mexico and Central America. This task has involved examining the political economy of religion as well as the ways in which religious ideology is shaped by and reshapes community politics and economics.

A common thread to all of the pieces is an emphasis on human agency in the creation of the complex social reality of Mexico and Central America which links together religion and politics. We have chosen the term "popular religion" to emphasize those religious activities that occur outside of institutionalized religion or those that, if carried on within the framework of institutionalized religion, offer a critique of that framework and of large political and economic inequalities. We believe that the arena of popular religion is dynamic and an integral part of the grassroots political process.

The original contributors were joined by Leigh Binford and James Greenberg, expert Mesoamericanists whose contributions we were fortunate to receive. Frank Cancian updated material for another chapter whose only previous presentation was in Spanish. Through a process of writing, talking with the authors, and communicating through electronic mail, James Dow and I edited the collection into a cohesive whole.

Jeffrey Ehrenreich, the Editor of the Society for Latin American Anthropology and General Editor of the SLAA Publication Series of which this volume is a part, has been extremely important in supporting this project since its inception. He not only provided intellectual feedback and suggestions, but took on the ambitious task of producing camera-ready copy. We cannot thank him enough for his efforts. We are indebted to the Society for Latin American Anthropology for their original support of the panel and for their continuing support of this publication. In addition we would like to acknowledge the important contribution of Deborah Szobel, Editorial Associate of the College of Arts and Sciences at Oakland University, whose crafted pen is responsible for smoothing out the rough edges that appear in a collective work. We also would like to thank Duncan Earle for his valuable contribution in co-organizing the panel from which this book emerged.

The introduction and conclusions of this book have benefitted greatly from Jim Howe's editorial suggestions and insightful regional and historical perspective. My ongoing conversations with Neil Harvey, Enrique Semo, and Maria Teresa Korack, fellow colleagues during my stay at the Center for U.S.-Mexican Studies, were extremely helpful to my writing. My participation in this project would not have been possible without the post-doctoral fellowship I received in 1989 from the Center for U.S.-Mexican Studies. James Dow also gratefully acknowledges the support of his department at Oakland University.

Finally, we would like to thank all of the authors for their willingness to rewrite their papers incorporating content, editorial, and copy editing suggestions.

Lynn Stephen
Boston, July 1990

CHAPTER ONE

Introduction: Popular Religion in Mexico and Central America

Lynn Stephen
Northeastern University

&

James Dow
Oakland University

INTRODUCTION

Local religious institutions in Mexico and Central America both respond to and influence larger political and economic forces. During previous periods of colonial and neocolonial domination, Middle American peasants established local religio-political systems in reaction to the lack of opportunities for direct participation in national political and economic systems. These local systems were continually influenced by the changing political and economic mandates of the Spanish and later independent states. Nevertheless, indigenous peoples, peasants, urban workers, and other marginalized sectors of Middle American societies continue to use religious forms and institutions to organize on a local level in response to the political and economic forces which influence their communities.

Acknowledging that secular proletarianization and modern party politics play a central role in the political lives of Mexicans and Central Americans today, the cases discussed here clarify the continuing place of religion in

1

shaping local and regional politics and economics, emphasizing the active role of community members in this process. They also focus on the role of class differentiation in shaping local religious participation and on the ways in which popular religious activities can bring together varied sectors of a population for political action or break them apart along class lines. While formal community political systems have been heavily influenced by the state in many parts of Middle America, local religious forms often operate semi-independently from the state and reflect political, economic, and ethnic conflict more openly than formal political systems.

Religion remains an active force in Middle America. The information presented in this volume does not support the idea that contemporary Middle American societies are becoming secularized. Rather, popular religion remains a vital mechanism in shaping social and political organization. We found that in order to understand how popular religion operates in Middle America it must be analyzed in relation to capitalist development and class relations, state intervention in local political systems, and struggles for local political and economic autonomy. Where capitalist development has stimulated class differentiation, popular religious forms may be transformed, but do not seem to disappear. For example, where wealth differences result in a status hierarchy outside of religious *cargo* sponsorship, rural communities may leave behind religious sponsorship, but religion still plays an important part in the political system. In addition, ritual consumption and prestige-producing ritual can take on other forms that are not directly related to religious *cargo* systems or *mayordomía* sponsorship.

While earlier anthropological analysis examined popular or "folk" religion in terms of its defensive functions, we found a more active process in which urban popular classes, indigenous peoples, and peasants can use religion under certain circumstances to try and realize their own agendas. This does not necessarily mean continued isolation from the centers of economic and political power, but a conscious attempt to influence the larger political and economic structures by which they have been historically dominated. In some cases, there may be a return to traditional forms of *cargo* sponsorship as communities lose control of resources to colonizing outsiders. Popular religious forms may also reinforce the ethnic solidarity of a village or region and serve as a basis for grassroots opposition. In other cases, religious forms will be used by local *caciques* or class fractions to defend their interests and highlight both economically class-based and ethnically class-based antagonisms.

When missionaries side with the politically and economically marginalized, they can organize opposition to state control, as in the case of Nicaragua under Somoza. Or missionaries may have little impact on indigenous populations who categorize them as outsiders. At other times, as in Guatemala under Ríos Montt, new religious forms can be aligned with government policies aimed at severely restricting the autonomy of indigenous and peasant populations. The final acceptance or rejection of missionaries by local populations depends largely on the political consequences of the new religion.

Thus, we conclude that Middle America is not being secularized, but that there is an ongoing, dynamic relationship between religion and politics. While significant economic, cultural, and political differences exist in the areas discussed here, we believe that it is important to look at the issue of popular religion in the region of Middle America because religion is a primary vehicle for political action. The cases examined here provide not only important ethnographic and historical detail about the role of popular religion in particular societies, but, taken as a whole, they can help us understand the regional importance of religion in shaping Mexican and Central American politics today, both locally and nationally.

DEFINITIONS

In order to situate our discussion, we need to clarify some concepts used in this introduction and in the chapters that follow. These include (1) Middle America; (2) peasants; (3) Indian versus indigenous; (4) popular classes and popular culture; and (5) religious syncretism.

1. Middle America: The case studies of popular religion included here are focused on the mainland region of Middle America, often referred to as Mexico and Central America. The area includes the countries of Mexico, Guatemala, Belize, El Salvador, Nicaragua, Costa Rica, Honduras, and Panama. The area of this region can be divided into three cultural sectors: (a) Mesoamerica, the areas of early civilization with large indigenous populations at the time of the Spanish conquest and with a marked influence of indigenous peoples on modern culture (Southeastern Mexico, Guatemala, Western Honduras, and El Salvador);[1] (b) Mestizo Middle America, the areas with less indigenous influence and a more Hispanicized modern culture (Nicaragua, Panama, Central Mexico, eastern El Salvador, and eastern Honduras); and (c) European Middle America, the areas settled primarily by people with a Spanish background who were influenced little by indigenous cultures (Costa Rica, Northern Mexico) (West and Augelli 1966:12-16).

It should also be noted that lower Central American societies shared historical experiences which differentiate them from the Mesoamerican heartland. Early contact with Spanish explorers, contact with pirates, interactions with the British and Germans, the settling of black slaves and freemen, and coastal land distinguish the area (Loveland 1982: xii). Religion therefore differs in its forms and its relation to politics in these cultural sectors due to historical differences in cultural, political, and economic relations before and during the colonial period. In particular, the colonial economic system in lower Central America did not depend to nearly the same extent on stable, accessible indigenous communities as a reliable and largely self-feeding labor pool such as that available in Mesoamerica.

The lands occupied by the people of mainland Middle America vary from desert rangeland in the north of Mexico to tropical coastal plains in the state of Veracruz and along the coasts of the Central American republics. Mountains are everywhere. The heartland of Mexico is a high plateau at about 7,000 feet above sea level where Mexico City is located. The Mexico City area is rapidly becoming the largest urban complex in the world, with ecological problems reaching dangerous proportions (Gold 1982:394; Pezzoli 1989).

MAP 1.1. MIDDLE AMERICA

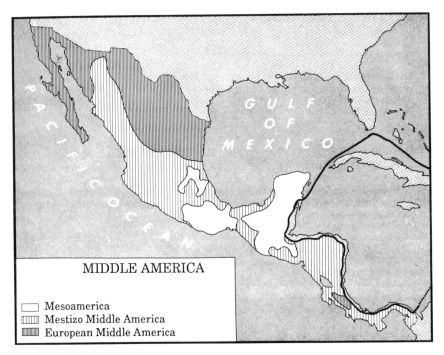

MIDDLE AMERICA

Mesoamerica
Mestizo Middle America
European Middle America

(Adapted from West and Augelli 1966:12)

To the south, the land lowers gradually. The state of Oaxaca is covered by the lower, hotter Sierra Madre and, in the narrowest part of Mexico, the Isthmus of Tehuantepec is a flat plain. Beyond Mexico, the mountains rise again in the Central American Highlands in Guatemala. In other parts of Central America, mountains crop up in the center of northern and southern coastal plains. The higher mountain ridges of Nicaragua reach 3,000 to 6,500 feet. All the way in the southeast end of Central America is Panama. Part of Columbia until 1903, some scholars still prefer to regard it as part of South America.

2. Peasants: Who are they? The colonial experience in Middle America has resulted in regional differences in political and economic formations which make it difficult to generalize about the nature of community social organization and economic relations. Many of the case studies included here focus on peasant communities. In discussing the use of the term peasant, two primary questions are important to the wide range of populations discussed here. First, to what degree is class differentiation and/or ethnic identity critical in framing the political potential of religious activities and institutions? Second, what is the historical and current relationship of the communities examined here to the larger political economy of nation states?

Positions vary on these two questions as reflected by the contributing authors. In general, we maintain that class is a critical variable in understanding the social and political dynamics of religion in peasant communities. While there may be varying degrees of class differentiation found among the cases explored here, the relations of production (particularly the categories of laborer and employer) as well as ownership of land and other productive means are keys to local power relations. In some communities described here, class relations closely follow ethnic lines with indigenous community members being relegated to a lower class by a *mestizo* minority with a monopoly on economic resources and political power. In other cases indigenous communities are characterized by internal stratification stemming from capital accumulation in association with commercial production of crops and/or artisanry.

In many cases here, the primary reason for use of the term "peasant" comes from the fact that these agrarian communities all share a marginalized status vis-à-vis larger society. Despite the fact of internal stratification in many communities, as a whole they have been placed in a subordinate status, both currently and historically, in larger political and economic relations. This framework of historical subordination is the focal point for this book and for a working definition of peasants. Here a peasant loosely refers to an agrarian-based individual who, while unavoidably participating in wider social, economic, and political relationships, is simultaneously active in local political, economic, and religious institutions. These institutions maintain an internal dynamic that is responsive to, yet not solely determined by, the state, national, and international economies.

Economically we cannot define a peasant as an individual who participates solely in agriculture, either for subsistence or commercial purposes. In reality, most peasant individuals and households engage in multi-stranded strategies of employment, mixing wage labor, subsistence agriculture, craft production, migration, and other work forms in order to make a living.

Rather than see the peasant as a subsistence farmer on his or her way to becoming a full-time landless wage laborer or petty capitalist (DeJanvry 1981; Lenin 1962), or as simply preoccupied with producing a surplus only large enough to satisfy family consumption needs (Chayanov 1966), we view peasants as manipulating labor and resources for the purposes of economic and social mobility in both class and non-class relations (Bennet and Kannel 1983; Deere 1986). Here we focus on those relations in extra-household religious and ritual institutions which are focal points for community autonomy.

3. Indian versus indigenous: The embeddedness of the multiple economic and non-economic processes in which the peasantry participates requires that our discussion of popular religion include not only economic class relations, but those of ethnicity as well, specifically indigenous ethnic identities. The historical position of subordination shared by peasant communities is also relevant in distinguishing between the terms "Indian" and "indigenous." The basic distinction between a self-chosen ethnic identity of particular "indigenous" groups and that of an imposed "Indian" identity is discussed by Smith in his analysis of ethnic federations, peasant unions, and Indianist movements in the Andean republics. He characterizes Indian identity as a "political and racial label imposed on the indigenous population irrespective of tribal identity marking a hierarchical relationship" (Smith 1985:9).

A self-chosen ethnic identity is usually based on (a) a claim to historical autonomy, and (b) perceived cultural, natural, or physical traits which are emphasized as a primary source of identity which is recognized internally as well as externally (Barth 1981; Stearns 1987; Stephen n.d.; Adams 1988). Adams states that the sociological salience of an ethnic group emerges most importantly "when it is both self-identified and externally identified, when its existence is significant both to members and outsiders" (1988:11). Adams maintains that such groups are, by definition, political beings (1988:11). Looking at the juncture of class and ethnicity in the Andes, Stearns describes presumed cultural and physical traits as drawing social boundaries which do not necessarily coincide with class boundaries and which may serve to link grievances of peasants and non-peasants (1988:15-16).

Noting that "Indian" is a colonial category for one who is dominated and that it is not usually a self-chosen label, we refer to particular peoples whose popular religious forms and institutions we are describing as "indigenous" people. Whenever possible we use the self-chosen ethnic identity of a particular people to refer to them. We have encouraged the other authors in this volume to do the same. The distinction between "Indian" and a self-chosen indigenous identity is important in keeping with the conceptual basis of "popular religion" defined below.

4. Popular classes and popular culture: While most of the chapters which follow focus on indigenous peasant communities, several include references to urban populations and one focuses on marginal urban populations in Oaxaca, Mexico and Managua, Nicaragua. The outlying *colonias* of Oaxaca city which originated with land invasions and the poor, urban neighborhoods of Managua share a common political and economic position with indigenous peasant communities—that of political and economic marginalization. As part of a broader political economy, these neighborhoods are referred to as *colonias*

populares (popular neighborhoods) and their members as part of the urban popular classes (Ramirez Saiz 1986:30).

In a description of the socioeconomic composition of people found in various *colonias populares* in Mexico, Ramirez Saiz estimates that about 50-60 percent are fully employed in small- and medium-sized industry or in the service sector, 30-40 percent are part-time or seasonal workers in the industrial reserve army, a small percentage (3-5) are part of an impoverished petty bourgeoisie (artisans, small merchants, self-employed workers), and 1-3 percent are part of the lumpenproletariat or informal sector–those with the least job security (1986:30-31). Ramirez Saiz uses these descriptions as a basis for explaining people's participation in popular urban movements. He maintains that although such movements include people from different classes and class fractions, they all share a common situation of economic exploitation and political domination which creates objective conditions for a shared class consciousness–the basis for their participation in an urban social movement.

Other authors have taken the idea of common marginalization and used it to link together a wider range of disenfranchised groups in the Mexican political and economic system, calling them popular classes (Garcia Canclini 1982; Higgins *intra*). These include indigenous populations, peasants, the urban poor, urban workers, and the marginally employed and unemployed. While the popular urban movement groups of Mexico such as La Coordinación del Movimiento Urbano Popular (CONAMUP) and the Sandinista Revolution in Managua were able to pull together a range of urban class sectors into social and revolutionary movements through the creation of a common popular culture and skilled political organizing, the popular classes elsewhere are not always so easily bound together. Popular culture and popular classes are examined here in terms of (a) how religious activities and symbols can serve as a way of linking together various class and ethnic sectors of the population, along with the extent to which such symbols and activities can be the basis for establishing political autonomy (Higgins, Earle, Kane, Stephen, Chance, Greenberg), and (b) how, on the other hand, common religious activities are used to reinforce socioeconomic differentiation and are used by particular individuals and class-based groups to augment their influence, power, and resources (Binford, Earle, Howe, Greenberg, Cancian).

5. Religious syncretism: When looking at religion in Middle America, we must realize that the present is not a pure expression of one historical unified belief system, but an amalgam of beliefs and rituals patched together from different historical sources and experiences. Middle America is a place where literate religions, including both Mayan and Aztec as well as Catholic and Protestant, have clashed and merged with local indigenous religions, including both shamanistic and magical traditions. This historical process began well before the colonial period. Thus, the religious forms we are examining have many and complex origins.

We should not be surprised to find that Catholic religious beliefs in Middle America are different from those in other parts of the world. Many Catholic saints have lost their saintly character (Madsen 1967: 381). They are human-like figures with powers and weaknesses that can be manipulated by people, perhaps seeming more like pre-Columbian gods than Catholic ones. However, most of the people are still devoted to the Catholic church and will show alarm at any suggestion that they are not firmly marching in the phalanxes of that faith, albeit it interpreted in an individualistic manner.

Studies of Catholic saints have centered primarily on *mayordomía* sponsorship in relation to civil-religious *cargo* systems in Mexico and Guatemala. Gudeman, however, also noted the importance of Saint's day celebrations or fiestas in *campesino* Panama (1976a:43-63, 1976b). He describes a yearly fiesta calendar which is not tied to formal sponsorship, but does share some common features with peasant and indigenous ritual calendars in Mexico and Guatemala. He emphasizes the fact that the saint's days are celebrated among the laity and are removed from the official sphere of the church, suggesting that such fiestas fall into the realm of popular religion as defined here (1976:726-727). His description of religion in *campesino* Panama differs from Emberá and Kuna religions which maintain many pre-Colombian elements.

Flexibility in the adoption of different ideas and beliefs is part of most religious systems. The most important aspect of religious syncretism in Middle America is that it creates a flexibility that allows religious rituals and beliefs to be molded around political processes in the past and present. We are not dealing with purists, but with people who know how to combine faith with practical thinking about political power.

THE CONCEPTUAL BASIS FOR THE STUDY OF MIDDLE AMERICAN POPULAR RELIGION

The cases presented here suggest that religion is a vital mode for articulating social ideas and political action in Middle America. Middle American religious systems are not religious throwbacks in the evolution of militaristic states from earlier theocratic ones, but are instead the result of modern political dynamics, specifically dynamics of class and ethnic conflict. In contemporary Mexico and Central America, as in the past, class conflict, capitalist development, political organization, and religion are inextricably linked.

Popular Religion

In a major critical essay on the anthropology of religion, Talal Assad proposes that we approach the study of religion by asking what historical conditions (movements, classes, institutions, ideologies) are necessary for the existence of particular religious practices and discourses (1983:252). How do particular social forces come together at particular historical moments to make particular religious discourses, practices, events, and spaces possible? These broad questions posed by Assad provide a general framework for the approach taken here for the study of popular religion. By popular religion, we mean religious or ritual activities consciously practiced outside of or in opposition to dominant institutionalized religion or those religious activities which, although carried on within the framework of institutionalized religion, offer a critique of that framework and of larger political and economic inequities (see Berryman 1984:380-381). Popular religious activities and practices are not necessarily the sole province of experts or specialists, but can be participated in by all people. In conjunction with the religious syncretism found in much of popular religion, we are concerned with the religions of the masses which appear in varied forms uniting indigenous elements with the literate traditions brought by missionaries.

While some formulations of the power politics of religion overemphasize the role of institutionalized religion as a means of instilling obedience in subordinate populations (Assad 1983), other examinations of local religious structures reiterate Ingham's comments on the construction of local religion in Mexico. He states that although folk Catholicism formulates and sanctifies positive sociality, it provides an idiom for critical commentary on negative social relations. He proposes that, ultimately, folk Catholicism in Mexico is as much a peasant construction as the product of elite clergy (1986:2).

This position portrays Middle American peasants as effective participants in the construction of religious institutions, events, and discourses. This participation is seen both in terms of peasant appropriation of local religious forms and institutions as a means of asserting local autonomy and by the use of institutional religious structures in political struggles to transform the socio-economic position of peasants in larger society. An example of the latter in Mexico is a troupe of 4,000 indigenous catechists who, in conjunction with Catholic Bishop Ruiz headquartered in San Cristobal de Las Casas, have formed Christian base communities, co-ops that market corn, women's groups, health brigades, and farmer's defense organizations throughout the 25,000-square-mile diocese (Latin America Press 1988:7).

In Guatemala, the 100,000-member Asociación Nacional Campesina Pro-Tierra (National Pro-land Peasant Association) under the leadership of the Catholic priest Andrés Jesús Girón de León, is one of the strongest agrarian movements in Guatemala which continues to occupy land and press for land redistribution in the face of continuing government oppression (Cambranes 1986:9-10). This movement, like that in Chiapas, is clearly related to the popular religious ideals projected in the Christian base communities of Nicaragua and El Salvador (see Berryman 1983:22-24; Pearce 1985). While most of the cases examined here do not focus on liberation theology, the self-determination and critique of dominant political and economic structures projected in indigenous peasant movements such as that of Padre Girón is also interwoven with the alternative authority structures of religious hierarchies (see Greenberg *intra;* Stephen *intra;* Earle *intra*), shamanism (Kane *intra*), and indigenous efforts at resisting and manipulating missionaries (Howe *intra*).

Anthropological Discussions of Religion in Mexico and Guatemala

Traditionally, anthropological discussions of religion in Mesoamerica have centered on debates concerning the nature of civil-religious *cargo* systems in Mexico and Guatemala (see Greenberg 1981 for a synopsis), and missionization and Protestant conversion, focusing on how religion affects community social organization. Later analyses of civil-religious hierarchies and Protestant missionization move beyond the scope of community and examine the role of economic change and national political policy in relation to changing local religious systems (Russ and Wasserstrom 1980; Greenberg 1981; Taussig 1987). The integration of national political and economic policy with community studies has also led anthropologists recently to begin to consider the role of liberation theology in local social interaction.

Religious Cargo Systems

Until recently, most anthropological discussion of religious institutions in Mesoamerica, particularly in Mexico and Guatemala, focused on the changing form, structure, and meaning of religious *cargo* systems. Following Chance (*intra*), we distinguish between (a) a *cargo* system as a hierarchy of ranked offices which individuals or male-female couples ascend and (b) a fiesta system in which prestige is attained through ceremonial sponsorship in the absence of any fixed hierarchy of positions. While earlier discussions focused on whether or not the function of civil-religious hierarchies was to level wealth differences (Tax 1937; Wolf 1955), reinforce and justify existing wealth differences (Cancian 1965), maintain a system of reciprocity and redistribution within communities (Dow 1977; Aguirre 1967), or serve as a means of extracting wealth from indigenous communities (Harris 1964), more recent analyses of *cargo* systems take a historical approach, looking at the changing form and function of *cargo* systems in relation to economic change and changes in state and church policy (Wasserstrom 1983; Chance and Taylor 1985; Chance *intra*). Such historical analyses of religious *cargo* systems have illuminated how changes in ritual activities were structurally organized and how such changes have affected not only individual peasant households, but the nature of the relationship between indigenous peasant communities and the state.

Recent ethnohistorical work, including essays in this volume, reveals ways in which particular communities have resisted changes in church and state policy regarding the functioning of religious *cargo* systems. Peasants have used local *cargo* systems as a way of asserting a political position in relation to the state (Chance, Stephen, Greenberg *intra*,) or as a way of maintaining local autonomy in a municipal hierarchy (Cancian *intra*; Wasserstrom 1978).

One of the most important contributions of recent historical work has been to correct the prevalent image in Mexican and Guatemalan ethnography of the "classical form" of the civil-religious hierarchy which is described as an intertwining hierarchy of civil and religious offices. The work of Chance and Taylor (1985), Chance (*intra*), Wasserstrom (1983), and others has shown that early colonial hierarchies were civil. Religious *cargo* systems originated in *cofradía* systems, religious corporations founded to pay for the cult of local saints. *Cofradías* owned land and herds, the proceeds of which paid for local cult celebrations. Only after *cofradía* property was expropriated by the church and state sanctions against religious festivals appeared did individual households begin to sponsor cult celebrations for local saints. The individualization of religious *cargo* responsibilities took place during the eighteenth century and resulted in the meshing of religious with civil *cargos*.

As Chance points out (*intra*), this form of civil-religious hierarchy was also a historical phase. Chance's comparison of 23 ethnographic sources and other recent studies of *cargo* systems show that, in fact, civil-religious hierarchies have undergone a structural shift in response to increasing integration of community political structures with those of state and national governments. This has resulted in a variety of institutional ritual forms.   Current ethnographic literature describes several contemporary forms of the religious side of former civil-religious hierarchies.   Chance (*intra*) focuses on what he calls "religious *cargo* systems," those systems which maintain a hierarchy of public offices for the express purpose of serving local saints.   He states that such hierarchies may consist of *cofradías* or single position *mayordomías*, but in either case position is hierarchically ranked.   He finds this to be the dominant trend in current literature on *cargo* systems.

Three other contemporary possibilities are also described in the literature. One is the complete disappearance of any type of *cargo* system.   Another variety reflects back on the communal support for cult celebrations offered by *cofradías* during the earlier colonial era.   Brandes (1981, 1988) and others (Smith 1977; Good 1988) describe a system of community-wide collections, usually carried out by specially appointed committees, which support community celebrations in association with particular saints, essentially replacing household sponsored *mayordomías*.   In some communities church committees, which were put in place as early as the 1920s as part of the municipal government structure, are also instrumental in taking up collections and organizing community rituals which were formerly planned and organized by *mayordomos* (Stephen *intra*).

Another local response to the uncoupling of civil from religious hierarchies has been to continue the sponsorship of sporadic *mayordomías,* but to transfer the ritual content and form of *mayordomías* to life cycle rituals such as baptisms, confirmations, engagements, weddings, and funerals.   Sponsorship is still household-based and continues to mobilize reciprocal goods and labor exchange networks, but towards a different purpose (Stephen *intra*; Good 1988; Warman 1980).

At the center of anthropological discussions on religious hierarchies are questions about the relationship between class differentiation, politics, and religious *cargo* systems.   Previously this has been posed as a debate between those who see the nature of Mesoamerican peasant society being largely determined by national and international political and economic forces (Smith 1977; Wasserstrom 1983) and those who emphasize the internal dynamics of reciprocity and redistribution as well (Dow 1974; Greenberg 1981).   Writing in the 1970s in the idiom of modernism, Smith proposes that socioeconomic integration which results in either poverty or relative affluence is associated with the collapse of what he calls "sponsored ceremonials" (1977:6-7).   He states that ritual consumption "tends to occur where economies are rural and traditional rather than urban and dynamic and where people are not subject to the investor-consumer pressure of the market" (1977:17).   He suggests that fiesta systems are viable only in situations of moderate economic prosperity (1977:7).   In a careful reading of Smith, Greenberg points out an apparent contradiction in Smith's work where he follows the extraction hypothesis of Harris.   On the one hand, Smith argues that fiesta systems did not isolate indigenous peoples from exploitation, that they fragmented indigenous societies, and that they drained money from communities.   On the other hand, however, he maintains that such systems flourished in communities that were isolated from the colonial market (Greenberg 1981:14).

Wasserstrom, who follows Smith's lead in looking to wider economic and political factors as primary forces in shaping the historical trajectories of *cofradías* and fiesta systems, indirectly challenges Smith's conclusions. Wasserstrom maintains that religious *cargo* systems and fiesta sponsorship have flourished in those regions closest to political and commercial centers of power. His careful enthnohistorical analysis of Chamula and Zinacanteco populations demonstrates that they have long been integrated into the national economy as commercial farmers, cattle ranchers, and primarily as wage laborers (Wasserstrom 1983). He outlines how, beginning in the 1930s, control of offices in religious hierarchies among the Chamula was taken over by local petty capitalists aligned with the interests of commercial agriculture and cattle ranching.

Wasserstrom's emphasis on the determinative power of expanding agrarian capitalism coordinated with state policy causes him to conclude that ethnic differences throughout the region have become submerged beneath "the more fundamental differences of wealth, property, and power" (1983:213). While he emphasizes the importance of capital accumulation and class differentiation within Chamula and Zinacantan communities, he does not reflect on how changing local class alliances may shift position in relation to the state and change internally. The final result is a level of analysis which allows for little agency among local Chamula and Zinacantecos in challenging the century-old alliance between land owners and the state.

Writing in the early 1970s, Dow painted a very different picture of peasant economies, religious hierarchies, and the economic results and rationale for fiesta sponsorship. Maintaining that the economic subsystem instituted in fiesta systems is separate from the commercial economic sector, Dow argued that fiesta sponsorship encourages the accumulation of a surplus which does not lead to capital accumulation, but which governs "only the production of subsistence goods benefitting the whole group" (1974:221). He proposed that religious ceremonies integrate peasant economies through coordinating production, redistribution, and consumption of surpluses. While Dow's analysis suggests that the redistributive exchange characteristic of indigenous rituals keeps the Otomí "non-capitalistic," his argument also hints at the interactive effect of indigenous communities on larger society through "indigenous institutions that are a successful means of establishing economic and political processes that resist exploitation..." (1974:225).

Greenberg's analysis of previous interpretations of fiesta systems and religious hierarchies offers a good stepping stone for bridging the positions of those focused on the determinative power of the international political economy in influencing local religious institutions and those who emphasize the importance of internal community dynamics. In the 1980s, Middle American anthropology evolved to a point where national economic and political systems, as well as local social, political, and economic organization in historical context, must be addressed in order to provide a sufficient analysis of popular religious participation. Critical of the reductionist dependency theory of Frank (1967), Greenberg (1981) offers us a combination of Laclau's (1971) emphasis on differences in relations of production and exchange which frame community-state relations and Taussig's (1980) emphasis on the importance of peasant ritual, cosmology, and ideology as a tableau evaluating social change from a past to a present perspective (1981:17-19). Taussig's characterization of fiesta systems and economies suggests a dialectical approach to understanding indigenous peasant communities:

> On the one hand, Indian communities have retained in varying degrees a cosmology and egalitarian ideology built upon the principles of reciprocity and redistribution. These principles are embedded in social and ritual relations. On the other hand, such a system of reciprocal obligations tends to be converted in the dialectic of an Indian community with a capitalist metropolis into 'individualism' and a vertical ladder of class forms based on unbalanced exchange. Wealth, of course, is increasingly extracted as unequal exchange and class relations penetrate the community. The religious system, albeit with varying degrees of success, attempts to mediate these contradictions... (1981:20-21).

As religious systems mediate the contradictions between reciprocity and redistribution on the one hand, and unequal exchange and class differentiation on the other, they become highly politicized. In many of the cases here, the political mediation of local religious institutions is associated with forms of cultural resistance to outside state and economic domination. Such resistance may not only involve direct confrontations such as the agrarian movement of Padre Girón in Guatemala, but it also occurs when local forms change and adapt to externally imposed conditions. The culture and institutions which are created out of such interactions can involve new cultural forms which combine the structure and content of older forms with new social and political reality, what Diamond (1951) refers to as genuine culture after Sapir (1954). Civil-religious hierarchies such as that described for the Chatino by Greenberg (*intra*) support the idea of ritual and religion as mediating institutions which both act upon and are acted upon by government policy and the dynamics of capitalist development.

The cases in this volume clearly demonstrate that the degree to which religious forms control or are controlled by extra-community political and economic interests is historically and regionally dependent. Earle, for example, shows that in the same Chamula *municipios* where Wasserstrom documented a long-standing rule by bilingual scribes aligned with the state government, a majority of community members recently removed a *cacique*-supported president and reestablished popular control of the *municipio*. As national politics and economics shift, so do local politics in relation to them.

Anthropological Discussions of Missionization in Middle America

In sharp contrast with their fixation on *cargo* systems, anthropologists have yet to give contemporary missionization the attention it deserves. The present period, in which Catholic and Protestant missionaries have been rapidly converting and reconverting rural peoples throughout Middle America, undoubtedly will be seen as an era of religious change almost as far reaching as the early colonial period. Recent ethnographies, biographies, and histories, especially those on Guatemala, almost invariably devote a few scattered pages to Protestantism. Polemical works, for example, those focusing on the missionary work of groups such as the controversial Summer

Institute of Linguistics, have appeared, but only a few of them are illuminating or informative. Serious studies of the process and effects of missionization are still lacking.

Anthropologists have perhaps most often focused on differentiation between Protestants, traditionalists, and reconverted Catholics, dissecting communities in economic and social terms to account for conversion or opposition and demonstrating differences in orientation, life paths, and economic success. The neo-Weberian study by Annis (1987) of San Antonio, Guatemala displays the strengths of this approach. Because traditional ethnographic censusing lends itself to interpretations such as that Catholics have "n" percent more land than Protestants, they are feasible as well as revealing, if incomplete.

Histories of prosyletization and religious struggle (Warren 1978; Brintnall 1979) are central to our understanding of the dynamics of local and national politics, however difficult it may be to collect data for them. In this volume, Howe presents a case of three way religious factionalism from lower Central America very similar to recent events in Guatemalan *municipios*, except that here Panamanian traditionalists follow a pre-Colombian religion rather than syncretic Catholicism. Howe insists that local events must be set within a frame of national politics, a point underlined by Riós Montt's presidency in Guatemala.

Histories of missionization, which typically involve starkly antagonistic interactions between cultural systems, with aggressive attempts to replace one with another, raise issues of cultural articulation and differences in consciousness (Warren 1978). In this volume, Kane dramatically illustrates the wide gap between the consciousness of Emberá Chocó and that of even the most tolerant missionaries who see themselves as defending the Emberá from oppression. In a different light, Howe shows that missionaries seeking to convert the Kuna affected the thinking of secular administrators and policemen more than they did that of the Kuna themselves.

Anthropological studies of missionization on other continents have begun to focus on the missionaries and their culture (Boutillier, Hughes, and Tiffany 1978; Beidelman 1982; Schneider and Lindenbaum 1987), something largely missing from Mesoamerican ethnography. Although the hostility and secretiveness of some missionaries may make close observation difficult, many sects continue to produce documents of the sort used by Howe in this volume, including memoirs, newsletters, and tracts of various kinds. Though fascinating in their own right, such materials most lend themselves to a form of historical and cultural interpretation that gives equal analytical weight to both missionized and missionizers, making sense of the articulation of contending world-views (Bowden 1981; Axtell 1985; Comaroff 1985; Comaroff and Comaroff 1986).

Activist Missionization: Liberation Theology in Middle America

In Middle America, the Catholic Church has articulated religion with the state since the conquest. In the nineteenth century and in part of the twentieth century while the church occasionally attempted to defend indigenous populations and the poor against the state, it was most often a conservative force inhibiting social reform. However, in recent decades, a shift has occurred linking elements of the Catholic and some Protestant churches with popular reform movements among the poorer classes. In many cases the churches have instigated such movements and can claim credit for them, a fact that has not passed unnoticed by the repressive oligarchies of Central America, who have sometimes brutally persecuted the radical clergy and missionary workers (Bermudez 1986; Bonpane 1985:41-43).

The Christian activists who have organized peasant Bible study groups and cooperatives in Middle America express the struggles of the poor and peasant classes primarily in Christian theological terms. While such terms may be neutral in relation to the Bible, such activists also come armed with a political agenda. The process of articulating popular protest proceeds often through the expression of "voices," expressions of the thoughts and feelings of groups whose needs are ignored by neo-colonial authorities and state bureaucracies. In Nicaragua, El Salvador, and Guatemala, missionaries and clergy have encouraged such voices as a response to Christ's teaching that the poor are especially beloved by God. Such clergy are, however, highly politicized individuals. After articulation by literate theologians, these ideas have become a genuine "liberation theology" (Boff and Boff 1986; Sobrino 1987) with a significant impact on the Church. Higgins (intra) notes how, in Nicaragua, Christian ideas in the form of liberation theology are vocabulary for articulating the needs of the poor.

In Mesoamerica, Christian activism does not seem to be inhibited by the presence of religious cargo systems. Interestingly, Warren (1978) suggests that during the nineteenth century, Guatemalan cargo systems flourished in part because anticlericalism at the national level kept priests away from indigenous communities. Now the priests have returned, but with a message which departs from that of the earlier institutionalized Catholic church.

In Guatemala, Christian activism has taken place in areas where traditional cargo systems are also found (Sierra 1983; Berryman 1984:171-180; Bonpane 1985:24-30). There seems to be a greater correlation between Christian activism and repressive state governments than with the presence or absence of cargo systems. Since Christian activism has been catalyzed by literate priests and missionary workers, we might expect it to be more accepted in communities more open to urban influences than in more closed indigenous communities. However, Christian activism contains many of the same communal values, such as feeding the poor and performing collective work, as does traditional service to the saints in a cargo system. Furthermore, it is a reaction to the exploitative power of capitalism, as many scholars believe cargo systems to be (cf. Earle intra and Chance intra).

For example, Bonpane (1985:25-30) found that Quiche communities in Guatemala were more open to revolutionary help than were equally poor Ladino communities. Several factors seemed to be responsible for this acceptance: local reverence for priests, the stable political structure of the community, the absence of internal conflicts, and the absence of Ladinos with government connections. The government of Guatemala has no way of stopping a revolutionary process in indigenous communities such of those of the Quiche, which are closed to Ladino influence, except by extreme military oppression. Tragically, military force has been used extensively in

Guatemala. In the long run, however, popular indigenous religion has aided rather than impeded the adoption of Christian activist ideas in Guatemala.

The role of Protestant churches in political change in Middle America has varied. Earle (*intra*) shows how protestantism can be linked with a traditional Mesoamerican *cargo* system to increase resistance to a Catholic Church that is aligned with capitalist interests. However, in Guatemala, North American Protestantism has been used to control peasant communities (Peck 1984). Protestant evangelical churches in Guatemala formed the organization FUNDAPI (Foundation for Aid to the Indian People) which supported food relief, Food-for-Work, road construction, and the model village programs that were part of the army's counter insurgency plan during the 1980s (Manz 1988:98). President Riós-Montt, a Protestant "born-again Christian," was linked to the Protestant Gospel Outreach in Eureka, California which funnelled money, material aid, and missionaries from the "born-again" movement to the oppressive Guatemalan government in 1982 and 1983 (Manz 1988:252; Frank and Wheaton 1984:73). While the connection of Riós-Montt and the activities he carried out cannot be generalized to most evangelical Protestants in Middle America, it does demonstrate an extreme of how institutional religion can be used by a modern state as part of an apparently genocidal policy. On the other hand, in Mexico, Earle's case (*intra*) and others suggest that the Protestant Church can be a leading force in peasant autonomy (Garma 1984). The varied role of Protestant sects suggests that peasant communities are able to pick and choose from various missionary groups and enlist their support to accomplish their own agendas when such groups are not directly coordinated with the political programs of national governments.

Shamanism

While shamanism is not a central focus here, Kane's discussion of it raises an important issue in relation to religion as a source of cultural resistance. Although shamanism articulates a set of beliefs that are removed from those of the Catholic Church or any other imported religious system, they can be integrated to varying degrees into the public ceremonies of indigenous communities. For example, Oakes (1951) describes a Mayan village in which a shaman acts as a priest for the entire village. Sierra Otomí shamans perform public rain ceremonies (Sandstrom 1981:56), and they act as priests to small flocks of devotees (Dow 1986:63-73). A considerable amount of evidence indicates that shamans in Mesoamerica have important priestly functions and can at times represent an entire community, making them important actors in local political processes (Tedlock 1982:47-53).

The important political difference between shamans and other politically powerful people in indigenous communities is in the means by which they acquire influence. Shamans rely on a belief in their magical powers. In Mesoamerica, other people acquire influence by the conspicuous sponsorship of fiestas, by establishing important links of political patronage, by utilizing wealth in a controlling fashion, or by organizing grassroots political groups. The shaman's influence depends on his or her ability to correctly express the best moral values of the community and to give these values expression in magical ritual. Although it is an alternative path to prestige and power, shamanism is not a common route to political leadership. Yet it can provide an opportunity for the development of charismatic leaders. In some ways shamanism, with its open recruitment of practitioners, is a threat to the local political system as well as to the state system.

OVERVIEW OF CHAPTERS

Throughout the history of Latin America, the church, ritual, and religion have been at the center of local and national politics. A careful examination of the historical dialogue between religious institutions and peasants reveals an ongoing tension between Catholic and Protestant religious authorities, community-based religious institutions, and the different strata of peasant communities. This volume documents that dialogue primarily from within peasant communities, looking outward at the effects of changing economic, political, and cultural circumstances on local religious forms. While many of these essays stress peasant use of religious forms and institutions as evidence of resistance to the state and outside institutions, they demonstrate as well how peasants can use institutionalized religion as a vehicle for self-identified goals. Through presenting the recent and historical dynamics of popular religion in Mexico and Central America, these essays reveal a central motor in the ongoing political struggles in the region.

The book is divided into five parts. Part I focuses on the long-term effects of state policy, regional politics, and local economic development on religious hierarchies. The remainder of the book deals with more recent religious responses to changing political and economic forces. Part II focuses on how changes in local religious systems are linked to changes in peasant economic relations. Part III focuses on political conflict, emphasizing how religion can be an important means of regulating factions within a community and unifying them for political purposes or breaking them apart. Part IV explores the role that organized churches, particularly missionaries and liberation theology, play in structuring popular religion at the local level.   Part V summarizes the work and draws conclusions for further research.

The historical view presented in Part I suggests that political systems articulating state power at the local level have caused religious hierarchies and fiesta systems to take on a more religious character and to disconnect from civil hierarchies. In addition, state political intrusions and the commercialization of local economies can result in the transfer of prestige from *mayordomías* to life cycle rituals. Structural changes in civil-religious *cargo* systems are analyzed with regard to internal community politics and the political relationship which indigenous peasant communities have with state and national political and economic institutions. Chance and Stephen both argue that changes in local religious hierarchies took place in response to state intervention and increasing integration of civil municipal governments with official state bureaucracies. Retrenchment and separation of religious from civil *cargo* systems are seen to preserve a limited level of community autonomy and internal systems of authority and prestige, often in situations of increasing class differentiation. Stephen maintains that relocation of the form and content of *mayordomía* ceremonies to life cycle rituals can have a similar purpose.

In the next two parts, Greenberg, Cancian, Earle, and Binford describe how religious *cargo* systems and ceremonial sponsorship are related to economic stratification and, in some cases, are mediums for political discourse. The cases of Cancian, Binford, Earle, and Greenberg all point out the impact of increasing economic stratification, and political loyalties and challenges to the state, on local religious institutions.

In Part II, Binford and Cancian suggest that as wealth is created in peasant communities through new opportunities for wage labor and profit-making enterprises, religious systems express these changes. Cancian documents how opportunities for small-scale capitalist development can result in increases and then decreases in *cargo* system participation. He states that in the highland Maya community of Zinacantan, both wage laborers and elite Zinacantecos involved in new capitalist enterprises are deciding not to take on religious *cargos* for different reasons. Wage laborers in Zinacantan may consider a day of *cargo* service to be a day of lost wages, while elites prefer to invest in trucks and other capital goods in order to build up family enterprises.

Binford notes that among Zapotec peasants in the Isthmus of Tehuantepec, increasingly fewer members of poorer households formally join *vela* associations because of the prohibitively high cost of membership. He also describes how two different *velas* became associated with two political groups like the Chamula described by Earle, and how participation in religious politics is becoming circumscribed by wealth.

Part III, emphasizing conflict, suggests that when confrontations within and between peasant communities are violent, religiously created consensus can be politically effective because it is less easily manipulated from the outside. Earle documents how civil-religious authorities among the Chamula used their political leverage as a way of assuring local loyalty to the PRI, the ruling political party in Mexico. Elite Chamula authorities threw out 7,000 people who were Protestants aligned with a conservative opposition party (PAN), or reform Catholics challenging the ruling PRI from the position of liberation theology. Greenberg also describes party loyalty being played out through conflicts between traditional elders who gain authority from their religious positions, and civil *cargo* authorities who derive their legitimation from their association with the PRI.

Part IV of the book focuses on the role of institutional religion and local politics. The first two chapters emphasize Protestant and Catholic missionization. Howe's historical essay suggests that Catholic and Protestant missionaries represent Latin American and North American culture to indigenous peoples, and make indigenous communities battlegrounds for ideological allegiance. In addition, he suggests that missionization is part of a larger process of political change that involves alliance with nonindigenous political groups. He shows how the religious fate of the Kuna relates to conflicts within national politics and between North American and Panamanian culture. The cultural gap blocking communication between missionaries and the people they seek to convert also extends to liberation theology, as suggested by Kane. In her discourse analysis of a shamanic voyage and a liberation theologian's call for class unity, Kane demonstrates the historical meaning for the Emberá attached to white man's religion, no matter what its form. The teachings of liberation theologians are filtered through Emberá consciousness, to be accepted or rejected according to their own view of history and political reality.

In contrast, Higgins shows in his chapter how the Catholicism of liberation theology can provide symbols for articulating the social needs of the poor, particularly through the use of revolutionary martyrdom. In Nicaragua, there was an active attempt on the part of the Sandinista state as well as by autonomous peasant and popular urban organizations to merge the theological practices of popular religion with those of the revolution. By contrasting popular religion in urban Managua with the folk Catholicism of urban Oaxaca, Higgins demonstrates the different ways in which marginalized populations appropriate institutional religious symbols for political and personal purposes.

CONCLUSIONS

The region of Mexico and Central America now holds a prominent position in international consciousness as reports of guerilla movements, civil wars, drug trade, debt, immigration, and human tragedy flash across television screens on a regular basis. Usually devoid of the historical complexity of class and ethnicity, our knowledge of the region often has been filtered through either romantic nostalgia for authentic "Indian" communities or through a reductionist vision of politics as a succession of dictators, and/or dominant political parties, with the exception of Costa Rica. The essays here seek to build on current public interest in political conflict and economic development in Mexico and Central America and to illuminate the role of popular religion in these processes, emphasizing the interplay of ethnicity and class through the lens of religion and politics. The essays emphasize community reaction to state intervention and economic development as reflected in local religious structures. They seek to portray indigenous peoples and peasants not only as constrained by the forces of state policy and capitalist development, but also as actively involved in building community autonomy and social movements which counteract and in turn affect such forces.

The arena of popular religion provides a rich opportunity to explore the complicated dynamics of class and ethnicity in Middle American politics. When viewed as part of a political process, religiously based institutions, events, and movements allow us to see how both ethnic identity and class, which exist in historically specific structural and material realities, are also ideologically reconstructed in relation to the changing political agendas of states, peasant communities, and the disparate individuals and factions within communities. On a larger level, the chapters here provide a conceptual basis for helping us to understand how cultural forms and institutions are integrated with the material and economic factors of local level politics in peasant communities.

NOTES

Acknowledgments. We would like to acknowledge the helpful criticism and input of James Howe in writing this introduction.

1. Adams (n.d.) notes that the indigenous population of Guatemala (about 50%) and El Salvador (probably less than 20%) have considerably more influence on their Ladino states than in other Central American countries. He notes the importance of the Miskito in Nicaragua as well, but on a smaller scale.

REFERENCES

Adams, Richard
  1988 "Ethnic Images and Strategies in 1944." Pre-publication working paper of the Institute of Latin American Studies, University of Texas at Austin. Paper No. 88-06. Austin: University of Texas, Center for Latin American Studies
  n.d. "Strategies of Ethnic Survival in Latin America." Unpublished manuscript.
Aguirre Beltrán, Gonzalo
  1967 *Regiones de refugio: el desarrollo de la comunidad y el proceso dominical en mestizo América.* Instituto Nacional Indigenista, Serie de Antropología Social, No. 17. Mexico.
Annis, Sheldon
  1987 *God and Production in a Guatemalan Town.* Austin: University of Texas Press.
Assad, Talal
  1983 "Anthropological Conceptions of Religion: Reflections of Geertz." *Man* 18 (2): 237-259.
Axtell, James
  1985 *The Invasion Within: The Contest of Cultures in Colonial North America.* New York: Oxford University Press.
Barth, Fredrick
  1981 "Ethnic Groups and Boundaries." In *Process and Form in Social Life, Selected Essays of Fredrik Barth: Volume I*, pp. 198-227. London: Routledge and Kegan Paul.
Beidelman, T.O.
  1982 *Colonial Evangelism: A Socio-historical Study of an East African Mission at the Grassroots.* Bloomington: University of Indiana Press.
Bennet, John W. and Don Kanel
  1983 "Agricultural Economics and Economic Anthropology: Confrontation and Accommodation." In *Economic Anthropology.* S. Ortiz, editor, pp. 201-248. New York: University Press of America.
Bermudez, Fernando
  1986 *Death and Resurrection in Guatemala.* Maryknoll, NY: Orbis Books.
Berryman, Philip
  1984 *The Religious Roots of Rebellion: Christians in Central American Revolutions.* Maryknoll, NY: Orbis Books.
Boff, Leonardo and Clodovis Boff
  1986 *Introducing Liberation Theology.* Maryknoll, NY: Orbis Books.
Bonpane, Blaise
  1985 *Guerrillas of Peace: Liberation Theology and the Central American Revolution.* Boston: South End Press.
Boutelier, James, Daniel Hughes and Sharon Tiffany
  1978 *Mission, Church, and Sect in Oceania.* ASAO Monograph 6. Lanham: University Press of America.

Bowden, Henry Warner
  1981 *American Indians and Christian Missions: Studies in Cultural Conflict.* Chicago: University of Chicago Press.
Brintnall, Douglas
  1979 *Revolt against the Dead: The Modernization of a Mayan Community in the Highlands of Guatemala.* New York: Gordon & Breach.
Brandes, Stanley
  1981 "Cargos Versus Cost Sharing in Mesoamerican Fiestas with Special Reference to Tzintzuntzan." *Journal of Anthropological Research* 37(3):209-225.
  1988 *Power and Persuasion: Fiestas and Social Control in Rural Mexico.* Philadelphia: University of Pennsylvania Press.
Cambranes, J.C.
  1986 *Agrarismo en Guatemala.* Guatemala: Serviprensa Centroamericana.
Cancian, Frank
  1965 *Economics and Prestige in a Mayan Community.* Stanford: Stanford University Press.
Chance, John K. and William B. Taylor
  1985 "Cofradías and Cargos: An Historical Perspective on the Mesoamerican Civil-Religious Hierarchy." *American Ethnologist* 12(1):1-26.
Chayanov, A.V.
  1966 *The Development of Peasant Economy.* Illinois: Homewood.
Comaroff, Jean
  1985 *Body of Power, Spirit of Resistance: The Culture and History of a South African People.* Chicago: University of Chicago Press.
Comaroff, Jean and John Comaroff
  1986 "Christianity and Colonialism in South Africa." *American Ethnologist* 13(1): 1-22.
Deere, Carmen Diana
  1986 "The Peasantry in Political Economy." Paper presented at The Thirteenth International Congress of the Latin American Studies Association. Boston, MA, October 23-25, 1986.
de Janvry, Alain
  1981 *The Agrarian Question and Reformism in Latin America.* Baltimore: The Johns Hopkins University Press.
Diamond, Stanley
  1951 *Dahomey: A Proto-state in West Africa.* Ph.D. dissertation, Columbia University. Ann Arbor: University Microfilms.
Dow, James
  1977 "Religion in the Organization of a Mexican Peasant Economy." In *Peasant Livelihood: Studies in Economic Anthropology and Cultural Ecology.* Rhoda Halperin and James Dow, editors, pp. 215-226. New York: St. Martin's Press.
  1986 *The Shaman's Touch: Otomí Indian Symbolic Healing.* Salt Lake City: University of Utah Press.
Frank, Andre Gunder
  1967 *Capitalism and Underdevelopment in Latin America: Historical Studies of Chile and Brazil.* New York: Monthly Review Press.
Frank, Luisa and Philip Wheaton
  1984 *Indian Guatemala: Path to Liberation.* Washington DC: EPICA Task Force
Garma Navarro, Carlos
  1984 "Liderazgo protestante en una lucha campesina en Mexico." *America Indigena* 44(1):127-141.
Gold, Harry
  1982 *The Sociology of Urban Life.* Englewood Cliffs, NJ: Prentice-Hall.

Good, Catharine Eshelman
   1988   *Haciendo La Lucha: Arte y Comercio Nahuas de Guererro*. Mexico DF: Fondo de Cultura Economica.
Greenberg, James
   1981   *Santiagos's Sword: Chatino Peasant Religion and Economics*.   Berkeley: University of California Press.
Gudeman, Stephen
   1976a   *Relationships, residence and the individual: A rural Panamanian Community*. Minneapolis: University of Minnesota Press.
   1976b   "Saints, Symbols, and Ceremonies." *American Ethnologist* 3(4):709-730.
Harris, Marvin
   1964   *Patterns of Race in the Americas*. New York: Walker.
Hermite, M. Esther
   1970   *Poder sobrenatural y control social en un pueblo maya contemporaneo*. Ediciones Especiales 57. Mexico City: Instituto Indigenista Interamericano
Ingham, John M.
   1986   *Mary, Michael and Lucifer: Folk Catholicism in Central Mexico*. Austin: University of Texas Press.
Laclau, Ernesto
   1971   "Feudalism and Capitalism in Latin America." *New Left Review* 67:19-38.
Lenin, Vladimir I.
   1962   *The Development of Capitalism in Russia*. Moscow: Progress Publishers.
Loveland, Christine
   1982   "Introduction."   In *Sex Roles and Social Change in Native Lower Central American Societies*. C. Loveland and F. Loveland, editors, pp. xi-xix. Urbana: University of Illinois Press.
Madsen, William
   1967   "Religious Syncretism." In *Handbook of Middle American Indians*. Volume 6. R. Wauchope, editor, pp. 369-391. Austin: University of Texas Press.
Manz, Beatriz
   1988   *Refugees of a Hidden War: The Aftermath of Counterinsurgency in Guatemala*. Albany: State University of New York Press.
Nash, June
   1963   "Protestantism in an Indian Village in the Western Highlands of Guatemala." *Southwestern Journal of Anthropology* 19:131-148.
Oakes, Maude
   1951   *The Two Crosses of Todos Santos: Survivals of Mayan Religious Ritual*. Princeton: Princeton University Press.
Pezzoli, Keith
   1989   *Irregular Settlement and Politics of Land Allocation in Mexico City: The Case of Ajusco*. Ph.D. dissertation, Department of Urban Planning, Univeristy of California, Los Angeles.
Peck, Jane Cary
   1984   "Reflections from Costa Rica on Protestantism's Dependence and Nonliberative Social Function." *Journal of Ecumenical Studies* 21:181-198.
Pearce, Jenny
   1986   *Promised Land: Peasant Rebellion in Chalatenango, El Salvador*. London: Latin America Bureau.
Ramírez Saiz, Juan Manual
   1986   *El movimiento urbano popular en Mexico*. Mexico DF: Siglo Veintiuno Editores.
Redfield, Robert and Alfonso Villa Rojas
   1962   [1934] *Chan Kom: A Mayan Village*. Chicago: University of Chicago Press.

Ross, John
    1988   "Mexico's Southern Prelates Firmly Defend Indian Flock." *Latinamerica Press*,
            24 March, 1988, pp. 6-7.
Russ, Jan and Robert Wasserstrom
    1980   "Civil-religious Hierarchies in Central Chiapas: A Critical Perspective."
            American Ethnologist 7(3):466-478.
Saler, Benson
    1965   "Religious Conversion and Self-Aggrandizement: A Guatemalan Case." *Practical
            Anthropology* 12:107-149.
Sandstrom, Alan
    1981   *Traditional Curing and Crop Fertility Rituals among Otomí Indians of the Sierra
            de Puebla, Mexico: The López Manuscripts.*   Bloomington: Indiana University
            Museum.
Sapir, Edward
    1966   "Culture, Genuine and Spurious." In *Culture, Language, and Personality*.   David
            Mandelbaum, editor, pp. 78-119. Berkeley: University of California Press.
Schneider, Jane and Shirley Lindenbaum, editors
    1987   *Frontiers of Christian Evangelism*. Special issue of *American Ethnologist* 3(1).
Serra Pop, Oscar R.
    1983   "The Church and Social Conflicts in Guatemala." *Social Compass* 30(2-3):317-348
Smith, Richard Chase
    1985   "A Search for Unity Within Diversity: Peasant Unions, Ethnic Federations, and
            Indianist Movements in the Andean Republics." In *Native Peoples and Economic
            Development*. Theodore MacDonald, Jr., editor, pp. 5-38. Cambridge, MA: Cultural
            Survival, Inc.
Smith, Waldemar
    1977   *The Fiesta System and Economic Change*. New York: Columbia University Press.
Sobrino
    1987   *Jesus in Latin America*. Maryknoll, NY: Orbis Books.
Stephen, Lynn
    n.d.   "Culture as a Resource: Four Cases of Self-Managed Indigenous Craft Production."
            Economic Development and Cultural Change. In Press.
Stern, Stephen
    1987   "New Approaches to the Study of Peasant Rebellion and Consciousness:
            Implications of the Andean Experience." In *Resistance, Rebellion, and
            Consciousness in the Andean Peasant World, 18th to 20th Centuries*. Stephen Stern,
            editor, pp. 3-25. Madison: University of Wisconsin Press.
Stoll, David
    1982   *Fishers of Men or Founders of Empire: The Wycliffe Bible Translators in Latin
            America*. London: Zed Press.
Tax, Sol
    1937   "The Municipio of the Western Highlands of Guatemala." *American
            Anthropologist* 39:423-444.
Taussig, Michael
    1987   *Shamanism, Colonialism, and the Wild Man: A Study in Terror and Healing*.
            Chicago: University of Chicago Press.
    1980   *The Devil and Commodity Fetishism in South America*. Chapel Hill: University of
            North Carolina Press.
Tedlock, Barbara
    1982   *Time and the Highland Maya*. Albuquerque: University of New Mexico Press.
Warman, Arturo
    1980   *We Come to Object*. Baltimore: Johns Hopkins University Press.

Warren, Kay B.
    1978   *The Symbolism of Subordination: Indian Identity in a Guatemalan Town.* Austin: University of Texas Press.
Wasserstrom, Robert
    1983   *Class and Society in Central Chiapas.* Berkeley: University of California Press.
West, Robert C. and John P. Augelli
    1966   *Middle America, Its Lands and Peoples.* Englewood Cliffs, NJ: Prentice Hall.
Wolf, Eric
    1955   "Types of Latin American Peasantry: A Preliminary Discussion." *American Anthropologist* 57:452-471.

Part I:
The Impact of State Politics and Economic Development on Religious Hierarchies

CHAPTER TWO

Changes in Twentieth-Century Mesoamerican *Cargo* Systems

John K. Chance
Arizona State University

INTRODUCTION

During the last 50 years, ethnographers of Mesoamerica have placed special emphasis on the civil-religious hierarchy or *cargo* system as the key to understanding indigenous communities and their relationships with the national societies of Mexico and Guatemala. In sheer volume, more pages of ethnographic description and analysis probably have been devoted to *cargo* systems than to any other aspect of village life. The so-called "traditional" or "classic" form of the system as described ethnographically consists of a hierarchy of ranked offices that together comprise a community's public civil and religious administration. The civil offices articulate the community with regional and national political systems, while the religious *cargos* are associated with the worship of the local saints (and normally are only tenuously linked to the external church hierarchy). Individuals or couples representing different households ascend this ladder of service during their lifetimes, alternating back and forth between civil and religious posts. Men with the resources and longevity to make it to the top join a select group of *principales*, or elders, who often are very influential in local politics. A central feature of the system is the private sponsorship of fiestas in honor of the saints by holders of religious *cargos*. Considerable amounts of wealth may thus be expended as an individual or couple ascends the hierarchy in search of influence and prestige in the eyes of fellow villagers.[1]

The vast majority of contemporary ethnographic descriptions of Mesoamerican civil-religious hierarchies come from the Oaxaca region and the Maya highlands of Chiapas, Mexico and Guatemala (see DeWalt 1975:88 and Table 2.1 below). Michoacán has not yielded any examples in the twentieth century, though there may have been civil-religious hierarchies there in the past (Carrasco 1952). Tzintzuntzan, one of the most thoroughly studied of all Mesoamerican communities, had a *cargo* system prior to 1925, but it lacked a civil component and was comprised entirely of religious offices (Foster 1967; Brandes 1988). The Yucatan peninsula likewise seems to be lacking in civil-religious systems, despite the interesting account by Grant Jones (1981) of a "fiesta system"—which is not the same thing—in nineteenth-century northern Belize.[2] Equally anomalous is the dearth of civil-religious systems in Nahuatl-speaking central Mexico, where *cargo* systems today are usually religious in structure (Table 2.1, but see also Montoya Briones 1964). Explanation of this regional variation must await future ethnohistorical research.

In this paper I will confine my attention to the central and southern highlands and argue that in twentieth century indigenous communities which still maintain functioning *cargo* systems, civil-religious hierarchies are being transformed into religious hierarchies. Supporting data come from 23 ethnographic case studies published since 1965, the year that marked the appearance of Frank Cancian's landmark study of the religious *cargo* system of Zinacantan, Chiapas. As William Taylor and I have previously noted (Chance and Taylor 1985: 20), analytical gains can be made by breaking down the civil-religious hierarchy into its three component parts—the civil hierarchy, the religious hierarchy, and the practice of fiesta sponsorship by individuals or couples (as representatives of households). The analysis that follows builds on this lead, and takes the primary defining characteristic of a *cargo* system to be the existence of a hierarchy of ranked public offices through which individuals are expected to pass in a certain order. It also assumes that ascending this ladder brings prestige. The nature of the offices themselves (civil or religious, etc.), whether or not they involve celebration of fiestas, and the practices surrounding fiesta financing are all secondary characteristics.

Discussions of the factors that promote change and breakdown in *cargo* systems are nearly as voluminous as the descriptive literature on the system itself. Many ethnographers, faced with faded or defunct *cargo* systems, have alluded to the local events which led up to their demise. Frank Cancian (1967:293-296) and Waldemar Smith (1977), on a more general level, posit that weakening or breakdown of *cargo* systems may be brought about by "*ladinoization*," direct political action by national governments, increasing poverty, increasing prosperity, and a reduction or increase in population. Billie DeWalt (1975:95, 100-102) stresses increasing "contact with the outside world"[3] and occupational specialization as correlates of the process of breakdown. James Greenberg (1981:159) singles out changes in modes of production and changing metropolis-satellite relations as causative forces. In this paper I neither endorse nor dispute any of these accounts, but rather take up the issue of *structural* change in the system. Despite the extensive debates over the origins and functions of the hierarchies (see Chance and Taylor 1985 for a summary), relatively little attention has been paid to the formal shape of *cargo* systems and the kinds of offices they contain. DeWalt (1975) offers a useful fourfold typology of forms, but fails to connect it convincingly with a theory of systemic change. In contrast, in this paper I utilize a broader typology and attempt to sketch a general process of change that has surfaced in many communities since the 1920s. To understand this process, it is necessary to place it in historical perspective and relate it to other changes in Mesoamerican *cargo* systems which have occurred during the last three centuries.

FROM CIVIL TO CIVIL-RELIGIOUS HIERARCHIES

In a previous paper, Taylor and I (Chance and Taylor 1985) challenged the long-held assumption that the civil-religious hierarchy has its origins in the early colonial period. We argue that such an assumption errs in projecting a twentieth-century ethnographic present back into the colonial past. Drawing on primary and secondary sources for Jalisco, Michoacán, the central Mexican highlands, the Valley of Oaxaca, the Sierra Zapoteca of Oaxaca, and Chiapas, we have suggested that the earliest form of the *cargo* system was a *civil* hierarchy, that it emerged in the sixteenth century, and that it was comprised of the political offices making up the municipal *cabildo* (town council). While some of the lower offices had indigenous names and probably dated from pre-Hispanic times, the higher *cargos* all carried Spanish titles and were filled by annual elections as required by colonial law.

Religious offices in colonial indigenous towns were centered in *cofradías,* religious sodalities founded to organize support for the cult of local saints and pay for its expenses. These sodalities, however, were a relatively late colonial development—most were founded in the seventeenth and eighteenth centuries. Furthermore, the evidence indicates that for most of the colonial period, these religious offices existed separately from the civil *cargo* systems, that is, that there were no unified civil-religious hierarchies. The custom of household sponsorship of fiestas, so important to twentieth-century *cargo* systems, was more the exception than the rule during colonial times when most fiestas were sponsored corporately by the *cofradías* themselves. Proceeds from their own cornfields or cattle herds were a primary means of financing fiestas. The civil-religious *cargo* system of the type recorded by ethnographers first emerged in the late eighteenth century and proliferated during the nineteenth, due to expropriations of *cofradía* property by the church and prohibition of communal support of religious fiestas by some Spanish political officials. These pressures brought about a shift from collective to household fiesta sponsorship. At the same time, the colonial status differences between indigenous nobles and commoners were being dismantled and there was growing concern in the villages that each household should help shoulder the burden of maintaining the cult of the saints. The historical outcome of these factors was the "classic" form of the civil-religious hierarchy.

If our ethnohistorical analysis is correct, major structural changes in village *cargo* systems can be expected to occur at times when direct political interference and external pressure on local resources are high. Civil *cargo* hierarchies arose initially in the sixteenth century as a local response to Spanish efforts to impose political control on indigenous communities via a European-derived model of town government. Likewise, the transformation from a civil to a civil-religious system came at a time when the corporate holdings of *cofradías* were under heavy attack from external powerholders. Here I extend this line of reasoning into the twentieth century and argue that another structural change has been brought about by new external political pressures.

FROM CIVIL-RELIGIOUS TO RELIGIOUS HIERARCHIES

In reference to Guatemalan *cargo* systems in the 1950s, Manning Nash (1958:67) noted that the twin political and religious ladders

> are tied together by common symbols, and in virtue of the fact that men in office alternate between posts in each of the ladders. The difference between the two ladders is conceptual. Indians tend to think of them as one system. And the term civil-religious hierarchy recognizes this fact of interrelation.

A decade later, following his fieldwork in Zinacantan, Chiapas, Cancian (1967:284) claimed that

> In other communities—apparently where national governments have recently imposed a new system of civil offices—the differentiation is clear, and the civil offices may even be excluded from the formal hierarchy of service.

Such is the case in Zinacantan, and Cancian (1965) subtitled his study of the hierarchy in that community *The Religious Cargo System in Zinacantan*. Table 2.1 lists published case studies since 1965 that provide evidence of functioning *cargo* systems. I make no claims for completeness; a number of works had to be excluded because they failed to provide sufficient data on the relationships between the civil and religious components of the hierarchies. But I believe the cases in Table 2.1 stand as a reasonably accurate representation of accumulated ethnographic knowledge between 1965 and 1986.

On the whole, these 23 examples show that while the old colonial civil hierarchies have passed from the scene (no cases are reported), civil-religious hierarchies are now themselves in the minority. The most prominent trend in recent ethnography is the proliferation of *religious cargo* systems, which are now twice as common as those of the civil-religious type. (The five "transitional" systems will be discussed below.) I define religious *cargo* systems as those which maintain a hierarchy of public offices for the manifest purpose of serving the local saints. Such hierarchies may consist of sodalities (*cofradías*), or as is common today in Mexico, single positions (*mayordomías*), but in either case offices are usually ranked hierarchically in a more or less clear-cut order.[4]   In communities with religious *cargo* systems, the civil offices have become in large measure formally divorced from the traditional

TABLE 2.1.   ETHNOGRAPHIES OF MESOAMERICAN *CARGO* SYSTEMS, 1965 TO 1986

Community and Type of System	Ethnolinguistic Group	Source
Civil-Religious Systems:		
Sta. María Yolotepec, Oaxaca	Chatino	Bartolomé and Barabas 1982
Yaitepec, Oaxaca	Chatino	Greenberg 1981
San Mateo del Mar, Oaxaca	Huave	Signorini 1979
San Pedro Yolox, Oaxaca	Chinantec	Gwaltney 1970
Chinautla, Guatemala	Pokomam	Reina 1966
Momostenango, Guatemala	Quiché	Tedlock 1982
Transitional Systems:		
Tlalchiyahualica, Hidalgo	Nahua	Schryer n.d.
Xalpatláhuac, Guerrero	Nahua	Dehouve 1976
Tlacoapa, Guerrero	Tlapanec	Oettinger 1980
Tlahuitoltepec, Oaxaca	Mixe	Kuroda 1984
Amatenango, Chiapas	Tzeltal	J. Nash 1970
Religious Systems:		
Atempan, Puebla	Nahua	Buchler 1967
Tlaxcalancingo, Puebla	Nahua	Olivera 1967
Chignautla, Puebla	Nahua	Slade 1973
Eastern Morelos region	Nahua	Warman 1980
Tlayacapan, Morelos	Nahua	Ingham 1986
San Bernardino Contla, Tlaxcala	Nahua	Nutini 1968
San Rafael Tepetlaxco, Tlaxcala	Nahua	Chick 1981
Santa Monica, Hidalgo	Otomí	Dow 1977
Ihuatzio, Michoacán	Tarascan	Zantwijk 1967
Jamiltepec, Oaxaca	Mixtec	Flanet 1977
"San Miguel," Oaxaca	Zapotec	Mathews 1985
Zinacantan, Chiapas	Tzotzil	Cancian 1965

prestige hierarchy. This is, I would argue, the most fundamental structural change in twentieth-century *cargo* systems.

Before proceeding to examine this change in more detail, DeWalt's (1975) alternative typology deserves consideration. He surveyed 26 published case studies dating from the 1930s to the mid 1970s and sorted them into four types: civil-religious (10 cases), ornate religious (3), acephalous (5), and faded (8). DeWalt's "ornate religious" type is the same as that which I call "religious." By acephalous hierarchies he means those in which the "highest civil offices no longer require passage through the rest of the system as a prerequisite" (DeWalt 1975:91). Shortcuts are available for those who are literate in Spanish and possess other desirable skills, causing the civil side of the hierarchy to break down at the top. I regard such systems as "transitional." DeWalt's "faded" hierarchies are those in which only individual *mayordomos* remain. They may still sponsor fiestas, but are no longer part of a clear-cut hierarchy of religious offices. In my analysis, these cases do not qualify as functioning *cargo* systems, since the key defining element—a hierarchy of public offices— is no longer present.

In DeWalt's survey, more cases are of the "traditional" civil-religious type than any other. Yet it is significant that the data in six of the ten cases were obtained in the 1930s and 1940s. (And, not surprisingly, eight of the ten cases come from Oaxaca and Guatemala.) In contrast, all three of his "ornate religious" cases derive from studies done in the 1960s. These three appear in my Table 2.1 (Atempan, Contla, and Zinacantan), along with nine more, seven of which have appeared since DeWalt's survey. Clearly, the trend is away from a civil-religious to an essentially religious structure. This direction of change is also reflected in DeWalt's typology itself. His fourfold classification masks the fact that all 16 of his cases that deviate from the "traditional" civil-religious structure (i.e., the 3 ornate religious, 5 acephalous, and 8 faded) are similar in that they display either a weakening, breakdown, or sloughing off of the civil rungs of the older system. In all of these instances, community government has come to operate partly, if not entirely, outside the confines of the hierarchy.

There are, of course, other sorts of changes and other possible outcomes. Indeed, the most common variant of all is the collapse of the entire system, as the local prestige hierarchy gives way to more cosmopolitan modes of status seeking and status validation. Indigenous villages which support active *cargo* systems of any kind now comprise a dwindling minority. Quite frequently, what DeWalt terms "faded" systems may survive by replacing household fiesta sponsorship with a church committee or a collection of voluntary contributions (DeWalt 1975; Smith 1977; Brandes 1988). But in such cases the local prestige hierarchy may cease to function effectively, at least in the ritual context.

Yet a third response is well documented by Stephen (1987, *intra*) for the Zapotec town of Teotitlán del Valle in the Valley of Oaxaca. Here the religious hierarchy associated with the *mayordomías* has declined, but the ritual content and form of the system, instead of disappearing, have been relocated to the life cycle rituals. By transferring fiestas from *mayordomías* to occasions such as baptisms, confirmations, and birthdays, Teotitecos have, Stephen argues, "transformed domestic rituals into public celebrations" (*intra*). This adaptation may well prove to be widespread among the more open communities which are highly integrated with the market system through commercial agriculture and craft production for export. But while the continuities in such cases may be striking, whether they can be regarded as *cargo* systems is an open question. To view them as such, it would have to be shown that household-based fiestas for life cycle events can support a recognized community prestige hierarchy. This question lies beyond the scope of this paper. The present analysis is intended to apply only to the more closed, conservative communities which still maintain functioning *cargo* hierarchies.

Fundamentally, the structural shift from a civil-religious to a religious hierarchy is symptomatic of increasing community integration into the structures of state and national government. As the legally appointed town governments come to operate more independently of the *cargo* systems, the hierarchies themselves become more occupied than before with internal ritual activities and less concerned with representing the community to the outside. The political pressures that bring about the change from a civil-religious to a religious system are most evident in the transitional cases listed in Table 2.1. These are communities where (using the ethnographic present) the civil and religious sides of the hierarchy are in tension and growing further apart, but have not yet been sundered. A good example is Danièle Dehouve's (1976:220-239) analysis of the increasing power of the Mexican state in the affairs of the Nahuatl-speaking village of Xalpatláhuac, Guerrero. New political *cargos* resulting from government reforms after 1930 have not been incorporated into the hierarchy, but exist outside of it and have stimulated considerable factionalism. A similar situation can be found in Amatenango, Chiapas where a civil-religious hierarchy still exists, although the high political *cargos* of *presidente, síndico,* and *secretario* are excluded from it and filled by young men who are literate in Spanish. As for the lower civil *cargos*, they are mainly ceremonial and ambitious individuals may bypass them altogether (J. Nash 1970:159-196). In the Tlapanec community of Tlacoapa, Guerrero, civil and religious affairs are also becoming estranged. The civil-religious hierarchy is no longer well defined and there is little alternation between civil and religious posts (Oettinger 1980:99-104). A further example of how the civil-religious hierarchy is bifurcated is succinctly summarized by Frans Schryer (n.d.:317) for Nahuatl-speaking Tlalchiyahualica, located in the *municipio* (township) of Yahualica, Hidalgo:

> Most civil posts (beyond the lowest rank of *topile*) are highly regulated by the national system and all top posts (*juez* and *comisariado*) must be confirmed by the *presidente municipal* or the Land Reform bureaucracy. In contrast, the religious posts represent a parallel but unofficial structure which provides prestige, but little real power.

The transition to a full-blown religious *cargo* system has important implications not only for the administration of political affairs and the exercise of power, but also for cultural integration in the community. One of the fullest accounts available is Doren Slade's (1973) description of the religious *cargo* system in Chignautla, a Nahuatl-speaking town in Puebla's Sierra Norte. Here the distinction between civil and religious administrations—the *ayuntamiento municipal* and the *autoridad eclesiástica*—is the most basic principle in the organization of public life. According to Slade:

To Chignautecos...the most significant differentiation of *cargos* is on the basis of which authority appoints the individuals who hold them and controls their activities, and not on the basis of duties performed. In essence, there are two systems, a moral system and a legal system paralleling a difference between religious life and civil life which does not always coincide with the administration process, but operates in terms of the ultimate locus of authority in each system.

At the basis of the moral system is a belief that God created the ideals and norms for human behavior....in the legal system, the ultimate authority is the legal code of the state which may be manipulated and to which one must answer only if caught (1973:194-196).

I suggest that the growing estrangement between the formal civil and religious ladders in the transitional systems described above is the first step in the evolution of an explicitly religious *cargo* system of the type found in Chignautla. There are, of course, a host of local factors that have a bearing on the direction of change in each case, but the evident commonalities in the ethnographic record indicate that there are also more general socio-historical processes at work. The principal factors involved in the emergence of religious *cargo* systems are not at all mysterious, but they acquire a special significance when we consider the history of the institution and that the first *cargo* systems were *civil* systems which linked indigenous communities to the colonial Spanish regime. Only in the twentieth century have state and national governments acted to replace colonial forms of local government with new systems more in line with national priorities. The nineteenth century is the least understood period in the ethnohistory of Mesoamerican village politics, but if Ronald Spores's (1984) work on Oaxaca is at all representative, there was surprisingly little change in the structure of local level government during the turbulent years following Mexican Independence. He says:

What may be most remarkable is that despite the great political upheavals of the [nineteenth] century, local level government and relations between local, state, and national levels ended essentially as they began. A practical and basically effective system which evolved during the colonial period survived and persisted through a series of experiments in government (1984: 168).

All this began to change significantly following revolutionary movements in the twentieth century. Drawing on a number of case studies, Richard Adams (1957) has shown that the pivotal events in Guatemala followed on the heels of the Revolution of 1944. The promotion of political parties and competitive local elections brought fundamental changes in community government, among them the weakening and destruction of many civil-religious hierarchies. The corresponding triggering event in Mexico came earlier, in the form of the Revolution of 1910. One of the most important revolutionary products was the Mexican Constitution of 1917 that called for a new system of local political offices, subject to regulation by individual state laws, to replace the older colonial forms.

Especially important were the attempts of the Mexican government to apply the new constitution between 1920 and 1940. Despite the revolutionary rhetoric supporting the concept of the *municipio libre* (the free municipio, or township), the Obregón, Calles, and Cárdenas governments actively sought to limit the autonomy of the local community and integrate it in new ways into national society (see Greenberg *intra*). The formation of a national revolutionary political party in 1929 (The Partido Nacional Revolucionario, precursor of today's Partido Revolucionario Institucional, or PRI) had important repercussions at the local level, even in seemingly remote areas. A federal school system by the state was begun and the anticlericalism of the Calles administration posed a threat to many local ritual traditions. These penetrations into local community spread to different regions of Mexico at different rates, but the general trend is clear and few, if any, villages appear to have remained unaffected. Despite some communities' ability to incorporate the newer political offices into their civil-religious hierarchies (see Table 2.1), many others have failed to do so effectively. Such failure may lead to a total breakdown of a preexisting *cargo* system or to the formation of a religious hierarchy which excludes the new political offices. A common result in either case is a decrease in local level autonomy and an increase in community dependency on state and federal governments. Political brokering by local officials becomes an important source of community income, and individuals who are literate in Spanish and equipped to deal with outsiders respond to these demands. In the process they frequently violate the rules of the civil-religious hierarchy by going quickly to the top of the civil ladder instead of passing through the ranks in the traditional way. Such activity is a sign that tension between the civil and religious spheres of public life has begun to build (in addition to the transitional cases discussed above, see also Kuroda 1984:63, 153; Mathews 1985:291-292; Signorini 1979:93-121; and others cited in DeWalt 1975:95).

Certainly there are exceptions to this trend toward decreasing local autonomy. Lynn Stephen's work (1987; 1988; n.d.) in Teotitlán del Valle suggests that a relatively affluent community able to fund public works projects is less in need of political brokers than are poorer communities. Teotitlán can *afford* to fill civil *cargo* posts with people who are more concerned with local priorities than with external political affairs. Commercial development in this town (centered around the tourist-oriented weaving industry) has led to class tensions between merchant and weaving households, yet class-based criteria for prestige must still compete with those based on community ethnic solidarity. This slower growth of class relations may be due to the fact that Teotitlán's development as a weaving town explicitly builds on its indigenous cultural heritage. Stephen (n.d.) points to a dual ethnic identity in the community: one identity produced for outside consumers of Teotitlán's textiles and indigenous culture (tourists, importers, state officials, etc.), and another defined from within, accessible only to those who participate in local social networks and institutions. This analysis perhaps could be extended to other economically successful tourist and craft communities, but there are not many of them. Overall, the number of indigenous communities able to retain this sort of quasi-independence from government funding is decreasing.

Most twentieth-century civil-religious hierarchies, when confronted with state interference, have adapted by retrenching, by transforming themselves into more overtly religious hierarchies, and by turning inward and emphasizing local ritual matters. Communities that choose this path give up some of their political autonomy, but are apt to retain strong local identities. In other cases, of course, civil-religious hierarchies have failed to adapt to external political pressures and have collapsed altogether.

A number of ethnographers have noted that the *cargo* systems in the villages they studied began to unravel in the 1920s (see, for example, Acheson 1970:245; Foster 1967:194-211; J. Nash 1970:230). The timing is significant, given the pressure exerted on municipalities by the revolutionary governments, as discussed above. Not only does state encroachment drive a wedge between the civil and religious spheres of traditional hierarchies, but it also can polarize them and place them in competition with each other. Kate Young (1976) gives a vivid account of political struggles in a highland Zapotec village in Oaxaca between 1920 and 1940, in which progressive and conservative factions mirrored the civil and religious sides of the *cargo* system. She shows how the PRI, its precursor parties, and the Oaxaca state government, working through local officials, effectively polarized the community for twenty years and ultimately destroyed its civil-religious hierarchy:

> The President at the beginning of the 1920s was always an elderly man (usually near 60); nowadays he is generally in his thirties. The streaming of *cargos*...has also had the effect of channelling the important posts in the village administration to men who tend on the whole to be more oriented toward the national culture. They are also possibly more malleable, that is they are less likely to reject out of hand improvements such as installing a telegraph office. At the same time there is no longer a single system of ranking with which the allocation of prestige is articulated; rather the emphasis on youth, education and wealth is in direct opposition to the former emphasis on age, service to the gods and the fulfillment of obligations to the community.
>
> By taking political power away from the elders, the local administrative apparatus was restructured in such a way as to be more responsive to pressure from the centre—either the state or the federal government. The undermining of the elders' authority also played an important part in freeing people from the bonds of the previous system so that they could participate in the new type of social and economic relations which were developing throughout the period (Young 1976:260-261).

It is important to note that the process Young describes was not an unplanned consequence or by-product of national government reforms, but rather the outcome of deliberate efforts by particular Oaxaca politicians to destroy the traditional hierarchies in this and other villages. Stephen (1987; *intra*) recounts a similar chain of events that unfolded in Teotitlán del Valle during the same period, and further shows how the decline of the *mayordomía* system there was linked to the anti-church policies of the Calles presidency. While Teotitlán's status as a craft village and higher level of market integration make it different in many respects from the poorer highland community described by Young, the exogenous forces penetrating each town in the 1920s were quite similar.

Another significant, if less dramatic, example of polarization between civil and religious sectors comes from Arturo Warman's work in several towns in eastern Morelos. Religious *cargo* systems prevail there, but they are on the defensive—they are important only in small satellite villages which have few civil officials to challenge their authority. *Cabeceras* (municipal head towns) with a full complement of civil officials, and frequently a resident priest as well, have weak religious *cargo* systems. Thus the hierarchies are being driven out of the nodes of formal power in eastern Morelos, and are taking refuge in smaller places where they can partially and informally fill the political vacuum.   In some towns, community *mayordomos* have been replaced by committees and the religious hierarchies have retreated to the level of the *barrio* (neighborhood).   In these instances, autonomy is sacrificed at the community level, but retained at lower levels through fragmentation (Warman 1980:291-293).

While the Oaxaca and Morelos examples have overtones of conflict between church and state, the fundamental contradiction is really between the state and the local community.   In Young's highland Zapotec case, the community lost the battle when its religious hierarchy collapsed in 1940 and out-migration began its upward spiral.   But this is, after all, just a single village.   Teotitlán, more favored economically, has been able to hold its own.   Warman's Morelos study shows that at the regional level the confrontation may proceed slowly and perhaps more gradually.

One of the most elusive aspects of the rise of religious hierarchies is its relationship to the changing distribution of power, both within particular communities and between those communities and the state.   The divorce of civil positions from a *cargo* system does not mean that local power will be concentrated entirely in the hands of the formally constituted civil authorities. The balance of power may indeed tilt toward the civil administration (see Flanet 1977:42-49; Schryer n.d.:317; Olivera 1967:70; Warman 1980:291-293), but some can be expected to remain in the hands of the religious *cargo* holders. The problem lies in determining how the balance is struck.   In Chignautla, Puebla, for example, Slade (1973:221) shows that as far as the indigenous community members are concerned, civil *cargos*–held by *mestizos*–carry authority, but very little legitimacy.   Power in this community is shared by mestizo civil authorities and indigenous community members of high ritual status who have participated in the religious *cargo* system, though Slade does not assign them a relative weighting.

More revealing of trends over time is June Nash's assessment of the balance of power between *principales* and civil officials in Amatenango, Chiapas in the 1960s.   Amatenango retains a civil-religious hierarchy, but it should be understood as "transitional" because there have been important changes.   According to Nash, the *principales* have been rendered nearly powerless in the face of strong support for an independent civil authority. While the overt form of political organization–the civil-religious hierarchy– remains the same, there has been a shift in the balance of power "from leaders whose authority rested on guardianship linked with the ancestors to leaders who can deal with the external power structure"(J. Nash 1970:266).

I would hypothesize that the shift from a civil-religious to a religious *cargo* system can be expected to carry with it a decrease in the power and functions of the *principales*.   The extent of the decrease, and whether or not the *principales* will come to share power with other groups, will vary from town to town, as the comparison of Chignautla with Amatenango suggests.   Another case in point comes from the District of Jamiltepec in Oaxaca, where Mixtec communities support civil-religious hierarchies and powerful groups of elders (De Cicco 1966:372).   In the head town of Jamiltepec itself, however, civil offices are controlled by *mestizos* and the indigenous community members maintain a religious *cargo* system with a much weaker array of elders (Flanet 1977:42-49).[5]

I would further suggest that the replacement of civil-religious hierarchies with religious hierarchies and separate civil offices entails a fragmentation of local power centers and an overall loss of community power vis-à-vis the state. Guillermo de la Peña (1981:240) notes the significant fragmentation which has occurred in Tlayacapan, Morelos (a town with a religious *cargo* system; see Ingham 1986:92-95). Most striking is the multiplicity of agencies in Tlayacapan (and many other Mexican villages) concerned with the maintenance of order, administration of justice, and implementation of public goals. In addition to the *ayuntamiento* (municipal council), there are the *ejido* land committee, the communal land committee, the village auxiliary officers, the public works committee, and the PRI committee. There is also considerable interference by district level officials, including the police, the courts, the district deputy, and the tax collector. According to de la Peña:

> All these agencies compete with one another for control of local environments; and it is only through the dependence on patrons in higher political spheres that a partial (never a total) control over environments is achieved...

> Loyalty and the perception of their own powerlessness are related to the participation by the local authorities in a series of activities which further reinforce their subordination and dependence (1981:240, 245).

Tlayacapan may well represent one extreme on a continuum of local dependency on state and regional structures. It is difficult to say whether de la Peña's analysis would apply to southern communities with religious hierarchies such as Zinacantan. June Nash (1970:265) argues convincingly that while Amatenango has experienced an internal shift in power groups, the town as a whole has ceded little autonomy to external political authorities. But Amatenango is a transitional community, and it is clear that a major instrument for the maintenance of its autonomy is the preservation of its civil-religious hierarchy.

Another possible method of preserving local power, of course, is *cacique* rule. Henning Siverts (1981:53) describes how in Chiapas powerful *caciques* sometimes emerge in communities where parallel indigenous and ladino administrative systems are in conflict. James Dow (personal communication) suggests that *caciquismo* is best adapted to times of war and that a community may oscillate between a *cacique* system and a *cargo* system as conditions change. These are important issues, but necessarily remain beyond the scope of this paper.

It would be erroneous to view religious *cargo* systems in purely expressive terms and deny them a role in village political life. They can perhaps most accurately be seen as part of the process of fragmentation of local power alluded to above. In this sense a religious hierarchy is likely to be just one of several local groups competing for power. From the external point of view, however, it is also clear that the political spoils to be had in such communities are meager. Religious *cargo* systems thus simultaneously constitute a recognition of decreased village autonomy and power relative to the state, as well as an attempt to prevent yet further losses.

CONCLUSION

Preservation of a local *cargo* system of any kind is a conservative strategy, an attempt to assert local autonomy and community identity in the face of external pressures. As national governments penetrate more deeply into community political life, religious *cargo* systems may form to stave off further erosion of village autonomy. Religious hierarchies are at best compromise solutions, at once products of the political penetration of community boundaries and weapons with which to combat further penetration.

Linking ethnography to ethnohistory, it is now possible to sketch the trajectory of structural change in Mesoamerican *cargo* systems over four centuries and observe how they have responded to historical episodes when communities were under particularly heavy pressure from external political and religious authorities. Early *civil cargo* systems, I have argued, were a direct result of the imposition of the Spanish model of town government in indigenous communities in the sixteenth century. They amounted to a reshaping of Spanish offices by indigenous community members to make them fit their own circumstances. These civil hierarchies facilitated colonial economic exploitation from the outside and rechanneled indigenous status aspirations on the inside. At the same time, they helped maintain the indigenous social strata of nobles and commoners that were recognized by the Spanish colonial legal system.

The change from a civil to a *civil-religious* structure was an adaptation to nineteenth-century attacks by government and the church on the corporate property holdings that had supported local religious ceremonies. During this period, household sponsorship of fiestas became institutionalized, while civil and religious offices were fused into a unified ladder of *cargos*. Economic burdens rested more directly on individual households, and the old colonial stratification between nobles and commoners crumbled. This civil-religious structure entailed a new emphasis on internal activities. These systems were more inward-looking, more involved with local ritual and local identity, and less concerned than their civil predecessors with representing the community to the outside (Chance and Taylor 1985).

Finally, in the twentieth century, revolution and political reforms for the first time opposed the whole concept of the politically autonomous indigenous community, and state and federal governments have attempted to incorporate local leadership into higher level bureaucratic and party hierarchies. Where these efforts have been successful, local civil hierarchies have become divorced from religious offices and in a sense have left the community and become appendages of higher-level systems. This process has effectively destroyed many civil-religious hierarchies, but a significant number have adapted by transforming themselves into primarily religious systems. Such changes have meant yet another step inward and a renewed emphasis on internal ritual affairs.

NOTES

Acknowledgments. This is a revised and expanded version of a paper presented at the 86th annual meeting of the American Anthropological Association, Chicago, November 18-22, 1987, as part of a symposium on "The Political Economy of Religion in Mexico and Central America." I wish to thank Frans Schryer for generously providing me with his unpublished manuscript and Frank Cancian, Pedro Carrasco, James Dow, Stephen Gudeman, and Lynn Stephen for their comments on earlier drafts of this paper. Any errors that remain are entirely my own.

1. In some communities, fiesta sponsorship is undertaken not by individuals, but by male and female pairs, often, but not always, consisting of husband and wife (Mathews 1985; Reina 1966; Stephen 1988). This pattern may well represent the norm. I believe most anthropologists would agree, however, that whether sponsorship is undertaken by individuals or by couples, they act as representatives of households.

2. I find it useful to distinguish between a *cargo* system, a hierarchy of ranked offices which individuals or couples ascend, and a fiesta system in which prestige is attained through ceremonial sponsorship in the absence of any fixed hierarchy of positions. *Cargo* systems often involve fiesta sponsorship, especially in the twentieth century, but Taylor and I have argued that colonial civil *cargo* systems lacked this feature (Chance and Taylor 1985).

3. As measured by a high degree of geographical mobility, location near a large city, economic and social ties with large cities, supplementary wage labor in other regions, and variety of transportation facilities (DeWalt 1975:95).

4. Some studies note that the rank order of offices is not well defined or even nonexistent (Chick 1981:227; Dehouve 1976:220-239; Oettinger 1980:99; Slade 1973:106-113). The importance of these observations is unclear. Perhaps a muddled ranking is linked to the growing bifurcation of civil and religious positions.

5. The District of Jamiltepec also seems to exhibit the same sort of polarization between civil and religious authority noted above for eastern Morelos (Warman 1980).

REFERENCES

Acheson, James
    1970 "Where Opportunity Knocked: Social and Economic Change in the Tarascan Pueblo of Cuanajo, Michoacán." Ph.D. dissertation, University of Rochester.
Adams, Richard N.
    1957 "Changing Political Relationships in Guatemala." In *Political Changes in Guatemalan Indian Communities*. Richard N. Adams, editor, pp. 48-54. Middle American Research Institute Publication 24. New Orleans: Tulane University.
Bartolomé, Miguel A. and Alicia M. Barabas
    1982 *Tierra de la palabra: historia y etnografía de los chatinos de Oaxaca*. Mexico City: INAH. Colección Científica No. 108.
Brandes, Stanley
    1988 *Power and Persuasion: Fiestas and Social Control in Rural Mexico*. Philadelphia: University of Pennsylvania Press.
Buchler, Ira R.
    1967 "La organización ceremonial de una aldea mexicana." *América Indígena* 27(2):237-263.
Cancian, Frank
    1965 *Economics and Prestige in a Maya Community: The Religious Cargo System in Zinacantan*. Stanford: Stanford University Press.
    1967 "Political and Religious Organization." In *Handbook of Middle American Indians*, Volume 6. Robert Wauchope, general editor, pp. 283-298. Austin: University of Texas Press.

Carrasco, Pedro
  1952   *Tarascan Folk Religion: An Analysis of Economic, Social, and Religious Interactions.* Middle American Research Institute, Publication 17. New Orleans: Tulane University.
Chance, John K. and William B. Taylor
  1985   "Cofradías and Cargos: An Historical Perspective on the Mesoamerican Civil-Religious Hierarchy." *American Ethnologist* 12(1):1-26.
Chick, Garry E.
  1981   "Concept and Behavior in a Tlaxcalan Cargo Hierarchy." *Ethnology* 20(3):217-228.
De Cicco, Gabriel
  1966   "Systems of Civil Authority in the Mixteca Baja: Patterns and Conflicts." In *Summa anthropologica en homenaje a Roberto J. Weitlaner.* Pp. 371-374. Mexico City: Secretaría de Educación Pública and INAH.
Dehouve, Danièle
  1976   *El tequio de los santos y la competencia entre los mercaderes.* Mexico City: Instituto Nacional Indigenista.
de la Peña, Guillermo
  1981   *A Legacy of Promises.* Austin: University of Texas Press.
DeWalt, Billie R.
  1975   "Changes in the Cargo Systems of Mesoamerica." *Anthropological Quarterly* 48:87-105.
Dow, James
  1977   "Religion in the Organization of a Mexican Peasant Economy." In *Peasant Livelihood: Studies in Economic Anthropology and Cultural Ecology.* Rhoda Halperin and James Dow, editors, pp. 215-226. New York: St. Martin's.
Flanet, Veronique
  1977   *Viveré si Dios quiere.* Mexico City: Instituto Nacional Indigenista.
Foster, George
  1967   *Tzintzuntzan: Mexican Peasants in a Changing World.* Boston: Little, Brown.
Greenberg, James B.
  1981   *Santiago's Sword: Chatino Peasant Religion and Economics.* Berkeley: University of California Press.
Gwaltney, John L.
  1970   *The Thrice Shy.* New York: Columbia University Press.
Ingham, John M.
  1986   *Mary, Michael, and Lucifer: Folk Catholicism in Central Mexico.* Austin: University of Texas Press.
Jones, Grant D.
  1981   "Symbolic Dramas of Ethnic Stratification: The Yucatecan Fiesta System on a Colonial Frontier." *University of Oklahoma Papers in Anthropology* 22(1):131-155.
Kuroda, Etsuko
  1984   "Under Mt. Zempoaltépetl: Highland Mixe Society and Ritual." *Senri Ethnological Studies,* No. 12. Osaka, Japan: National Museum of Ethnology.
Mathews, Holly F.
  1985   "'We are Mayordomo': A Reinterpretation of Women's Roles in the Mexican Cargo System." *American Ethnologist* 12(2):285-301.
Montoya Briones, José de Jesús
  1964   *Atla; etnografía de un pueblo náhuatl.* Mexico City: INAH.
Nash, June
  1970   *In the Eyes of the Ancestors.* New Haven: Yale University Press.
Nash, Manning
  1958   "Political Relations in Guatemala." *Social and Economic Studies* 7:65-75.
Nutini, Hugo G.
  1968   *San Bernardino Contla.* Pittsburgh: University of Pittsburgh Press.

Oettinger, Marion
    1980 *Una comunidad tlapaneca.* Mexico City: Instituto Nacional Indigenista.
Olivera de V., Mercedes
    1967 *Tlaxcalancingo.* Mexico City: INAH, Departamento de Investigaciones Antropológicos, Pub. No. 18.
Reina, Ruben E.
    1966 *The Law of the Saints.* Indianapolis: Bobbs-Merrill.
Schryer, Frans J.
    n.d. "Class Conflict and Ethnicity in Rural Mexico: Peasant Revolt in a Nahua Region." Unpublished manuscript. University of Guelph, Canada.
Signorini, Italo
    1979 *Los Huaves de San Mateo del Mar.* Mexico City: Instituto Nacional Indigenista.
Siverts, Henning
    1981 "Stability and Change in Highland Chiapas, Mexico." *University of Bergen, Occasional Papers in Social Anthropology*, No. 4. Bergen, Norway.
Slade, Doren L.
    1973 "The Mayordomos of San Mateo: Political Economy of a Religious System." Ph.D. dissertation, University of Pittsburgh.
Smith, Waldemar R.
    1977 *The Fiesta System and Economic Change.* New York: Columbia University Press.
Spores, Ronald
    1984 "Multi-Level Government in Nineteenth-Century Oaxaca." In *Five Centuries of Law and Politics in Central Mexico.* Ronald Spores and Ross Hassig, editors, pp. 145-172. Nashville: Vanderbilt University Publications in Anthropology, No. 30.
Stephen, Lynn
    1987 *Weaving Changes: Economic Development and Gender Roles in Zapotec Ritual and Production.* Ph.D. dissertation, Brandeis University. Ann Arbor: University Microfilms.
    1988 "Zapotec Gender Politics: The Creation of Political Arenas by and for Peasant Women." Paper presented at the 87th annual meeting of the American Anthropological Association, November 16-20, Phoenix, Arizona.
    n.d. "Culture as a Resource: Four Cases of Self-Managed Indigenous Craft Production." *Economic Development and Cultural Change*. In Press.
Tedlock, Barbara
    1982 *Time and the Highland Maya.* Albuquerque: University of New Mexico Press.
Warman, Arturo
    1980 *We Come to Object.* Baltimore: Johns Hopkins University Press.
Young, Kate
    1976 "The Social Setting of Migration." Ph.D. dissertation, London University.
Zantwijk, R.A.M. Van
    1967 *Servants of the Saints.* Assen, The Netherlands: Van Gorcum.

CHAPTER THREE

The Politics of Ritual: The Mexican State and Zapotec Autonomy, 1926-1989.

Lynn Stephen
Northeastern University

Since the writing of the 1917 Constitution, the Mexican state has actively tried to shake the power and presence of the Catholic church at all levels of Mexican society. In 1988, not surprisingly, the maintenance of a secular state was one of the main demands of the Corriente Democratico, which led a left-of-center opposition campaign against PRI presidential candidate and now president, Salinas de Gortari. The ways in which religion still informs both national and local politics are also deeply woven into the local histories of peasant communities. As seen in the case of Teotitlán del Valle and other Oaxacan communities highlighted here, municipal archives reveal an ongoing battle between local authorities, state level political parties, governors, national officials, and peasants to control the nature of religious institutions and ritual participation in peasant communities. Local interpretations and reshaping of national policy, however, often result in unintended consequences and institutional forms which can subvert the state's goal of centralization and furthering the integration of indigenous populations into a national identity.

One of the best documented areas of peasant community and state interaction is the decline of *mayordomías* associated with the religious hierarchies in civil-religious *cargo* systems. The historical events which brought about the decline of *mayordomías* in some Oaxacan communities included: (1) the appointment beginning in 1926 of local church committees as part of civil municipal governments, bringing local churches and their property under direct state control, and (2) political campaigns by local branches of the national party in the 1920s and 1930s to eliminate obligatory *mayordomías* in the name of progressive economic change. These events, as well as the particular details of local history, help explain the current structure and function of ritual activity and institutions in indigenous communities.

Here changes in local religious organization among the Zapotec of central Oaxaca emphasize the mediating roles of religious institutions in ongoing tensions between class differentiation and local ethnic solidarity. The discussion highlights postrevolutionary local and national political and economic events which changed the basis for ritual institutionalization and participation in Teotitlán del Valle. In this community, the steady decline of *mayordomías* has not resulted in a lack of ritual activities and the secularization of cultural activities. Instead, the decline of *mayordomía* activity in Teotitlán has been accompanied by a transfer of the ritual form, content, and supporting institutions of *mayordomías* to life cycle ritual events such as weddings, baptisms, engagement ceremonies, and funerals.

The institutions which supported a rich *mayordomía* system, such as kin-*compadrazgo* networks[1] and reciprocal forms of exchange, have been maintained and perhaps even strengthened through this reworking of *mayordomía* ritual content in Teotitlán. As such, they stand in stark contrast to local merchant enterprises which (because they accumulate capital) are tangible reminders of political authority backed by money and property, standards which resonate with national class-based and secular definitions of power and importance. The presence of kin-based ritual activity in the context of economic differentiation links the entire community in reciprocal relationships which crosscut class conflicts based in the relations of weaving production. Such a process can provide a basis for community autonomy and, if circumstances are ripe, a basis for local political organization, as suggested in the case of Juchitán, Oaxaca. I will begin my discussion by outlining the role of the postrevolutionary Mexican nation-state in restructuring religious hierarchies and campaigning against *mayordomías*.

COMMUNITY RESPONSE TO STATE INTERVENTION AND THE ANTI-*MAYORDOMIA* CAMPAIGN OF THE 1920s

As described by Chance and Taylor (1985), civil-religious hierarchies, that is, a system of ranked civil and religious administrative offices, were a post-independence development of the nineteenth century. This system, called traditional in most anthropological texts, administered the community's civil affairs through one side. The other side of the hierarchy regulated the ritual life of the community. While many local churches were staffed by priests, the ritual calendar of the community was organized by a group of *mayordomos*, pairs of men and women who either volunteered or were appointed by village elders to sponsor the cult feasts (*mayordomías*) for the saints and virgins in the village's pantheon of gods (Mathews 1985). While the civil offices[2] of the hierarchy were tied to the state through their functions, such as census taking, tax collection, and negotiation for state funds and resources, the religious offices in the hierarchy remained under the exclusive control of the community. Shortly after the Mexican Revolution, however, the autonomy of local religious administration was challenged by state intervention. Ritual sponsorship, which translated into political authority and leadership outside of official administrative structures, could only be controlled through eliminating ritual sponsorship in the form of *mayordomías* and bringing all aspects of religious leadership under state control.

Since Mexican independence, the church and the state had been locked in a struggle fueled by the large amounts of wealth and land accumulated by the church throughout the colonial period. By the time the Revolution was over, the national state's struggle was no longer to cut back the wealth of the church which had already lost large quantities of land. Instead, the focus of state policy was explicitly to loosen the ideological control of the church over Mexican citizens. The attack which was launched against the Catholic church by the postrevolutionary state was more serious than any previous exhibition of anticlericalism. It threatened the survival of the Catholic church as a major influence in the lives of all Mexicans, urban populations and rural peasants alike.

As noted by historians, the Mexican Constitution of 1917 is a hallmark in the state's relationship with peasant communities. The 1917 document called for a new system of political offices subject to control by individual state laws. These are the civil offices associated with the *ayuntamiento* (government) and *juzgado mayor* (judicial branch) of all community governance systems (see note 2). The constitution also contained several blatantly anticlerical articles and regulations for how local churches were to be administered. When these articles were enforced under the Calles administration in 1926, they not only caused major changes in the structure of the Catholic church in Mexico, but profoundly altered the state's relationship with ritual institutions in indigenous communities. Additional government decrees by Calles obligating communities to organize secular *juntas vecinales* to care for churches placed community ritual activity under direct state power in 1926.

Under the Calles administration, the national government strictly limited the powers of the Catholic church. Article Three declared that instruction in all public institutions be free and secular. In addition, no religious corporation or member of the clergy was allowed to establish or direct a primary school. Article Five prohibited monastic orders, while Article Twenty-four declared that the government had the right to supervise public worship. Article Thirty gave each state legislature the authority to determine the number of clergy permitted in its territory, specified that only Mexican nationals could practice religious professions, prohibited members of the clergy from holding public office, voting, or assembling for public purposes, and outlawed the construction of new churches without government consent. Under Article Twenty-seven, all places of public worship and other properties used for religious purposes were defined as property of the state. The same article prohibited religious institutions from owning land (Archivo del Estado 1926a:1-4; Brown 1969:115).

Beyond the constitutional articles of prohibition, Calles issued a decree in July 1926 that stipulated penalties for noncompliance with the anticlerical articles of the 1917 constitution. The decree severely undercut the position of the Catholic church in Mexico and was met with active opposition from many quarters both within the church hierarchy and within rural and urban communities (see Quirk 1973; Bailey 1974). While clerical compliance with the decree varied from place to place, Rome supported the active resistance of Mexican bishops, and on August 1, 1926, no priest mounted the altar (Bailey 1974:82). The standoff between the Catholic church and the state lasted for three years, and many of Mexico's churches closed down.

The action of the priests was an opening for local communities to demonstrate their resistance to the anticlerical policies of the Calles administration. Within a few days of the August 1, 1926 action, Catholics began to take up arms. In the states of Zacatecas, Jalisco, Michoacan, Naryarit, Puebla, and in a few places in Oaxaca, groups of armed men rebelled against Calles in what is known as the movement of Cristo Rey (Quirk 1973:188). The state of Jalisco was the center of the movement.

While most communities in Oaxaca were not a part of the Cristo Rey rebellion, they were strongly affected by the Calles decree which had prompted it. In some indigenous peasant communities, local churches were not under the direct control of local priests. They were run primarily by local *mayordomos* and ritual practitioners who hired the services of a priest when needed. In other cases, local priests were constantly competing with the administrative powers of local elders (former *mayordomos* who had a long record of ritual sponsorship). Greenberg (*intra*) describes a contemporary version of this power dynamic. While communities such as Teotitlán did not participate directly in the uprising, they no doubt were affected by local news about the uprising and the fact that large numbers of peasants in neighboring Chiapas were participating in armed resistance. Trade routes taken by local muleteers and traders brought significant numbers of people from the community into frequent contact with indigenous communities in Chiapas.[3] In contrast to the Cristeros of Chiapas, however, the forms of resistance in Teotitlán were more subtle and involved noncompliance with the mandates of the governor of Oaxaca, specifically around increased government control of the administration of churches.

In 1926, the Calles government ordered municipalities to create *juntas vecinales* (neighborhood committees) as part of a new municipal structure. This move had a lasting effect on the organization of ritual in some communities, as it set up an alternate administrative structure for local churches which in actuality were run by *mayordomos* and former *mayordomos* who were village elders. Correspondence from the Teotitlán archives indicates that community officials appointed the first *junta vecinal* in 1926 in response to an order by the governor of Oaxaca. A letter from 1927, written by the *presidente* of Teotitlán to the governor of Oaxaca, states that members of the newly named *junta vecinal* refused to take on their new *cargos* until receiving a new order, in writing, from the government of Oaxaca (Archivo Municipal de Teotitlán del Valle, 1927). In 1928, a national government order circulated by the governor of Oaxaca outlined the exact duties of the newly formed committees, including overseeing the inventory of objects belonging to the churches and the expenditure of alms collected on altars (Archivo Municipal de Teotitlán del Valle, 1928). By the early 1930s, the *junta vecinal* became a branch of the local government system in Teotitlán, appointed on a rotating basis like civil *cargos*. Now called the *comité de la iglesia*, it still manages the church and also organizes major celebrations for community saints, a task done formerly by *mayordomos*.

While the creation of *juntas vecinales* to administer local churches did not appear to be designed specifically to compete with the duties of *mayordomos*, in reality it did, particularly when piggybacked with a political strategy on the part of several Oaxaca governors to control autonomous religious organization in the form of *mayordomías*. My ethnohistorical research in Teotitlán del Valle, Kate Young's work in the Sierra Juarez, and a review of correspondence to the governor in the Oaxaca version of the national government's news organ (*Periódico Oficial*) suggest that the Oaxaca state government used local branches of political parties to carry out an anti-*mayordomía* campaign as well as to oppose *mayordomías* in official Oaxaca state media. If *mayordomías* could be eliminated, then the basis for ritually-based political power in indigenous communities also could be undermined.

An item in the *Periódico Oficial* of 1926 provides an interesting glimpse into state policy on *mayordomías* (Archivo del Estado 1926b:27-28). The headline reads "Memorandum from the Municipal Authorities of San Juan, Teitipác, Tlacolula Asking the Governor of the State to Dictate Measures Conducive to the Suppression of Mayordomías." The interchange suggests, as in Young's case described below, that some local officials seeking to align themselves with the anti-*mayordomía* line of the official party were using *mayordomías* as a political issue to further their own careers. The governor's official response is instructive here as it reveals his position on *mayordomías*. The memorandum complained about the fact that village authorities of Teitipác had to carry out annual festivities associated with their office. They pleaded for permission to eliminate *mayordomías* altogether:

> ...given that such customs ruin the scarce patrimony which they (municipal authorities) have and leave them in conditions even more disastrous so that next year they will constitute a weight for our families and for society (my translation).[4]

The response from governor Genaro Vasquez clarified the Oaxaca state's position on *mayordomías*. He said:

> I see with satisfaction the proposition which you have to rectify the customs in our towns which produce ruin or stagnancy of the moral and economic patrimony of the community (my translation).[5]

The Oaxaca government's apparent anti-*mayordomía* policy in conjuntion with the restructuring of the municipal administrative structure seems to have been aimed at limiting the autonomy of indigenous peasant communities. An informed strategy for limiting political autonomy would have taken into consideration ritually-based positions of power such as those emanating from the sponsorship of *mayordomías* which translated into permanent political status as community elders. The breaking down of *mayordomías* did result in a considerable realignment of local power and limitation of community autonomy in some cases, such as in the Sierra Zapotec community described by Kate Young. In Teotitlán, which underwent a similar sequence of events, the outcome of the anti-*mayordomía* campaign was somewhat different because of the specific political economy of the *mayordomía* system which was heavily tied into local peonage. There the elimination of obligatory *mayordomías* had the unintended result of also eliminating economic inequality tied to the ritual system. The two cases are compared below.

In her doctoral thesis, Young vividly describes a community's struggle over the abolition of the *mayordomía* system. The struggle was strongly influenced by the desire of a regional political *cacique*, Ibarra, to end the institution of *mayordomía*. In 1925, a faction of young men who fought under Isaac Ibarra returned to their native Sierra Zapotec town determined to abolish the *mayordomía* system in their community. Their mentor, Ibarra, was governor of Oaxaca briefly in 1924 and then a local *cacique* and Federal Deputy (Young 1976). He was always closely linked with the Calles administration. Young writes that this faction of young men aligned with Ibarra echoed the federal government's advice to peasants at this time, suggesting that the proceeds of *mayordomía tequios* (work parties) would be better spent on building a cooperative store than squandered on feasting and drinking (Young 1976:249).

The message also was reflected clearly in the agenda of state-sponsored political parties. The battle over *mayordomías* which Young describes took place largely within the local political system. The goal of the young followers of Ibarra was to take over municipal offices in order to control community ritual policy. When village elders attempted to bring the young leader of the anti-*mayordomía* Ibarra faction into line by making him undertake an expensive *cargo,* he refused, and the local *presidente* (mayor) put him in jail. Ibarra, however, severely reprimanded the *presidente*, threatening him with imprisonment for unlawful arrest. As a result of this political intervention, Young reports, the elders lost considerable authority (Young 1976:250).

During this same time, local politicians encouraged some of the followers of Ibarra to form a branch of the national political party, the *Partido Nacional Revolucionario.* Ibarra's followers joined with members of the PNR to organize a revolt against church tithes and first fruits. In 1939, the original leader of the young followers of Ibarra (who was previously jailed) was elected municipal president. After consulting with the then governor of Oaxaca, Chapital, he decreed that there were to be no *mayordomías*. The announcement resulted in an armed confrontation between pro- and anti-*mayordomía* factions in the community. Ultimately, the accepted resolution called for voluntary *mayordomías* (Young 1976:254).

While a similar sequence of events occurred in Teotitlán, the outcome differed significantly. Opposition to *mayordomías*, which was part of the platform of the local branch of the ruling national political party, coincided with widespread local discontent based on debt peonage associated with the forced appointment of *mayordomos* for fiesta sponsorship. The elimination of *mayordomías* occurred as a result of a popular demand in Teotitlán reinforced by external politics. It was not simply imposed by aspiring local authorities affiliated with Ibarra and the Calles administration as occurred in the Sierra case described by Young. In fact, resistance to terminating *mayordomías* was carried out primarily by a small group of large landholders who were profiting from indebted local peasants who took out large loans to finance their *mayordomía* expenses and worked off their debts as contracted laborers.

In Teotitlán, as in the Sierra Juarez community described by Young, obligatory *mayordomías* were causing high levels of tension by the 1920s. Economic resources were scarce after the Mexican Revolution. Many people faced certain economic hardship when they were forced to make the expenditures associated with sponsorship of a local saint. In Teotitlán, future *mayordomos* often sold their land or indentured themselves or their children to local merchants (1987:66-68). This situation made obligatory *mayordomía* ripe as a political issue in the community.

In 1926, the *Partido Socialista* of Oaxaca formed a small branch in Teotitlán (Stephen 1987:71). In 1929, this branch became a part of the *Partido Nacional Revolucionario* (precursor to the PRI), the same party Young mentions in association with a local confrontation over *mayordomías*. The party was blatantly anticlerical and urged all members to liberate themselves from the oppression of church control in Teotitlán. Although the *Partido Socialista* and the later *Partido Nacional Revolucionario* never gained a wide base of support in Teotitlán, their demands for an end to *mayordomías* had a major impact on community politics and ritual organization. People, primarily from younger households and who had not yet been appointed *mayordomos*, supported the demand for an end to obligatory *mayordomías*. They had not yet served as *mayordomos* and wanted to avoid going into debt from ceremonial expenses. Village elders, those who had already made the personal sacrifices necessary to be *mayordomos*, and merchants who profited from the hasty sale of land and indentured labor, however, opposed ending obligatory *mayordomía*.

After 1928, many couples appointed as *mayordomos* by the municipal president of Teotitlán refused to carry out their sponsorship duties, declining to pay for and organize the rituals and fiestas for which they were responsible. As a result, the municipal president of Teotitlán declared an end to obligatory *mayordomía* in 1931. Community elders and local merchant families protested, but they were soon overruled by the majority of the community. The community demand for voluntary *mayordomías,* which began in the early 1930s, resulted in the continuance of most *mayordomía* posts until the 1960s when they began to decline in number and frequency.

While the cases of Teotitlán, Teitipác, and Young's Sierra Juarez community are limited in scope, they do nevertheless provide evidence of the interest that the postrevolutionary Mexican state had in controlling community religious and ritual institutions by attempting to structure ritual organization into municipal governments and by actively opposing the continuation of *mayordomía* sponsorship. The case of Teotitlán is important in that while official federal and state policy advocated an end to *mayordomías* in all forms, obligatory or voluntary, the community of Teotitlán opted to continue with voluntary *mayordomías*. The nature of the community's resistance to and reworking of both federal and Oaxaca state policy designed to limit local political autonomy following the Mexican Revolution is important in understanding the more contemporary dynamics of community/state interaction which focus on economic as well as religious and political institutions.

THE ECONOMICS OF RESISTANCE:
EXPORT PRODUCTION, "INDIAN" IDENTITY, AND LOCAL AUTONOMY

State initiated policies regarding the functioning of local municipal governments can influence the ways in which religious hierarchies and ritual institutions function, but local level politics, economics, and history are equally important in structuring and restructuring religious institutions. In the case of Teotitlán del Valle, the expansion of the weaving industry from production for regional and local use to production for export has had a major impact on the ways in which the community responded to state efforts to control ritual authority through the civil government and limit the institution of *mayordomías*. The steady influx of cash which has come with the export of weavings has been invested in public works and local ceremonial life. An abundance of economic resources has decreased the community's dependence on the Oaxaca state government for basic infrastructure and resources. This in turn has limited the amount of political brokering the community must do to survive. Because of the nature of their economic production, however, the community became subject to other forms of state intervention beyond that described above.

Beginning in the late 1950s and 1960s, Teotitlán, along with other artisan communities, became the object of government development efforts as the indigenous identity reflected in craft products was packaged for sale to make Oaxaca attractive to tourists (Stephen 1987: 154-169). As the market for Teotiteco weavings moved toward export orientation in the 1980s, foreign importers and entrepreneurs joined state development officials in a campaign to define and publicize genuine Zapotec culture. This consisted of a continuous link with the past in which weaving production, ritual, and other traditions remained basically undisturbed by the passage of time. Teotitecos were active participants in this process, albeit with a different agenda from that of the state and foreign entrepreneurs.

The commoditization of indigenous culture also had a community-based dynamic. In the case of Teotitlán, the international marketing of local ethnicity, along with the long reach of the PRI and the national government into community politics, has prompted the redirection of most ritual activity to life cycle ceremonies. At a larger level this can be seen as due to the high level of financial resources present in the community and the cumulative results of state intrusion on local religious institutions. What is unique about this redirection of ritual activity is that life cycle ceremonies have not become increasingly privatized and secular. Instead, they have grown into large, public events which incorporate the very elements which made *mayordomías* into truly community-wide rituals. Although *mayordomías* were sponsored by pairs of individual men and women, usually but not always the heads of households, the extensive labor exchanges involved in carrying out the necessary ritual activities and accompanying feasting and dancing pulled together extended networks of kin and *compadres*. Now these same networks are mobilized in the name of celebrating weddings, funerals, birthdays, baptisms, and engagements along with the food, liquor, music, and dancing which accompanied them in *mayordomías*.

At a more abstract level, the transfer of *mayordomía* ritual content and form to life cycle events can be viewed as part of a continued effort on the part of indigenous communities such as Teotitlán to limit outside control of community political, economic, and ritual institutions (see Varese 1982, 1986; Bartolome y Barabas 1977; Barabas y Bartolome 1986; Garcia Canclini 1982; Bonfil Batalla 1981). While communities such as Teotitlán may attempt to preserve their autonomy, such efforts do not necessarily coincide with the existence of an egalitarian ethic within the community which prohibits individual accumulation of wealth and the use of wealth and entrepreneurial ability as a basis for claiming political authority. Both community solidarity and a process of economic differentiation can exist simultaneously. Significant wealth differences do exist within Teotitlán that are becoming important bases for contesting political authority based in ritual experience (Stephen n.d.b).

What the case of Teotitlán does signal is that even within the context of emerging class differences, communities can also sustain a local indigenous identity. In this case, the identity of Teotitlán Zapotec stands in opposition to state- sponsored "Indian" identities created for the sake of nationalism and the promotion of tourism. The reinforcement of life cycle rituals in the form and content of the fading *mayordomía* system is a part of a self-generated local Zapotec identity.

THE REDIRECTION OF RITUAL:
FROM *MAYORDOMIAS* TO LIFE CYCLE EVENTS

To facilitate a discussion of the integration of ritual activity identified with *mayordomías* into life cycle celebrations in Teotitlán, we need to place the household into a wider context with two networks of social interaction: (1) the "official" public network of the community, and (2) kin-*compadrazgo* networks. The first involves individuals appointed to *cargo* posts encompassing religious, legal, and local governing activities. This group is articulated with the state through the municipal government structure and is represented to visitors, both government bureaucrats and tourists, as the "formal" authority of the community. The second concerns networks which are mobilized through reciprocal labor exchanges every time a ritual event is sponsored by the municipal government or, most often, by individual households. Included at this level are ritual specialists such as *huehuetes*, who are called on to officiate based on their kin-*compadrazo* relationships with the initiators of the rituals.

Kin-*compadrazgo* networks work to support the "official" public network of the community most often presented to outsiders and government officials. Both of these networks are coordinated through the household which is the basis for recruitment into kin-*compadrazgo* networks and is also the source of men appointed to official *cargo* posts. As explained below, the labor of women and children replaces male labor lost to *cargos* and is also extremely important in the reciprocal labor exchanges which characterize kin-*compadrazgo* networks.

The household is a basic building block for the official public face of the community (the civil hierarchy of the municipal government) and kin-*compadrazgo* networks which support all ritual activity. While individual males are named to civil *cargo* positions, the entire household supports these positions through making up the domestic labor of the absent male as well as through providing additional labor for ceremonial events (Stephen 1987:62-63). Through the mobilization of labor in reciprocal labor exchanges based in extended kin and *compadrazgo* networks, the household is also the unit of ritual participation. When invitations are made to ceremonial events, people are invited by household. Ideally, at least one male and one female member provide labor for ritual events to which their household is invited. In reality, invited women end up working many more hours in ritual events than invited men. As such, the household is the basic unit of participation in both *mayordomías* and life cycle rituals.

While some 50 years have passed since the postrevolutionary Oaxacan state reorganized the structure of municipal government and tried to ban *mayordomías*, more recent intervention has focused on promotion of indigenous culture through advertising handicrafts and "traditional" rituals still to be found in Oaxaca's villages. Indigenous culture is a major drawing card for tourists in Oaxaca as well as in other parts of Mexico. In the process of attracting tourists to indigenous communities, local fiestas become public spectacles available for touristic consumption (Garcia Canclini 1982; Stephen n.d.a). In towns like Teotitlán del Valle, known for production of handloomed weavings, local ritual is an attraction for tourists and United States craft importers who use descriptions of local ceremonies to help market Mexican indigenous crafts in the United States and Europe (Stephen 1988a).

In Teotitlán, the rise in tourism in the 1950s overlapped with a gradual decline in the sponsorship of voluntary *mayordomías* which began in the 1930s. Sponsorship of cult celebrations for saints and virgins in Teotitlán continued through the 1950s, but by 1960 only six or seven *mayordomías* were functioning. By the 1970s that was reduced to four. Only two of the *mayordomías*, including the largest one, are currently active in Teotitlán. Most of the celebrations formerly associated with *mayordomías* are carried out by the *comité del templo* which appoints special committees to take up community collections to cover the costs of food, drink, dancing, music, and fireworks associated with the rituals. The *comité del templo*, begun under the Calles administration as a *junta vecinal*, is part of an effort to bring ritual leadership into the state-controlled civil sphere.

Catherine Good (1988) notes a similar pattern in the Nahua community of Ameyaltepec in Guerrero where craft production in the form of *amate* paper paintings has also resulted in an influx of wealth into the community. Like Teotitlán, Ameyaltepec retains only a small number of *mayordomos* and most Saints' days festivities are funded not individually, but cooperatively by tithing each household. Good notes that people recirculate a significant part of the profits they earn from marketing their paintings through the fiesta system.

In communities like Teotitlán and Ameyaltepec, where cult celebrations for local saints and virgins are no longer purely local affairs because of the continued presence of nonindigenous outsiders (tourists, importers, and government officials), such rituals are only part of the way in which local ethnic identity is celebrated. While Teotitlán has long served as a ritual center and indigenous peoples from other communities have attended local celebrations, the presence of nonindigenous outsiders has pushed expressions of ethnicity into more protected parts of community life not usually analyzed by ethnographers in relation to ritual. In fact it is the not-so-obvious mobilization of kin-*compadrazgo* networks that today forms an important part of local ethnic identity in Teotitlán and contains the seeds of ethnic solidarity.

Historically, such networks were not analyzed seriously by anthropologists because they included women and children, and because their activities were not emphasized publically. These networks are behind the "official" public network associated with individual males who, in name, hold positions of authority in civil and religious hierarchies. A focus on individual males not only led to a misunderstanding of the gendered aspects of ritual authority, but also rendered invisible much of the support structure which held together *mayordomías* and other ceremonial events. As is now well documented, women are key actors in these support structures and are granted authority on the basis of their participation (Mathews 1985; Chiñas 1987; Sault 1988; Stephen n.d.b; Warman 1980). In Teotitlán this continues to be the case in relation to life cycle events.

The fact that such networks materialize only during ritual events obscures their presence to outsiders who are not avid participants in the local ritual system. The continued presence of such networks and of economic systems of reciprocal exchange such as *guelaguetza*[6] in Oaxaca point to the resilience of the core institutions of the *mayordomía* system (see Diskin 1986). In some communities these institutions continue to service life cycle and other types of rituals such as celebrations for household saints, *posadas*, and *cuelgas* for the completion of a new home. Similarly, Warman describes several communities in Morelos in which large ritual expenditures and extensive social networks support reciprocal relationships of varying types and intensity, even though the *mayordomía* system has disappeared (1980:293). In her description of fiesta activities in Ameyaltepec, Good notes that, in addition to the official religious structure, a wide range of ceremonial activities which also operates in the context of an extensive web of socioeconomic relations, encompassing the entire community (1988).

Research into the size and duration of life cycle rituals in Teotitlán reveals that they became progressively longer and that consumption of food, drink, and music increased as the number of regularly celebrated *mayordomías* decreased (Stephen 1987). Celebrations such as birthdays, graduations, and confirmations, which formerly included only immediate family and godparents, now include large numbers of people. Such occasions also include the use of ritual speech, seating arrangements, dancing, and other activities formerly associated with *mayordomías*. Life cycle rituals such as elopement ceremonies, weddings, and funerals which involved ritual etiquette similar to that used in *mayordomías* continue to do so and have grown considerably in size since the 1960s. The influx of wealth into the community from weaving production beginning in the 1960s gave people more disposable income, some of which went into increased ritual consumption. Older informants discussing the expenses associated with the weddings of their children (expenses documented in *guelaguetza* notebooks) noted that with each successive child, parents were spending greater amounts of money and inviting more people in order to keep up with local standards. Parents recalled their own weddings as simple, one-day ceremonies with one ritual meal for ten people. Weddings currently involve hundreds of people celebrating for three days to two weeks. While such large wedding celebrations were occasionally held in the past by the rich, they are now a standard form.[7]

The incorporation of ritual form, content, and kin-*compadrazgo* networks associated with *mayordomías* into formerly simple life cycle events results in the creation of a public ritual space which is inaccessible to outsiders. This domestically identified yet "public" ritual space is clearly differentiated from the "public" space in the plaza accessible to all who enter the community. The space in the plaza is associated with the official public network of the community represented by local officials who hold civil *cargos,* in contrast to the public space created in life cycle rituals which is identified with kin-*compadrazgo* networks (Stephen n.d.b). A group of up to 200 people gathered in a household plot to celebrate a *mayordomía* or a large life cycle ritual is not just a domestic constellation. Membership in the group depends on the particular kin and *compadrazgo* ties of the sponsoring household. The resulting network represents different segments of the community and functions as a working group from three days to two weeks, working and celebrating together. The mobilization of this group towards a specific purpose results in the temporary creation of a public space for the duration of the ritual event.

FROM RITUAL TO POLITICS:
LOCAL RELIGIOUS INSTITUTIONS AND THE POLITICAL PROCESS

At the local level, the continued mobilization of kin-*compadrazgo* networks for life cycle events or other types of ceremonies results in an extra-domestic grouping which serves not only as a labor force for a particular ritual event, but as a potential focus for other types of activities, often political. In Teotitlán and many communities such networks are primary channels for political dialogue, and discussions at ceremonial events can be crucial in shaping local politics. Such networks also have the potential to provide underlying structures for social and political movements. Political mobilization in Oaxaca, particularly in municipal elections in Juchitán, also suggests the importance of ritually based networks of kin and *compadres* in the political process. This brings the dialogue on religion full circle, as peasant communities use their strongest institutions, often religious in nature, to facilitate the process of local opposition to state candidates and policies. I will discuss this process briefly by referring primarily to the case of Juchitán, a Zapotec town in the Isthmus. The case provides an illustration of how the politicization of ritual networks and the generation of opposition movements could work in settings such as Teotitlán.

The study of grassroots political movements shows that political organizations are more often than not built on existing networks, not through the creation of new ones. In an analysis of factors which contribute to grassroots organizing in Third World as well as western countries, Fox (1987) suggests that the prospects for democratic mobilization are most favorable in circumstances where distinct forms of self-identification overlap and reinforce one another (interests of locality, class, gender, ethnicity, religion, etc.). In a similar vein, Evans and Boyte emphasize the importance of "free spaces"— environments in which people can develop group identity and cooperation and learn public skills. They suggest religious organizations, clubs, mutual aid societies, and ethnic groups as such environments (1986:17-18).

The notion of political "free space" built around ritual and religious institutions is also suggested by Long and Roberts. Their work in Peru's Mantaro Valley revealed that the same kin-*compadrazgo* networks are used to organize fiestas and to mobilize political support (1978:311). In a different study of capitalist transition in the Mantaro valley, Florencia Mallon describes how relations of reciprocity and ritual kinship united disparate community factions. Although such alliances were fragile, she suggests that they did produce community cohesion in a context of merchant capitalism where villagers provided money, goods, and labor to the commercial economy (1983:33). In both Peruvian cases, participation in kin networks and reciprocal forms of exchanges provided a counter-balance to community divisions and channels for political activity.

The case of the COCEI (Isthmus Coalition of Workers, Peasants, and Students) in Juchitán, Oaxaca carries the integration of ritual networks and political mobilization a step further than that seen in the Mantaro valley in Peru. In Zapotec Juchitán, channels of ethnic solidarity and ritual networks have been critical in building a political opposition movement. During the 1970s, the COCEI fought for better living and working conditions, using primarily direct action tactics. In the 1980s, the COCEI has twice won offices in municipal elections (Rubin 1987:127). Rubin, who has analyzed the development of the COCEI into a mass organization, maintains that "class consciousness and support for the COCEI developed through ongoing, daily discussions over the course of years in family courtyards, in the context of fiestas and social obligations..." (1987:136).

Rubin is not the first to note the central role of ethnicity in the creation of the COCEI (see Lopez Monjardin 1983 and de la Cruz 1984). However, social scientists and Mexican politicians have been baffled by the the COCEI's success in using ethnicity as an organizing tool. My observations, along with Rubin's fieldwork, suggest that the kin and *compadrazgo* networks mobilized in Juchitán for fiestas, the form of the fiesta itself, and multi-class neighborhoods along with the physical layout of courtyards were key factors in the development of the COCEI as a large, independent leftist movement in the Isthmus.

In Juchitán, kin-*compadrazgo* networks provide not only a basis for organizing the rich ceremonial system focused on the celebration of *velas* –cult celebrations of neighborhood saints (see Binford *intra*)–but also channels for family and neighborhood politicization. Juchitán has 27 *velas* which are identified with saints, particular sites, occupations, and family names (Peterson-Royce 1975:143). The *vela* association is a corporate group from which a member household is chosen to sponsor annual *vela* celebrations. The sponsor takes a major planning and financial role in activities associated with the annual celebration. In addition to the celebration of *velas*, people in

Juchitán also participate extensively in lavish life cycle rituals, similar to those described for Teotitlán (see Chiñas 1983, 1987).

While the networks mobilized for *vela* and life cycle fiestas are not identical to the patterns of COCEI loyalty (some family members side with and others against the COCEI), they are a primary vehicle for political discussion and organizing (Rubin, personal communication). People in particular *velas* do not necessarily align with one political candidate or party. In contrast, Binford (*intra*) found that in communities outside of Juchitán, particular *velas* have taken on a complete political identity and have become associated with specific parties and candidates.

In Juchitán, COCEI political activities also use the form and content of local fiestas to promote ethnic and political solidarity. The use of fiesta dress, particularly by women, the Zapotec language, and the presence of ritual music, food, and gifts are a given at many COCEI political events. The COCEI has used preexisting ritual networks, and ritual form and content, as tools for forging a political opposition movement which has pulled together diverse sectors of the peasant and working population in Juchitán. The existence of Zapotec ritual channels, social groups, and forms has been critical to the success of the COCEI.

Juchitán is similar to Teotitlán, particularly in the number and sumptuousness of its ritual celebrations and the strength of its kin-*compadrazgo* networks. Both communities retain a strong sense of local ethnic solidarity in the context of increasing class differentiation. And in both, politics and economics are played out in conjunction with a rich ceremonial life. The political reality of the COCEI in Juchitán provides insight into how the covert historical resistance of Teotitlán to state intervention is transformed into overt, formally organized opposition under a different set of economic and political circumstances.

In Teotitlán del Valle, the continued existence of strong and vital ritual networks which remain outside state control or other outside interests are associated with continued efforts at autonomous self-improvement and an independent political relationship with the state and the PRI. In the 1988 presidential election, Teotitlán gave 63% of its votes to the opposition front of Cardenas, 28% to the PRI, and 9% to the PAN. In Juchitán, where the PRI ran the municipal government with an iron fist, a strong ritual system has provided channels for the politicization and organization of large segments of the community into a unified political opposition movement.

CONCLUSIONS

Civil-religious *cargo* systems in Oaxaca have undergone major changes in the twentieth century largely due to the 1917 Mexican constitution which reorganized government structures at the level of the *municipio* through the mandates of state governors. In some communities, an important result of this reorganization was that local church committees, named as part of the municipal government, assumed responsibility for church property and activities which previously had been undertaken by *mayordomos*. These constitutional changes, along with an overt anti-*mayordomía* policy on the part of the Calles and Obregon governments, had a major impact on the changing structure and function of religious hierarchies and the *mayordomías* associated with them. As seen in the case study of Teotitlán, however, local history and economic development are also critical in defining contemporary religious institutions and ritual participation.

In Teotitlán del Valle, expansion of weaving production for export, and state promotion of Indian identity and crafts for tourists, are associated with a retrenchment of ritual forms and institutions in a context of class differentiation. In this community, as well as in others, the decline of *mayordomías* has not signalled the death of indigenous ritual and the end of reciprocal relations. What emerges is a complex reality in which reciprocal labor and goods exchanges continue to occur for life cycle rituals instead of for *mayordomías*. This seeming anachronism is further complicated by the fact that reciprocal ritual obligations occur in a context of increasing social and economic differentiation. While this was not explored in detail here, it is important to realize that both reciprocal and class-based labor relations can and do coexist. This coexistence frames the social world of Teotitecos.

On a larger level, the ongoing historical dialogue between the state and peasant communities suggests that while indigenous peasant communities are certainly constrained by the larger political and economic frameworks of the Mexican national state and the divisive tendencies of class formation, many communities continue to build forms of social organization which resist further loss of community autonomy. In some cases today, these forms of social organization involve the maintenance of ritual institutions and networks which crosscut different sectors of the community. Through the continued maintenance and mobilization of kin-*compadrazdo* networks for ritual purposes, such communities have strengthened local ethnic identity and provided potential support structures for political activity.

NOTES

Acknowledgments. I would like to thank John Chance, James Dow, Cathy Winkler, and Ellen Herman for their many helpful suggestions and criticisms in writing this article. Research was supported by the Inter-American Foundation, The Wenner-Gren Foundation for Anthropological Research, and the Damon Fellowship of Brandeis University. Writing and revision was supported by a fellowship from the Center for U.S.-Mexican Studies, University of California, San Diego.

1. Kin-*compadrazgo* networks refer to networks of consanguinial, affinal, and ritual kin (*compadres*) who share a set of obligations and responsibilities involving ritual commitments and reciprocal labor exchanges.

2. Civil offices are divided into two main branches, the *ayuntamiento* and the *alcaldía* or *juzgado mayor*. Those offices which belong to the government branch or the *ayuntamiento* include posts such as *presidente* (mayor), *sindico* (legal advisor to the *presidente* and *ayuntamiento*), *regidores* (councilmen each in charge of dealing with a specific area such as water and land resources), treasurer, secretary, and local police. Offices which pertain to the judicial branch, *juzgado mayor* or *alcaldía*, include *alcaldes* (judges), their alternates, and assistants. The numbers and names of offices vary by community.

3. The local economies of Teotitlán del Valle, Santa Ana, Maquilzochitl, and Díaz Ordaz included the production and trading of wool blankets. Trade routes during the 1920s and 1930s involved the trading of first class blankets from Teotitlán and Santa Ana in Chiapas and the

Isthmus. Local census and oral histories revealed that from 8 to 16 traders from Teotitlán travelled regularly to Chiapas. Such individuals were also primary information sources for the community and were described by informants as being like the radio, bringing news from other places. Knowledge of the Cristero rebellion was spread in this way (see Stephen 1987:135-143).

4. The original document states in Spanish: "...puesto que dichas manifestaciones arruinan su escaso patrimonio y los dejan en las condiciones mas desastrosas al grado de que en el ano siguiente constituyen un lastre para sus familías y para la sóciedad."

5. The original Spanish read: "...ve con satisfacción los propositos que tienen de rectificar todas las costumbres que en nuestros pueblos producen la ruina o el estancamiento de su patrimonio moral y económico.

6. *Guelaguetza* refers to a system for the reciprocal exchange of goods and labor which is carried out in association with ritual events. See Stephen n.d.b for a detailed description.

7. Traditionally, large five-day weddings are called *za guili* ("with music"). These ceremonies involves several days of dancing in which not only the bride's and groom's families sponsor large meals and dancing, but the couple's *padrinos* (wedding godparents) do as well. Essentially, what was once the province of only the very well-off has become the norm.

REFERENCES

Archivo del Estado
    1926a Sección de Gobernación, *Diario Oficial*, Tomo XXXIV, No. 2:1-4.
    1926b Sección de Gobernación, *Periódico Oficial*, Tomo VIII, No. 4:27-28.
Archivo Municipal de Teotitlán del Valle
    1927 Copiador de Oficios, No. 17
    1928 Copiador de Circulares, No. 14
Bailey, David C.
    1974 *Viva Cristo Rey!* Austin: University of Texas Press.
Barabas, Alicia and Miguel Bartolome
    1986 *Etnicidad y pluralismo cultural: La dinámica etnica en Oaxaca.* Mexico, DF:INAH
    1977 *La resistencia Maya: Relaciónes interetnicas en el oriente de la Península de Yucatan.* Colección Científica No. 53. Mexico DF: Instituto Nacional de Antropología e Historia.
Bonfil Batalla, Guillermo
    1981 "Utopía y revolución: El pensamiento político contemporáneo de los Indios in America Latina." In *Utopía y Revolución.* Guillermo Bonfil Batalla, editor, pp. 11-53. Mexico DF: Editorial Nueva Imagen.
Brown, Lyle C.
    1969 "Mexico's Constitution in 1917." In *Revolution in Mexico: Years of Upheaval. 1910-1940,* J. Wilkie and A. Michaels, editors, pp. 112-116. New York: Alfred A. Knopf.
Chance, John K. and William B. Taylor
    1985 "Cofradias and Cargos: An Historical Perspective on the Mesoamerican Civil-Religious Hierarchy." *American Ethnologist* 12(1):1-26.
Chiñas, Beverly
    1987 "Women: The Heart of Isthmus Zapotec Ceremonial Exchange." Paper presented at the 86th Annual Meeting of the American Anthropological Association, November 18-22, Chicago, Illinois.
    1983 *The Isthmus Zapotecs,* 2d edition. Prospect Heights, IL: Waveland Press.

de la Cruz, Victor
  1984 "Hermanos o ciudadanos: dos lenguajes, dos proyectos políticos en el istmo." *Guchachi Reza* 21.
Dennis, Philip A.
  1987 *Intervillage Conflicts in Oaxaca.* New Brunswick: Rutgers University Press.
Diskin, Martin
  1986 "La economía de la comunidad étnico en Oaxaca." In *Etnicidad y pluralismo cultural: La dinámica étnica en Oaxaca.* Alicia Barabas and Miguel Bartolome, editors, pp. 259-297. Mexico DF: Instituto Nacional de Antropologia e Historia.
Evans, Sara and Harold Boyte.
  1986 *Free Spaces.* New York: Harper and Row.
Fox, Jonathan
  1987 "Grassroots Organizations vs. 'The Iron Law of Oligarchy': Reflections on a Research Agenda." Paper presented at Cambridge University Department of Geography Seminar on Local Leaders, Community Development and Participation, September 28-October 1, Cambridge, England.
Garcia Canclini, Nestor
  1982 *Las culturas populares en el capitalismo.* Mexico DF: Editorial Nueva Imagen.
Good, Catharine
  1988 *Haciendo la lucha: Arte y Comercio Nahuas de Guerrero.* Mexico DF: Fondo de Cultura Económica.
Long, Norman and Bryan R. Roberts
  1978 "Peasant Cooperation and Capitalist Expansion in Peru." In *Peasant Cooperation and Capitalist Expansion in Central Peru.* N. Long and B. Roberts, editors, pp. 297-328. Austin: University of Texas Press.
Lopez Monjardin, Adriana
  1983 "COCEI: Una Etnia Redefinida?" Paper presented at Mesa Redonda Sobre la Cuestión Etnica, Juchitán Oaxaca.
Mallon, Florencia
  1983 *The Defense of Community in Peru's Central Highlands.* Princeton: Princeton University Press.
Mathews, Holly H.
  1985 "'We are Mayordomo': a Reinterpretation of Women's Roles in the Mexican Cargo System." *American Ethnologist* 17:285-301.
Quirk, Robert E.
  1973 *The Mexican Revolution and the Catholic Church 1910-1929.* Bloomington: Indiana University Press.
Rubin, Jeffrey
  1987 "State Policies, Leftist Oppositions and Municipal Elections: The Case of the COCEI in Juchitán." In *Electoral Patterns and Perspective in Mexico.* Arturo Alvarado, editor, pp. 127-160. San Diego: Center for U.S.-Mexican Studies, Monograph Series No. 2, 22.
Sault, Nicole
  1988 "Patrons and Sponsors: The Network Strategies of Zapotec Women in the Oaxaca Valley." Paper Presented at the 87th Annual Meeting of the American Anthropological Association, November 16-20, Phoenix, Arizona.
Sacks, Karen
  1987 *Caring By the Hour.* Urbana: University of Illinois Press.
Stephen, Lynn
  1987 *Weaving Changes: Economic Development and Gender Roles in Zapotec Ritual and Production.* Ph.D. dissertation, Brandeis University. Ann Arbor: University Microfilms.
  1988a "Zapotec Picasso: The Weaving of an Export Culture." Paper presented at the International Congress of Americanists, July 4-8, Amsterdam, The Netherlands.

1988b "Zapotec Gender Politics." Paper presented at 87th Annual Meeting of the American Anthropological Association, November 16-20, Phoenix, Arizona.

n.d.a   "Indigenous Culture as a Positive Factor in Economic Development: Craft Production in Latin America." *Economic Development and Cultural Change.* In press.

n.d.b *Gender, Class, and Ethnicity in the Lives of Zapotec Women.* Austin: University of Texas Press. In press.

Varese, Stefano

1982 "Restoring Multiplicity: Indianties and the Civilizing Project in Latin America." In *Latin American Perspectives*, Vol. 9, No. 2:29-41.

1988 "Multi-ethnicity and Hegemonic Construction: Indian Projects and the Global Future." In *Ethnicities and Nations.* Francesco Bellizzi, editor, pp. 57-77. Austin: University of Texas Press.

Warman, Arturo

1980 *We Come to Object.* Baltimore: Johns Hopkins University Press.

Young, Kate

1976 "The Social Setting of Migration." Ph.D. dissertation, London University.

Part II:
Peasant Economic Relations and Changes in Local Religious Systems

CHAPTER FOUR

The Zinacantan *Cargo* Waiting Lists as a Reflection of Social, Political, and Economic Changes, 1952 to 1987

Frank Cancian
University of California, Irvine

At least since the conquest, the forces of social, political, and economic change in Chiapas, in Mexico, and in the rest of world have repeatedly transformed what constitutes life as a Zinacanteco. Yet, the relevance of Zinacantan as an ethnic identity and a social construct remains. Despite the enormous importance of outside influences, it still is useful to look at Zinacantan and Zinacantecos in terms of relations that are internal to the *municipio*.

In the last half century change has been dramatic. In this chapter, I will first paint with broad strokes both the internal and the external changes of the past 50 years, and then I will focus on some limited data resources that help to improve our understanding of the continuing transformation of internal relations in Zinacantan. In what follows, the ethnographic present is 1987.

Internal relations reflect the adaptation of Zinacantecos to external economic and political changes, to the dynamics of population growth within the *municipio*, and to the evolving definition of internal relations themselves. Slow change in some of the more stable elements in this complex (the *cargo* system and the waiting lists) is used here to help understand features that are changing more rapidly. Notably, the force and clarity of the rapid economic and demographic change should help us understand the evolution of the apparently more stable features like the *cargo* system and the waiting lists. Nothing in the situation is absolutely unchanging.

MAJOR CHANGES

Great shifts in the fundamental conditions of Zinacantan's economic life have taken place in the last 50 years (Wasserstrom 1983). By the 1930s and 1940s the Mexican Revolution and land reform made independent farmers of many Zinacantecos who had been heavily dependent on semifeudal arrangements, wage labor, and small-scale subsistence farming. This trend seemed to peak in the middle to late 1960s, just when the nation reached comfortable self-sufficiency in the production of basic grains (Barkin and Suarez 1981:154). During that period, most Zinacantecos spent an important part of their time as independent farmers (Cancian 1972). Since then the national economy has passed through a period of increased prosperity based on oil, but overall agricultural self-sufficiency has suffered (Barkin and Suarez 1981). At the local level the dominance of independent corn farming as the principal Zinacanteco male occupation gave way to a broad diversity that ranges from increased wage labor to occupations in commerce, transportation, education, and other government sponsored activities that were almost completely dominated by Ladinos as recently as twenty years ago (Cancian 1987).

In the last three decades, the physical space of Zinacantecos, both internal and external to the *municipio*, has been drastically altered by the construction of roads and the development of transportation (see Cancian 1972; Wasserstrom 1983). Schools have become available to all. Official figures show that the municipal population went from 6,312 in 1950, to 11,428 in 1970, and to 13,006 in 1980.

In sum, Zinacantecos have seen (1) greater wealth and greater diversity of occupations; (2) an accompanying shift from subsistence production of basic necessities to a monetized economy; (3) vastly improved transportation and education; and (4) a great increase in population. Neither space nor data resources allow for full details on these trends in this chapter. Rather, I wish to look at indications of how such trends have affected some aspects of internal relations in Zinacantan.

THE *CARGO* SYSTEM, AND THE ORIGIN OF THE WAITING LIST

In Zinacantan in 1960, a man's community-wide reputation was established in large part through service in the religious *cargo* system.[1] The *cargos* were and are yearlong offices whose incumbents sponsor religious fiestas at great personal expense. Similar systems have been described for many Middle American communities (Cancian 1967).

In the early 1960s the Zinacantan religious *cargo* system was made up of 55 *cargos* on four levels (Cancian 1965). The organization of the system is illustrated in simplified form in Figure 4.1. In order to reach the top level a man served in a yearlong position at each of the first three levels.[2]

FIGURE   4.1.   THE RELIGIOUS HIERACHY IN ZINACANTAN.
Shown are 55 *cargos* on four levels, and four types of Auxiliary
Personnel. (From Cancian 1965:29)

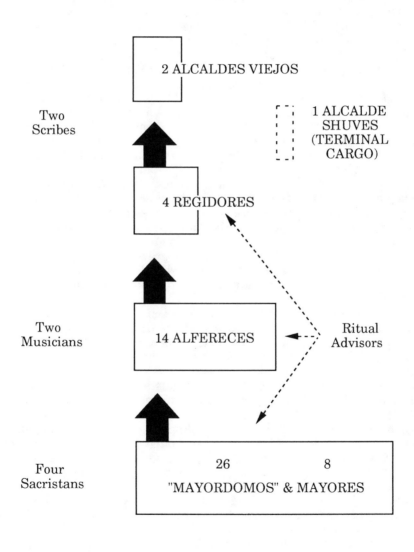

Customarily, he rested a number of years between periods of service. Thus a complete career, from first to fourth *cargo,* could take 20 years.

Figure 4.1 shows that many first level positions were available each year, but fewer were available at each succeeding level. Thus, while many entered the
system every year, only a few passed on to be an *alferez* some years later, and, of those, even fewer ever reached the fourth level of service. In 1960, virtually all the men in Zinacantan participated–at least to the degree of passing a first level *cargo* (Cancian 1965:127). During this era the *cargo* system provided the principle means of establishing a public identity within the community.

At about the same time, changes in (a) the population of Zinacantan, and (b) the regional economy began to threaten the apparent balance between the *cargos* available and the potential incumbents.   As the population of Zinacantan grew the number of men eligible for service increased greatly (Cancian 1965:162). During the same period, increasing economic prosperity led to greater numbers of men who sought to transform their wealth into the immediate enjoyment and the lingering prestige that comes with *cargo* service.   In combination, these factors greatly increased the demand for *cargos.*

For a time, the excess demand was accumulated on waiting lists which scribes began keeping in the 1940s. The waiting lists were administered by the *regidores* and *alcaldes viejos* whose responsibilities included assuring that all *cargos* were filled and properly carried out. These lists permitted a man to register his intention to serve a certain *cargo* one or more years before the actual service. As population and prosperity grew, so did the lists. By 1966, the list for the most popular *cargo* (which was also the most expensive one) was 22 years long. The scribes had registered incumbents for every year from 1966 through 1988.

The interpretation of these lists raises two issues for brief discussion before passing on to look at the detailed data that are the central concern here. The first concerns the function of the lists as a new institutional feature in Zinacantan public life. The second concerns the events and forces that led to the origin and growth of the lists.

The lists are not simply a backlog of requests for immediate service, as a ticket line at the movies represents people waiting for immediate service that cannot be given for lack of ample facilities. Rather, the lists also became a way in which men who had no desire to serve immediately might state their long-term intentions.   In some cases men responded to social pressure to serve immediately in a minor *cargo* by agreeing to serve in an expensive *cargo* in the future. That is, the lists became part of the service system, not just a reflection of the supply/demand imbalance in which the system found itself.

Working with data from the neighboring *municipio* of Chamula, Jan Rus and Robert Wasserstrom have made important discoveries about the events that led to the waiting lists in highland Chiapas in the 1940s.[3] They report that the lists were created out of a complex political struggle for control of Chamula. State officals were trying to install municipal political officials who spoke Spanish and were connected to the outside world. Chamula elders were trying to maintain a system in which important political officials could enter office only after they had served in a religious *cargo*. According to Rus and Wasserstrom:

> During this period, in fact, the community had two mayors: a traditional *cargo* holder designated by the elders, and a young scribe who had been named by state officials. Rather than force the issue, however, local progressives decided for the moment to conciliate the . . . (elders). Then, in late 1942, the government candidate requested that he be allowed to serve an expensive religious *cargo*—not immediately, but in five years' time. Simultaneously, the state government began to enforce a law, enacted in 1937, which effectively permitted only religious officials or those who would soon assume religious office to sell liquor in Indian communities—as a "way of paying the costs of service." Essentially, then, this regulation offered traditional authorities a new source of income to compensate for their loss of power—a source of income which depended upon their cooperation with the young presidents (1980:474).

Rus and Wasserstrom, reasonably enough, generalize this discovery to Zinacantan, where lists appeared during the same period. They conclude that the waiting lists ". . . appeared in both Zinacantan and Chamula for reasons which have little to do with demographic pressure" (1980:475). While their discoveries of the historical origins of the lists (in Chamula at least) are an important improvement over the vague functionalist interpretation of origin presented in my original study of the *cargo* system in Zinacantan (Cancian 1965:183), I see no contradiction between their documentation of historical origin and my emphasis on demand forces.[4]

They apparently see such a contradiction. Thus, it seems worth clarifying the issues before we look at the data on the waiting lists in Zinacantan. The presumed contradiction is between the primacy of political events and forces and the primacy of the inclinations of ordinary people that, under the right conditions, amount to supply/demand pressure for institutional change. However, the contradiction doesn't exist unless we believe, simplistically, that political history is exclusively the product of the political center or, just as simplistically, that ordinary people operate as preprogrammed isolates who are not influenced by political events. Neither of these alternatives is acceptable. Clearly, political events that appear to transform the organization of any community respond to a wide variety of pressures, including demographic and economic ones. Below we will see considerable evidence for the importance of demand pressures, as they operate in a complex of political, economic and demographic changes in the region and the *municipio* of Zinacantan. We also will see that these pressures do not have simple, direct, and continuous effects.

CHANGES IN THE WAITING LISTS, 1952 TO 1987

The trends for 1952 to 1966 are shown in Table 4.1, Part A.[5] The growth in the lists was continuous and dramatic during this period. More and more Zinacantecos added their names to the lists as the years went by. By 1966, 347 were on the lists for the 41 *cargos* administered by the *regidores* and *alcaldes viejos*. The backlog varied for different *cargos*. As noted above, the most

TABLE 4.1. REQUESTS FOR *CARGOS*

A: Requests for *Cargos* 1952 to 1966[a]

Year	Total Requests[c]	First Level	Second Level[b]	Higher Levels[b]	Last Year Listed	Length of List
1952	119	57	39	23	1962	10[c]
1958	247	138	66	43	1974	16
1961	310	180	86	44	1981	20
1966	347	222	80	45	1988	22

B: Requests for *Cargos* 1971 to 1987[a]

Year	Total Requests[c]	First Level	Second Level[b]	Higher Levels[b]	Last Year Listed	Length of List
1971	332	217	70	45	1991	20
1975	290	196	57	37	1992	17
1978	256	169	52	35	1995	17
1980[d]	222	144	50	28	1996	16
1983	217	127	58	32	1999	16
1987	193	94	64	35	2002	15

a. The name of a man who has requested a *cargo* is repeated on each new list until he serves. Thus rows repeat many of the men counted in previous years.

b. The second level includes the twelve *alfereces* usually served as second *cargos* (see Cancian 1965). The other two *alfereces* are included with the higher levels.

c. Total requests are for years after the year of use, e.g., for the 1952 lists the ten years are 1953 through 1962.

d. Probably slightly overcounted due to inconsistent recording practices used in field research.

popular *cargo* was requested through 1988. Ten or more *cargos* were requested for each year through 1980, fourteen years in the future, and five or more were requested for each year through 1984. This broad-based expansion of requests supports the demand argument for the growth of the lists, whatever the details of their origin.

Then something changed. As Table 4.1, Part B shows, the number of requests registered has steadily declined since the early 1970s. Population and prosperity in Zinacantan continued to grow during the period (at least until the current economic crisis began in 1982), but the lists declined in length. What happened to the demand for *cargos*?

Here I want to speculate about two areas of change that may provide the mechanics behind diminishing requests for *cargos*. The first involves broad socioeconomic trends in Zinacantan (especially occupational change); the second, the changing relations of the outlying hamlets to the municipal center. Both are related to changes in the Mexican political economy.

BROAD SOCIOECONOMIC TRENDS IN ZINACANTAN

The trend away from *cargo* service as the principal form of public service and public identity in Zinacantan seemed likely in the early 1960s when I made my original study of the *cargo* system. Then, the capacity of the *cargo* system to absorb prospective claimants to respect and authority in the community was diminishing relative to the number of adult men. Likewise, economic prosperity was increasing the proportion of the growing population that could aspire to high *cargo* service. It seemed then that alternative prestige systems would have to emerge, and that expensive *cargo* service might become less desirable as alternatives developed (Cancian 1965:187-194). It is hard to tell how much of the recent change in demand for *cargos* stems directly from the inability of the *cargo* system to include the increasing number of men who had wanted to serve.

In the intervening 20 years, the continuing integration of the state of Chiapas into the national economy has transformed the way Zinacantecos make their livings. In the 1960s, they were principally corn farmers with a peasant-like adaptation in which they kept expenses low and produced a substantial part of their household needs. Since then the increasing monetization of the economy has affected both rich and poor within the community.

Many elite Zinacantecos have become involved in transport and other new capitalistic enterprises. For example, in the early 1960s when most Zinacantecos were principally corn farmers, the many who were involved in commerce used their own mules or *ladino* trucks for transportation. There were two trucks in Zinacantan. By the mid-1970s, Wasserstrom found a maximum of 20 trucks owned by Zinacantecos (Wasserstrom 1983:200), and my 1981 census found 69 vehicles registered to Zinacantecos.

How has this affected demand for *cargos*? One interpretation is that demands of high investment in vehicles and other capital intensive technologies introduced by government programs will drain off potential participants in the *cargo* system. The declining total number of requests may reflect the division of the Zinacantan elite into modern, capitalistically involved individuals, and more traditional entrepreneurs. Since wealth is a crucial characteristic of both *cargo* holders and truck owners, it is not surprising that many vehicles are now owned by families of former *cargo* holders—usually with the younger generation taking the active roles in managing the vehicles. While younger truck owners may be drawn away from *cargo* service by the alternative demands for cash and by the intensive attention demanded by the great capital investment they have made, this trend is not yet certain. Another possibility is that the new economic elite will have extra earnings that will facilitate *cargo* service, and that they will continue to seek prominence in *cargo* service.

During this same period of diminishing requests for *cargos* many Zinacantecos have become increasingly dependent on wage labor. While a transport elite (truckers) has appeared at one end of the socioeconomic scale, proletarians have appeared in greater numbers at the other end. In 1967, four percent of household heads in one hamlet (Nachig) lacked corn fields. By 1983, they had grown to 40 percent of the population (Cancian 1987). Many of these men were heavily dependent on construction project wage labor (until August 1982 when massive layoffs accompanied the onset of the national economic crisis).

These proletarianized Zinacantecos probably have less economic security and fewer resources to permit them to serve *cargos*. The ceremonial calendar leaves most *cargo* holders free during the peak work periods of the agricultural cycle, so those who are farmers commonly arrange to continue corn production while in office. To the proletarian, a day of *cargo* service is a day of lost wages, at best. Thus, I speculate that proletarianization is an important cause of the diminishing requests for *cargos*.[6]

In sum, both truck owners, who usually must manage substantial indebtedness, and proletarians, who must worry about unemployment, are constrained by the direction of the larger society, especially its economy. The waiting lists, which offer some stability of meaning as an institutional form, simply permit us to see that some sort of radical transformation is taking place in Zinacantan. Much of the impetus for this transformation comes from outside Zinacantan, and its future will depend on events in the region and the nation.

Both Eric Wolf (1960), for Mexico, and G. William Skinner (1971), for China, have interpreted long-term historical trends in ways that may be adapted to explain the relation of the shifts in the length of the *cargo* waiting lists to changes in the Mexican political economy. They noted that ties to the local community weaken during periods of national stability and prosperity, and that rural people withdraw into the local community in times of national crisis. Thus, the attenuation of demand for *cargos* may be seen as a reflection of opportunities outside of Zinacantan. By the same token, if the Mexican economic crisis continues, it may lead to retrenchment that increases interest in local social life in a manner that slows or even reverses the declining demand for *cargos*. The slight increase in requests for second and higher level *cargos* in 1983 and 1987 (Table 4.1) may signify such a reversal.[7]

THE RELATION OF THE HAMLETS TO THE CENTER

The relation of the outlying hamlets (*parajes*) to the municipal Center (*cabecera*, ceremonial center) has long been an ambivalent one. On the one hand, ultimate political and religious power is located in the Center. The *presidente municipal* (mayor) is the final arbiter of disputes within the *municipio*, and the sacred mountains of the Center are the ultimate site of religious curing ceremonies. On the other hand, hamlet populations grew to the size that could support an independent level of administration, while new roads, wealth and education provided many hamlets with the means to govern themselves.

Two administrative changes reflect recent shifts in the struggle for greater independence. One is the increase in the number of hamlets with the official semi-autonomy implied by a local *agente municipal* (hamlet official). In the 1950s, no hamlet had an *agente municipal*. In the 1960s, one hamlet, Navenchauc, had an *agente*. In the 1970s, nine new *agentes*, including one for each of the large hamlets not bordering the Center, were named. Thus, formal political decentralization increased tremendously.

Second, and more relevant in the present context, are changes in the personnel that serve the *cargo* holders. While it was previously customary to recruit the two scribes associated with the *regidores* and *alcaldes viejos* and the four sacristans associated with the *mayordomos* from the population of the Center, in the late 1970s the hamlets insisted on a system of rotation that included candidates from outlying areas. Previously, the lack of transportation, and more importantly the concentration of schooling in the Center, had limited the possibilities. By the 1970s, however, the hamlets could provide plenty of literate, capable people to fill those traditional roles. Thus, the Center's population lost its distinctive character and its monopoly on certain roles.[8]

The construction of chapels in the hamlets was another sign of decentralization and independence, as many students have noted (Vogt 1976; Wasserstrom 1978; Bricker 1981). By the middle of the 1980s, chapels existed in ten hamlets (see Table 4.2, including the notes), and *cargos* had been established in most of them. Wasserstrom (1983:216-239) has documented and discussed the chapels and *cargos*. The establishment of local hamlet *cargos* meant, of course, that the number of first level *cargos* per capita varied from hamlet to hamlet. In some of the smaller hamlets the new *cargos* required the service of a very substantial proportion of the men of appropriate ages. In others the new positions were a much smaller part of the total first level service desired by local residents.

During the 1970s and the 1980s, political divisions in Zinacantan became more marked than they had been in the past. The PRI (single dominant national party) candidate for *presidente municipal* in 1976 was opposed by powerful people who eventually associated with PAN (the largest minority party at the time). In 1982, a large PRI faction supported the PAN candidate for *presidente municipal* and he won the election, thereby initiating greater instability and conflict. The political divisions influenced some changes in the *cargo* system.

The localism, the imbalances of *cargo* supply and hamlet populations, and the political divisions interacted and were reflected in the waiting lists. Table 4.3 indicates the relative number of requests for first level *cargos* served in the Center by the men of the major hamlets (and clusters of adjoining hamlets). The entries in Table 4.3 are ratios that would be 1.0 if the men of each hamlet requested *cargos* in the Center in exact proportion to their number in the municipal population.

In Apas and Paste, demand clearly grew very strong before local *cargos* were established (in 1961 and 1977, respectively). In both cases, I believe that a sense of competition with a neighboring hamlet (Navenchauc and Nachig respectively) that had recently established its own *cargos* encouraged the changes. In Apas, the pressure to fill the four local *cargos* from the limited population (plus the elimination of some candidates due to political divisions) led to lower participation on the waiting lists and eventual suspension (in 1987) of two of the hamlet's four *cargos*. As far as I can tell, the continuing, relatively high number of requests by Nachig men reflects great

TABLE 4.2. CHAPELS AND *CARGOS* IN THE HAMLETS[a]

Hamlet	Chapel Built	Cargos Begin	Number of *Cargos*
Salinas	c. 1859	c. 1850	1 *Mayordomo* 1 *Mayol*
Navenchauc	1950s	1957 1982	2 *Mayordomos* 2 *Mayordomos*
Apas[b, c]	1961	1961	2 *Mayordomos Reyes* 2 *Mexones*
Nachig	1967	1976	2 *Mayordomos*
Paste	1971	1977	2 *Mayordomos*
Elanvo[c]	1972	1979	2 *Mayordomos*
Chajtoj	1967	no *cargos*	
Cornfields area:			
Joigelito	1973	no *cargos*	
Jocchenom	1983	no *cargos*	
Zequentic	1971	no *cargos*	

a. These data correct errors in Cancian 1986, Table 4.2. Tierra Blanca, a mostly Ladino hamlet within Zinacantan, had its own chapel for many years and established a single *cargo* in 1968. Until 1987 when one man awaited an *alferez*, no Tierra Blanca man was on any of the lists covered in Table 4.1.

The twenty religious *cargos* served in the Center included no new ones. Thus, there were 24 religious *cargos* before 1960 (the Center, Salinas and Navenchauc), and 36 by 1980. Since the population of Zinacantan more than doubled between 1960 and 1980, for the *municipio* as a whole, there were fewer *cargos* per capita in 1980.

b. Apas had four *cargos* soon after its local system was established. The listing in Cancian 1965, p. 30, omitted two of them. There were really 57 *cargos* in 1965.

c. In 1987, both Elanvo *cargos* and two of the Apas *cargo* were suspended. That was the first reduction in *cargos* in at least 50 years (Tax *et al* 1947).

TABLE 4.3. FIRST LEVEL *CARGOS*

Requests for First Level *Cargos* by Hamlets, 1952-1987
(Ratio of Requests to Population[a])

Recorded in the Lists for the Year:

Hamlet[b]	1952	1958	1961	1966	1971	1975	1978	1980	1983	1987
Navenchuac	1.2*	1.0	1.3	1.6	1.0	1.1	1.0	1.0	1.3	1.4
Apas	1.0*	1.6	2.0	0.6	0.9	0.9	0.8	0.7*	0.5	0.6*
Nachig	1.6	1.1	1.0	1.5	1.4	1.3	2.0	2.5	2.9	2.6
Paste	1.9	1.4	1.2	1.6	2.4	2.6	2.2	1.9	1.2	0.8
Cornfields	0.9	1.5	1.5	1.3	1.0	0.8	0.8	0.6	0.5	0.4*
Center	0.7	0.8	0.6	0.6	0.6	0.5	0.5	0.6	0.8	1.1
Other	0.4*	0.1*	0.2*	0.1*	0.4	0.6	0.4	0.5	0.3*	0.3*

a. The entries in the cells are ratios of the hamlet's percentage of total first level *cargo* requests to percentage of total population.

b. Elanvo and other small hamlets are included in "Other." They include roughly 15 percent of Zinacantan's population.

*. Cell count is less than 10.

local prosperity and extraordinary effort by men in political factions that were defined in part by nonparticipation in local *cargos*. The slight increase in requests by men from the Center suggests that they turned to regular *cargos* as their monopoly on auxiliary roles was broken. Also, the decreasing participation of men from the Cornfields (the area furthest from the Center) parallels finalization of their area as a separate communal land district (*ejido*) and their major role in the split that upset PRI in the 1982 election.

Overall, Table 4.3 shows that the spread between the most active and the least active areas of the *municipio* grew substantially between 1952 and 1987. Before 1970, requests from Nachig men and men from the Cornfields were comparable. By the 1980s, however, Nachig men were at least five times as likely to ask for *cargos* in the Center and they also filled two local *cargos*, while men in the Cornfields organized less formal ways of caring for their chapels. Whether this increasing detachment from the common ritual system continues under the pressure of the national economic crisis remains to be seen. If the understanding of the waxing and waning of commitment to local communities suggested by both Wolf (1960) and Skinner (1971) is correct, we may see a resurgence of shared Zinacanteco identity.

SUMMARY AND CONCLUSIONS

The *cargo* waiting lists reflect basic changes in social, political, and economic life inside Zinacantan. The shortening of the lists in recent years reflects a shift away from the *cargo* system as the central and dominant institution in the community-wide social structure of Zinacantan. The patterns of requests by hamlet reflect the establishment of the hamlet *cargos* and the related decentralization of social and political organization. Additionally, a combination of factors, including open political turmoil that began in the mid-1970s, is reflected in the wide differences in participation rates by the men of different hamlets. All of these internal changes in turn reflect changes in the larger political economy.

The first version of this chapter was written for a congress that honored Evon Vogt's contributions to the anthropological study of highland Chiapas. In thinking about the future of the *cargo* system and the waiting lists in Zinacantan, it is appropriate to recall Professor Vogt's remarks in his forward to my study of the *cargo* system as it existed in 1960. He noted (Vogt 1965:viii) that our predictions for the future of the *cargo* system were different. I predicted that the system was likely to be destroyed as the institution on which community integration is based. He supported the possibility that community fission would lead to the development of additional *cargo* systems in parts of the municipality. There is support for both these views in the patterns described above.

NOTES

Acknowledgments. An earlier version of this chapter (Cancian 1986) included a preliminary analysis based on data from waiting lists through 1980 and general observations made through the early 1980s. Summer field research in 1981, 1982, 1983, and short visits in December 1982 and March 1983 were supported by the School of Social Sciences, the Mexico/Chicano Program, and the Faculty Research Committee at the University of California, Irvine. Fieldwork from April to August 1984 and short visits in 1985 and 1987 were supported by the National Science Foundation. Zinacantan is a Tzotzil-speaking Maya *municipio* in the highlands of Chiapas. Background information is found in the many publications of the Harvard Chiapas project (see Vogt 1979) and especially in Evon Z. Vogt's general books (1969, 1970).

1. Public life in Zinacantan is almost completely dominated by males. Female involvement in support roles is crucial.

2. The actual pattern of service is not as simple as the diagram (see Cancian 1965). The fact that two of the *alfereces* are usually served as third or fourth *cargos* is the most important complication for my purposes here. In this paper these two *alfereces* are classified with the third and fourth level *cargos*.

3. Similar lists in eighteenth-century Yucatan are discussed in Thompson 1978.

4. Whatever the specific origin of the lists in Zinacantan, by the 1960s there was no strict association between anticipated *cargo* service and the sale of liquor. In fact, most Zinacantecos who could manage it bought liquor produced clandestinely by Chamulas whose stills were, by then, hidden from the Ladino monopolists who aggressively supressed production by Indians.

5. I have been fortunate in my work on the waiting lists to have the cooperation of a number of people, including former *alcaldes viejos* who kindly allowed me to study the annual books of lists that remain in their possession as mementos after their year of service. These individuals include: Antonio Perez Shulumte of Apas; Pedro Uch, Domingo Santis Es, and Mariano Vaskis Shulhol of Navenchauc; Lorenzo Chicharon and Mariano Perez Lopez of Paste; Domingo and Manuel, sons of Juan Perez Hacienda, and Andres Ahte of the pueblo of Zinacantan; and Jose Hernandez Ko' of Patosil. Without their help, and that of many scribes and friends, this study would not have been possible.

6. I am currently preparing a study (Cancian n.d.) that will help answer some of the questions raised in this section.

7. The sharp decrease in requests for first level *cargos* is in part due to new first level *cargos* available in the hamlets (see Table 4.2, Note a). The new hamlet *cargos* make more men eligible for service in second level *cargos*.

8. The hamlet rotation system had broken down by 1984.

REFERENCES

Barkin, David and Blanca Suarez
    1981   *El Fin de la Autosuficiencia Alimentaria.* Mexico: Nueva Imagen.
Bricker, Victoria Reifler
    1981   *The Indian Christ, The Indian King: The Historical Substrate of Maya Myth and Ritual.* Austin: University of Texas Press.
Cancian, Frank
    1965   *Economics and Prestige in a Maya Community: The Religious Cargo System in Zinacantan.* Stanford: Stanford University Press.
    1967   "Political and Religious Organizations." In *The Handbook of Middle American Indians,* Robert Wauchope, editor. *Volume 6: Social Anthropology,* Manning Nash, editor, pp. 283-298. Austin: University of Texas Press.
    1972   *Change and Uncertainty in a Peasant Economy: The Maya Corn Farmers of Zinacantan.* Stanford: Stanford University Press.
    1986   "Las Listas de Espera en el Sistema de Cargos de Zinacantan: Cambios Sociales, Politicos y Economicos (1952-1980)." *America Indigena* 46:477-494.
    1987   "Proletarianization in Zinacantan, 1960-1983." In *Household Economies and Their Transformations.* Morgan Maclachlan, editor, pp. 131-142. Lanham, MD: University Press of America.
    n.d.   "The Decline of Community in Zinacantan: Economy and Public Life, 1960-1985." In preparation.
Rus, Jan and Robert Wasserstrom
    1980   "Civil-Religious Hierarchies in Central Chiapas: A Critical Perspective." *American Ethnologist* 7:466-478.
Skinner G. William
    1971   "Chinese Peasants and the Closed Community: An Open and Shut Case." *Comparative Studies in Society and History* 13:270-281.
Tax, Sol, *et al.*
    1947   "Notas sobre Zinacantan, Chiapas por Miembros de la Expedicion a Zinacantan— 1942-3 bajo la Direccion de Sol Tax." Microfilm Collection of Manuscripts on Middle American Cultural Anthropology, No. 20. Chicago: University of Chicago Library.
Thompson, Phillip Covington
    1978   *Tekanto in the Eighteenth Century.* Ph.D. dissertation, Tulane University. Ann Arbor: University Microfilms.

Vogt, Evon Z.

    1965   "Forward." In *Economics and Prestige in a Maya Community*.   Frank Cancian. Pp. vii-ix. Stanford: Stanford University Press.

    1969   *Zinacantan: A Maya Community in the Highlands of Chiapas.* Cambridge: Harvard University Press.

    1970   *The Zinacantecos of Mexico: A Modern Maya Life Way.* New York: Holt, Rinehart ßand Winston.

    1978   *Bibliography of the Harvard Chiapas Project: The First Twenty Years, 1957-1977.* Cambridge: The Peabody Museum of Archaeology and Ethnology, Harvard University.

Wasserstrom, Robert

    1978   "The Exchange of Saints in Zinacantan: The Socioeconomic Bases of Religious Change in Southern Mexico." *Ethnology* 17:197-210.

    1983   *Class and Society in Central Chiapas.* Berkeley: University of California Press.

Wolf, Eric R.

    1960   "The Indian in Mexican Society." *Alpha Kappa Deltan* 30:3-6.

CHAPTER FIVE

The Political Economy of the *Velas* in the Isthmus of Tehuantepec

Leigh Binford
University of Connecticut

INTRODUCTION

At least since the publication of *Mexico South* in 1947 by Miguel Covarrubias, the Zapotec of the Isthmus of Tehuantepec in the region of the Pacific Coast of Southern Oaxaca have been renowned for the beauty and pageantry of the Isthmus *vela* rituals, which combine religious ceremony, secular dances, parades and public gift-giving. In the late twentieth century, the traditions observed by Covarrubias have undergone substantial changes, related to changes in the socioeconomic class structure stimulated by state sponsored development schemes. As social and economic relations became more differentiated, and income and income disparities have increased, many pre-existing features of the *velas* dropped out, and the form (and perhaps the meaning) of the remaining practices altered. This paper examines the *vela* system in Espinal, located about three miles north of Juchitán. Apart from documenting correspondences between changes in the *vela* system and changes in the socioeconomic class structure, it will also address the political significance of the *velas* and their role as sites for class and ethnic struggles.[1] Although the *velas* do not usually alter the balance of power between contending forces, an examination of prior writing on and observations of the *velas* indicate that they do sometimes serve as channels through which contending political positions are articulated and differentiated, and through which political battle lines are drawn.

THE *VELA* TRADITION IN THE ISTHMUS

Although *vela* ceremonies have a form and content specific to and associated with the Isthmus Zapotec of the Southern Isthmus region, they are similar to other syncretistic forms which developed out of the complex fusion of Catholic and indigenous ceremonial systems following the Spanish conquest (Whitecotton 1977:216-218; 248-249). The *velas* juxtapose a belief in miracle-working saints, a system of economic *cargos* (burdens) assumed by volunteers (*mayordomos, capitanes* and *capitanas*), and a complex network of economic and social exchanges which link together many individuals and households. As Chiñas noted: "Every ritual contribution, voluntary or otherwise, represents either the payment of ritual obligations or the prepayment toward ritual obligations the household anticipates at some future date, an on-going system in which a balance is never struck" (1973:76-77). On the other hand, the *velas* have involved events of a secular nature, organized collectively by committees which have more in common with school or community improvement committees than with the civil-religious *cargo* system described in the anthropological literature (Smith 1977; Dewalt 1975). Thus Royce (1975:141) characterized the *velas* as activities of a predominantly social character but with a religious component, although there is substantial regional variation (e.g. Chiñas 1973).[2]

Everywhere, however, the *velas* have played a significant role in the expression and reproduction of neighborhood, community, and perhaps most importantly, ethnic identities. The Isthmus differs from other indigenous areas of Mexico in that its Zapotec inhabitants manifest an overt pride in their indigenous heritage. Particularly in the area around Juchitán, there was a long history of struggle for local and regional autonomy, and against outside interference in local affairs, whether perpetrated by Spanish conquerors, French invaders, or the mestizo dominated Mexican state apparatus (Campbell 1988:1-2). An idealized form of this history is now crystallized as part of regional identity and it has contributed to, even as it is to an extent a product of, the fact that Zapotecs control both economic and political spheres. Although most people are bilingual, the ability to speak Zapotec is an important symbol of ethnic affiliation, but participation in exchange networks, rituals such as the *velas*, and the wearing of regional dress by the women are also means of social positioning (Royce 1975).

ESPINAL'S *VELAS* IN THE PAST

Espinal had a 1980 population of about 8000. Although the vast majority of the adult inhabitants were conversant in Zapotec and regarded themselves as Zapotec (*"Somos Zapotecos aqui"*), the community had no pre-Hispanic existence, but developed in the seventeenth and eighteenth centuries around the cattle hacienda of San Antonio Sopiloapan. Largely agricultural during the first 60 years of the twentieth century, the occupational structure began to shift toward services and construction after the completion of the Benito

Juarez dam in the late 1950s and the inauguration of Federal Irrigation District No. 19 in 1962.

The following "reconstruction" of *vela* customs and institutions derives from ethnographic interviews with older informants and refers primarily to the period between 1930 and 1970. Due to the limitations of informant recall, the precise dates and even sequences in which the *velas* changed is difficult to establish. As shall be seen in a later section, ritual activity underwent a drastic transformation after 1970 and by 1980 had assumed a form which was almost unrecognizable to older informants.

In the early years of the twentieth century, the *vela* system paralleled the *barrio* or neighborhood system, each of four neighborhoods being associated with one of the following saints in the Catholic ritual calendar: San Marcos, San Lucas, San Juan, and San Mateo, moving from south to north. Ritual sites were marked with crosses until neighborhood chapels were constructed between 1935 and 1940. Vela San Lucas dropped out in 1950 and at about the same time, Vela San Marcos was renamed Vela Primera and then Vela Primavera, by which it is currently known. Along with these three survivors (Primavera, San Juan, San Mateo), another celebration, Vela Guidxi (referred to by its supporters as "The People's Vela"), was appended in 1979 for the specific purpose of raising money for the construction of a new market building, which the municipal administration wanted to postpone until the completion of a much more expensive drainage project.

The rituals associated with veneration of the neighborhood saint were under the charge of a *mayordomo*, who volunteered for the office (often years in advance) in fulfillment of promises made to the saint for his/her intervention in a family illness, failing marriage, injury, etc. Although the office called for substantial expenditure of personal resources, the candidate dispersed these in space and time through the recruitment of *padrinos* (males) and *madrinas* (females) to take charge of specific facets of the activity.[4] These persons, in turn, mobilized their friends and relatives so that large numbers of people eventually were drawn in, thus spreading the cost of the banquets, fireworks, liquor, and other items widely among the populace. Extensive mental and even written records were maintained of debts contracted and paid. The *padrino/madrina* (*compadrazgo*) system did not provide a substitute for the *mayordomo's* personal resources but did allow him or her to spread the cost widely over time and thus reduced, but did not eliminate, the need to amass substantial savings prior to the event. Also, as mentioned below, *mayordomos* were recipients of ritual gifts of food, goods, and money, only some of which, according to the rules governing the system, had to be repaid.

Vela practices involved the following events: (1) the production of candles (*labrada de cera*) in April, supervised by the *mayordomo*; (2) the "Grand Balls" or outdoor dances held for each *vela* on consecutive weekends in May and organized by directive boards composed of an elected or appointed president, vice president, secretary, treasurer, and several *vocales* (alternates); (3) a fruit giveaway, banquet, and mass (also the *mayordomo's* responsibility), the latter dedicated to the *vela's* patron saint, and held on a day corresponding to the saint's position in the Catholic ritual calendar; (4) a final dance, designated the "washing of the pots" (*lavada de ollas*), held the day after the Grand Ball and attended mainly by women whose physical and ritual labors were (and are) the keystone of the fiesta system. Such "pot washing" ceremonies occur during weddings and other extended festive occasions in the Isthmus and thus are not specific to the *velas*.

The *mayordomo's* main interventions occurred in April during production of beeswax candles, which were placed in the neighborhood chapels, and in May, when he/she sponsored a mass, community banquet, and dance on the saint's day. Both sets of activities occurred at the home within the neighborhood of the *mayordomo*. To assure that everything was carried out properly, office holders were aided by a *guzana-gola*, a female specialist in ritual etiquette, usually an elderly woman whose domestic responsibilities had declined to the point that they were no longer onerous. Royce (1975:141) claims that great honor is attached to the office which "represents the culminating point of many years of a very active social life."

The April candle production was accompanied by a feast of bread, beer, and a rich beef stew prepared only for important occasions. *Vela* members paid dues to help the *mayordomo* purchase the two bulls which went into the stew and to aid with the other expenses. *Vela* members then invited guests from their own or other neighborhoods. Apart from the dues, *vela* associates also were expected to provide the *mayordomo* with ritual gifts of money known as *limosnas*, and some people contributed food and drink—for example, three cartons of beer or a bushel of tomatoes—much of this organized via the *compadrazgo* system. Uninvited members of the community were welcome to purchase bowls of stew and pieces of bread.[5]

The April events actually were the opening round for the more grandiose May events, each *vela* occupying a different weekend. Festivities traditionally began Friday afternoon (the day before the Grand Ball) with a procession of *vela* associates led by the *guzana-gola* and the town band to the *barrio* chapel to set off fireworks in the form of a castle (or tower) and bull, purchased from artisans in Juchitán. On Saturday morning men smoothed and levelled the dance area, covered it with canvas, and erected a large tent over it. The female *guzana-gola* and her helpers decorated it with sheets, mirrors, lanterns, palm or banana leaves, and paper flags.[6] On Saturday afternoon the queen was crowned and the "fruit throw" was held. The fruit throw was preceded by a parade of *vela* associates and their helpers. Carrying the candles produced the previous month, the *mayordomo* led the procession and was followed in turn by musical bands, officials carrying elaborate banners portraying the patron saint of the *barrio*, and oxcarts (later replaced by automobiles and trucks) decorated with banana leaves, *carizo* (a bamboo-like plant), and colored tissue and foil. Bringing up the rear were long, double lines of women, some bearing baskets of fruit, clay toys, and kitchen utensils, and others carrying flowers or decorative plants for the church. In Tehuantepec, Covarrubias (1947:370) described how the women climbed to the church roof and hurled their fruits and other gifts to the expectant crowd gathered below. But in Espinal the fruit was thrown to the onlookers directly from the oxcarts and floats, as was the case in nearby Juchitán in the early 1970s (Royce 1975:149) and in Santiago Laollaga in 1987.[7] In communities in which the *tirada de frutas* (fruit throwing) is still practiced, however, the fruit has been mostly replaced by processed foods such as cookies and crackers and plastic items, e.g., toys, cups, bowls, and storage containers, indicative of recent changes in consumer preference and the increased availability of cash. In the postwar period the parade of oxcarts was supplemented (and in some communities replaced) by elaborate floats, decorated with Biblical allegories designed and executed by local artists or, more commonly, by *muxés'* (homosexual, bisexual, or transvestite males) of Juchitán, regional specialists in many types of artistic work, but best known for decorating floats and creating banners for fiesta celebrations.[8]

These preparations set the stage for the Grand Ball, the central event in the celebration. In fact, two dances were held in Espinal (and three in Tehuantepec in 1940, according to Covarrubias 1947:370-371), a large and elaborate one which began Saturday night and usually lasted until dawn, and a smaller "washing of the pots" on Monday which began in the afternoon and ended early in the evening. The Grand Ball was given over mostly to the youth, who dressed in their finest clothes. They danced to marimba music before the advent of electricity, and after to electronic music.

The Grand Ball was open to the public, as well as to the associates and their guests. Entry fees were charged at the door, although membership dues assessed the associates provided them with a certain number of free admissions per household.[9] The hosts provided their guests with drinks, but until recently the consumption of alcoholic beverages was restricted to the men, while women drank *horchata* made from milled rice, sugar, and cinnamon. At midnight guests accompanied their hosts home for a snack, perhaps to fortify themselves for the long night of revelry. The Monday "pot washing dance" was a mirror image of the Saturday night dance but on a much smaller scale and with fewer people in attendance. With the completion of this ceremony, the *mayordomo* had fulfilled his/her responsibilities, and the successor took over.

The above is a general "reconstruction," and by no means should be equated with "tradition." As with other cases of popular religious practices in Mexico and Central America, the *velas* clearly were subject to a continuous process of experimentation and change, in line with changes in other socioeconomic and cultural activities (Smith 1977:146; Wasserstrom 1983). Pre-existing intra-community political conflicts were, and continue to be, reproduced within them. Espinaleños recall that the members of each *vela* took a certain pride in their neighborhood and the ceremonies associated with it, shouting *vivas* (health) during the processions and dances. As neighborhoods were stratified by wealth, it is possible that *vela* competition reverberated with social tensions rooted in socioeconomic differentiation. Twenty to thirty years ago, however, social differentiation was, with the exception of a small number of wealthy and influential cattlemen and merchant/usurers, little more than incipient. The vast majority of the households in the community were poor, technically semi-proletarians, and thus incapable of generating in the course of a single growing season enough surplus crop to sustain themselves through the long October to March dry season. As Espinal never developed a substantial petty commodity industrial orientation as did nearby Ixtaltepec (pottery, fired bricks) or Juchitán (palm weaving, fireworks, hammocks), adult males were compelled to seek work in other areas. For example, they cut sugar cane in Hacienda Santa Cruz (until its expropriation in 1940) or Santo Domingo in the Isthmus, and in San Cristobal, San Juan Covarrubias and other towns in

Veracruz.   They also worked the cotton harvest on the southern coast of Chiapas (Binford 1983:91-92).[10]

THE *VELAS* PRACTICED IN 1981

By 1981 much of the ceremonial, including the fruit throwing, the processional with floats, and the fireworks tower and bulls had all but disappeared.   The fruit throwing and associated processionals were dropped between 1976 and 1979 because of a lack of interest and because many associates no longer were willing to foot the rapidly escalating costs of preparations.   In the case of Vela Primavera, the entire April celebration of the candle production and its accompanying pot-washing ceremony ceased in 1979 with the death of the *guzana-gola* who had overseen it.   Although many elderly people openly lamented its demise, there was little talk of resurrecting it.[11]

Velas still bear neighborhood associations, although these appear to be weakening.   Contributing to the apathy has been rapid population growth and a construction boom which has consumed much previously vacant urban space, leaving few areas in which large tents might be erected.   In 1979 the municipal president mandated relocation of the Grand Balls of all *velas* to a central concrete area in the town center, removing them from the sections of town with which they had been historically associated.

The cost of putting on these balls has risen rapidly, partly because of inflation but also because each *vela* seems intent upon "beating" the other *velas* as well as surpassing its own previous performance.   Directive Boards, with the permission of *vela* associates, now also seek to generate large surpluses which are donated to community projects, further adding to the costs.   For instance, Vela San Juan contributed 200,000 pesos (approximately $8000) to a drainage project in the late 1970s and early 1980s.   Vela Primavera, between 1980 and 1981, gave 30,000 pesos to the drainage project and 10,000 more toward the purchase of a municipal truck.[12]   Sponsoring dances to raise money for community projects has a long history in the Isthmus, and on occasion the *velas* have been strategically used as a forum for this purpose.   It does not appear, however, that the *velas* were ever profit oriented, as were those in Espinal in 1981.

Before generating surpluses, the Directive Boards must be certain that they have enough money to pay municipal taxes (10,000 pesos for permission to stage the event in 1981), electricity, use of the cement basketball court in the town center (constructed and owned by Vela San Juan), rental of tents where necessary, and the cost of erecting a wooden palisade around the perimeter of the area (since this is no longer carried out by volunteers).   The several hundred tables and chairs, ice, and ice chests are provided by one of the two major regional beer distributors (Corona and Carta Blanca) which compete to obtain monopoly rights on beer sales.   This leaves the orchestras.   The opening act is recruited from among well known Isthmus groups, while, if the *vela's* financial situation permits, a nationally known orchestra is sought to serve as the Saturday night headliner.   (Lesser-known, and thus cheaper, groups play on Monday afternoon.)   Here we encounter the main expense and the means by which inter-*vela* competition is carried on.   According to Covarrubias (1947:371), competition centered forty years ago around the number of oxcarts in the parades and the beauty of the women in attendance. Now it is focused upon the renown of the orchestra, the number of people who attend the ball, and the orchestra's ability to motivate them to dance. The better known the orchestra, the "more strongly it plays" (*toca más fuerte*), and the more successful its leaders are in stimulating the assembled crowd to dance, the better the evening (and, by extension, the more tickets sold and the greater the profits of the *vela*). The *velas*, in short, are critically judged by the quality of their entertainment. Groups of major stature do not come cheaply, and they do not come from the Isthmus but from Mexico City, Veracruz, and other areas. For instance, the Directive Board of Vela Primavera hired the Mexico City band, the Socios del Ritmo, for its May 2, 1981 ball at a cost of 250,000 pesos ($10,000) to play from about 10 p.m. until 4 a.m. The Vela San Juan, with fewer associates to underwrite the contract, spent 130,000 pesos ($5,200) for Chico Ché, another popular group specializing in "tropical" music.

The funds to pay for musical groups are generated from several sources. First, annual dues are assessed each member of the *vela* society. The amount is set, not without discussion and debate, by the Directive Board, and varies with projected costs. The more expensive the orchestra, the higher the dues. In 1981 dues varied from 600 to 1000 pesos ($24 to $40) per household. Evidence for their systematic escalation comes from records of Vela San Juan, which cost 25 pesos to join in 1970, 60 pesos in 1976, and 1000 pesos (plus 500 more to help with candle production) in 1981, a rate of increase far exceeding the general rise in consumer prices over the period.   Lack of resources is undoubtedly a major reason why many poor families now either stay home or pool available funds to send a single representative, usually a teenager or young adult who enjoys dancing.

Another source of funding is the money collected at the door. The events are open to the public and anyone can purchase a ticket, although only the guests of an associate are guaranteed a seat and free food and drink. Others must stand between dance numbers and purchase their food and drink outside from the numerous merchants and beer vendors who set up stands and stalls near the entrance to the palisade.[13] Women enter without charge, but adult males in 1981 were charged 200-300 pesos ($8 to $12) each, varying with the *vela*, an amount equivalent to the income from 1.0 to 1.5 days of wage work in agriculture. Interestingly, some of the Juchitán *velas*, locally categorized into rich and poor, still did not charge for admission as of 1981.

For associates who request tables and invite guests, the dues which they are assessed account for only a small proportion of their total expenditures. They usually purchase new clothing for the event, and they must rent chairs for their tables, pay for food and drink, and provide gifts for their guests, a custom introduced to replace the community giveaway associated with the defunct fruit-throwing ceremony. Those who attend the Monday wind-up dance incur additional expenses. The *vela* expenditures of a young widow, about 45 years old, who ran a clothing stall in the Juchitán market are itemized in Table 5.1 to illustrate the point.

With the exception of some uncertainty regarding chair rental during the

TABLE 5.1. EXAMPLE OF *VELA* EXPENSES *

Saturday			Monday		
Item		$ Cost	Item		$ Cost
12	Cartons beer @ $4.40 ea.	52.80	5	Cartons beer	22.00
2	Cases soda @ $8.00 ea.	16.00	1.5	Cases soda	12.00
1	Bottle liquor	12.00	1	Bottle liquor	8.00
16	Chairs @ $.60 ea.	9.60	?	Chairs	?
	Gifts for guests	28.00			
	Dues as associate	40.00			
	New clothes	44.00			
	Food	73.00		Food	16.00
TOTALS		**$276.20**			**$58.00**

* All costs in U.S. dollars

lavada de ollas on Monday, this record is fairly complete. It reveals that this merchant, representative of Espinal's middle-class petty bourgeoisie, spent 8355 pesos or over $330 to meet her perceived obligations. Of this total, $89 was spent on food for her table, a far cry from the days when guests accompanied their hosts home for a midnight snack. Costs would have been higher if not for contributions of beer and food by guests. Some people spent a great deal more, especially members of the local elite who feast their guests on shrimp, fete them with endless shots of brandy, and send them home with handsome gifts. The expenditures of another informant, who purchased 25 cartons of beer, 4 cartons of soda, and 6 bottles of brandy for Saturday night alone, were possibly double those of the widow. It is important to emphasize that these are customary expenses, typical of those that a majority of *Vela* associates might find themselves saddled with. These are simply costs of attending a *vela*. They do not apply to a *mayordomía* which an individual might host on only a few occasions during a lifetime.

In this context it is noteworthy that the total number of associates of the three principal *velas* numbered less than 500 households in 1981 in a community of more than 8000 people (about 1500 households). Although there is no comparable information from earlier years, it seems probable that even as the number of *vela* associates is rising, the proportion of households in the community that participate as associates is in decline. The rising cost of full participation, which is at least partly under the control of the Directive Board, has the unintended effect of excluding much of the remaining peasantry and many wage workers who simply can no longer afford the dues, the *limosnas*, and especially the expenses of wining and dining guests during the Grand Ball.

WATERING FIELDS AND FERTILIZING MINDS

As seen in the case of the *velas*, substantial differences developed in Espinal between the old and the new—the past as remembered by those who lived it and the present as it is currently lived. However, this statement holds not just for the ritual sphere, but for the economic sphere and the sphere of class relations as well. As mentioned above, the early 1960s was a watershed period because it was then that the canal network of Irrigation District No. 19 began to deliver water from the Benito Juarez dam to the previously-parched lands of Espinal. The double cropping of corn that irrigation made possible put an end to the dry season (October to March) migrations that had taken males away from home in a search for supplementary cash income. However, irrigation also raised ground rents and land values, and stimulated a land rush by wealthy landowners and merchants as well as immigrant speculators. Most of the acquisitions involved lands which composed the expanding agricultural frontier. Previously occupied land, however, also was concentrated through its purchase and sale. Many of the economically weaker peasants, without the financial resources or knowledge of the system to defend themselves, were dispossessed either because they fell into debt and were forced to sell, or because they were unable to prove to the satisfaction of state representatives that they were in fact the legal owners. The process of land concentration might have advanced farther had the state not engendered serious contradictions in the interpretation of the tenure situation (Binford 1985).

In the late 1960s and early 1970s, and at an increasing pace throughout the mid- and late 1970s, the state began to take an active role in the production process, which until then had been left to the discretion of local landholders. New crops (rice, sorghum, sugar cane, hybrid forms of corn, and improved pastures)
were introduced under the sponsorship of state agencies, which also controlled the technology deemed necessary to grow and process the crops (tractors, rice processing plant, sugar mill), and access to the credit required to pay for the technology. Agriculturalists were confronted with a very complex and contradictory situation. On the one hand, it became possible for the first time to plant large (by Isthmus standards) tracts of land in market crops with potentially high values and profits. On the other hand, the higher unit cost of production which was the complement of green revolution technology resulted in large losses when yields were low and/or market prices failed to obtain minimal levels. Corruption, mismanagement, and poor planning on the part of government promoters also contributed to the failure of most of the programs. Moreover, state agencies used their control over production inputs and processing technology to secure exclusive rights to the purchase of many crops (rice and sugar cane being the most important) at prices maintained deliberately low as a function of a long standing state policy of providing cheap food to the urban working classes (Sanderson 1986:47-48, 200-201, 243-245). The state assumed as well the right to organize the production process as a condition for financing the crops, though the landowners remained solely liable for losses when crop yields fell short of targets.

In Espinal and surrounding communities, peasants and a growing class of small capitalist farmers organized formally and informally to struggle for their economic interests against the agrarian banks, the irrigation authority and, most recently, the sugar mill. In the early 1980s, community, family, and ethnicity all played roles in the recruitment of individuals of discrepant socioeconomic class backgrounds to the populist discourse ("the people" versus "the state") which resulted. While the rising petty bourgeoisie of small capitalists, merchants, and professionals-cum-part-time-farmers led the struggle to secure the best possible conditions for capital accumulation, there developed in Juchitán a radical movement, the Isthmus Coalition of Workers, Peasants, and Students. Known by its acronym, the COCEI was supported nationally by the Mexican Communist Party, which struggled for a redistribution of land and economic resources from the large landowners to the small peasantry and those who had been dispossessed in the years following the completion of the irrigation project (see the excellent articles by Campbell 1989 and Rubin 1987 on the COCEI). Although the COCEI never made any headway in Espinal, local political life was nonetheless affected by its proximity to Juchitán.

Besides dedicating themselves to the production of edibles, Espinaleños have dedicated themselves to the development of minds. In the early decades of this century, most economically active males were peasant agriculturalists, with little use for formal education and little opportunity to obtain it. However, shortly after the founding in 1932 of an academy in nearby Comitancillo to train rural school teachers, first the elite and then people of lesser means began to make the sacrifices necessary to educate one or more of their offspring.[14] For reasons that are still unclear, Espinaleños grasped the economic and social potential of education at an earlier date and pursued it with greater intensity than inhabitants of other Isthmus communities. During the 1940s, 1950s and 1960s, but especially in the 1970s, increasing numbers of local youth studied to earn teaching credentials, accounting degrees, and technical certificates in schools from Chiapas to Mexico City and beyond. By 1980 a new ideology had come into existence: "Knock on any door," I was told, "and you will find that the family within counts at least one professional among its members." This turned out to be an exaggeration, but not by much! A 1981 door-to-door census conducted by Espinal's school teachers counted 302 male "professionals" among the 1316 men whose occupations were recorded, accounting for 22.9% of the total. The number was exceeded only by "peasants" (394 or 29.9%) and "wage laborers" (312 or 23.7%). Significantly, an inverse relationship existed between age and the likelihood of being a professional; the age group 21-30 years counted only 42 "peasants" among 325 occupations (12.9%) compared to 95 "wage laborers" (29.2%) and 145 "professionals" (44.6%). On the other hand, 127 (78.9%) of the 161 men over 60 identified themselves as "peasants" (c.f. Binford 1983:141 for complete figures).[15]

The prestige of post-secondary educations and the well-paying jobs that followed made for the formation of a new petty bourgeois class which inserted itself into local economic and political circuits, and gradually wrested control from the old merchant/rancher elite that had dominated politics for many decades. In 1968, one group of young modernizing professionals organized themselves into the Espinal Front for Unity and Progress (FUPE). In 1971 the FUPE candidate won election to the municipal presidency, and they have controlled the administration ever since. Although their principal opposition draws portions of its leadership from the declining peasantry, it too has a heterogeneous class and occupational composition, and counts teachers and other professionals, along with merchants and agriculturalists, among its militants and membership. Nonetheless, by 1981, these two basic political groups, both of which worked within and identified themselves as representatives of PRI (Mexico's ruling Institutional Revolutionary Party), were popularly designated as *"Los Maestros"* ("the teachers") and *"Los Campesinos"* ("the peasants"), respectively. In fact, a clear majority of the small and middle peasants supported the teacher faction and its political line of community service and "modernization" (by which they meant the provision of better schools, drainage projects, renovation of the municipal offices, etc.). Their support makes sense when it is recognized that many peasants (and ex-peasants) made tremendous economic sacrifices in order for their sons and daughters to study away from the community and to return with innovative ideas. Still, a certain percentage of people, mostly elderly, lamented the rapid social changes, the loss of "traditions," and the youth movement in politics. In 1980 and 1981, many aging peasants touted the advantages of practice (agricultural, political) over theory. Reinforced in their suspicions by the opposition leadership, they questioned the intentions of the new municipal government. What in effect occurred politically was the counterpart of the economic developments, which had led to a restructured class system characterized by rapid, though incomplete, social differentiation and, in the context of an overall rise of income, increased maldistribution. There can be no doubt that the "average" Espinaleño was better off in 1981 than in 1960. In the wake of a generalized growth of economic prosperity, however, many households were left behind. For those with little or no land, unable to obtain decent wage employment, and whose extended families were unable to help them out, life was only a little more secure (if that) than it had been before irrigation. Their marginalization is an index of the internal social differentiation of rural economies which are integrated into the capitalist-dominated market system (Cook and Binford 1986, 1988; Binford and Cook 1987).

THE POLITICS OF RITUAL

In 1981 the *velas* were, as always, an arena for the expression of political conflict. Despite the family traditions of *vela* membership, various *velas* by 1981 had become associated with distinct political groups: the Velas Primavera and San Mateo with "the teachers" and Vela San Juan with "the peasants." Furthermore, Vela Guidxi ("The People's *Vela*") was created by the "peasant" faction in 1979 as a means of raising money for the construction of a new market. Many Vela Guidxi members were also in the Vela San Juan, although the high cost of joining two *velas* led some people to drop their pre-existing *vela* membership in order to participate in Vela Guidxi. The leaders of the "teacher" faction encouraged their followers to boycott the festivities. Apart from a reticence to socialize with "the enemy," they also wished to deny their opposition the luxury of a well-attended dance which could be construed as a mandate of support or could generate profits that, subsidizing the construction of the new market, might be converted into political capital. As this example implies, joining and attending *velas* in Espinal in 1981 generally was equated with a declaration of political allegiance. Along the way, families divided, in some cases to the point where individuals ceased greeting their estranged relatives in public.

Always a stage for the playing out of political discourses, the *velas* have been shaped by the discourses as well. Covarrubias (1947:373-374) observed a conflict in Ixtepec between the followers of two political parties, the "Red" and the "Green," over whose representative would be crowned queen of the ball. Royce (1975:144), who worked in Juchitán, noted that Vela San Vicente split into two *velas* (Vela Grande of San Vicente Ferrer and Vela of San Vicente Goola) due to irreconcilable differences among the members regarding the candidates in the municipal election of 1968. Royce also observed that rich and poor have separate *velas*, a fact that some years later was put to use by the nascent COCEI in developing support for its cause (Rubin 1987:136). More recently, in Santiago Laollaga from June to August 1987, dissatisfaction over the appointment of the Directive Boards of the *velas* (of which there were three) and their assumed mishandling of funds resulted in the founding of a new *vela*, Vela Veinte (also referred to as "The People's *Vela*").[16] Almost all of the members of Vela Veinte were drawn from one of the two rival sections of PRI, an indication that more than *vela* politics was at stake.

New in this equation, however, is the restriction of participation in Espinal to those with an income level high enough to underwrite the escalating cost of membership. As noted above, an increasing number of people in poorer households participate only marginally, if at all. They have been swept aside by the new wealth which accompanied the irrigation project, the expansion of the rural school system (which provides many jobs for locally-born teachers), the regional expansion of trade, the construction and service sector, and the growing number of jobs which this wealth sustains. I do not attribute any inevitability to the fact that Espinal's *velas* are developing into orgies of conspicuous consumption, in which the beneficiaries of state-promoted capitalist development commune with one another while the "losers" in this regional drama enviously peruse the scene through the cracks in the palisade. Separate *velas* might have developed for the rich and the poor, as in Juchitán, or the *velas* might have been recast in the mold of the past, complete with wooden flutes, turtle shells, and other instruments that now are seen primarily in museums. That they shed so much ritual baggage so quickly says much, however, about the differences in perspective and influence of the older and younger generations. Many of the latter were educated in major Mexican cities. They have travelled and have a cosmopolitan outlook. While they are proud of their heritage, they seek to obtain for themselves first, and their community second, the amenities that they associate with modern life. It is these people who have determined the course of *vela* development. While wearing regional dress and dancing to Zapotec *sones* are important issues, dancing to a fine orchestra and treating their friends to a sumptuous feast is a way of saying to themselves and others that they have arrived. The problem, of course, is that not everyone arrived, nor, considering the increasing disparities of income, are they likely to in the future.

As the issue of the *velas* makes clear, rapid social differentiation in Espinal was not accompanied, as it was in Juchitán, by a politics opposing small peasants, petty merchants, and proletarians, to larger merchants, capitalists, and bureaucrats (and a smaller number of peasant and worker supporters). Perhaps because of the community's higher per capita wealth, the vast majority of Espinaleños believed that things had improved enormously in comparison to the pre-1960 era. To maintain these improvements they needed leaders who could negotiate with state authorities to provide jobs and investments, and to struggle when those investments did not result in the anticipated benefits. Political struggles were largely over which local faction could best secure these demands shared by most Espinaleños. The *velas* served as one arena for struggles between political factions, but the similarity in their newly transformed practices is also revealing of the degree to which they have come to articulate a single discourse of "modernization," "development," and materialism.

NOTES

1. Fieldwork was carried out in the Southern Isthmus region in 1980 to 1981 in collaboration with Nancy Churchill. Ms. Churchill graciously made available to me her field notes on the *vela* system, and read and commented on various drafts. The responsibility for any errors or omissions are my own.

2. There is great variation in the manner that the *velas* have been integrated into a larger ritual cycle. In some communities, such as Espinal and Tehuantepec, with distinct *barrio* (neighborhood) organizations, *velas* were (or still are) celebrations of neighborhood saints, distinct both from one another and from the festival celebrating the community patron saint. In Juchitán, which was more loosely organized into sections instead of distinct neighborhoods (Nader 1969:340-341), *velas* were named for saints, sacred locations, occupations (e.g., fishermen, beer sellers, fireworks makers), and even surnames, e.g., Pineda, López, etc. (see Royce 1975:143). In another variation, found in Santiago Laollaga, individual *velas* were independent of *barrios* and of one another as well, but were (and are) incorporated into a short but extremely intense ritual period of 10 or 12 days that also included the ceremonies dedicated to Santiago Apostol, Laollaga's patron saint. In short, the timing, associations and even practices of *vela* display a substantial degree of intra-regional variation.

3. *Velas* have long served as forums for raising money for community projects and for the expression of political conflict. For instance, Covarrubias (1947:367-368) noted how in 1940 a pro-school committee (Comité Pro-Escuela Ejidal del Barrio de Guichivere) took contributions from integrants at a table set up at the *mayordomo's* house during the festival to the patron saint of Guichuvere.

4. *Padrinos* and *madrinas* (*compadres*) translate as "godfather" and "godmother," respectively, usually in connection with baptism and the system of ritual co-parenthood known as *compradrazco*. In the Isthmus, however, the terms refer to a variety of relationships varying greatly in intensity and duration. For instance, birthdays involve the recruitment of *padrinos* who provide music and beer and *madrinas* charged with party favors and the birthday cake. Just about every ritual occasion which entails collective organization and celebration involves the recruitment of *padrinos* and *madrinas*. Since these persons often recruit an additional coterie of helpers and/or contributors, and since all of the aid is recorded mentally or in writing and must be repaid, Isthmus Zapotec males and especially females become immersed in extremely dense networks of ritually-based economic exchanges with important implications for non-ritual relationships of kinship and friendship.

5. Before construction of the chapels for the *barrio* saints, each *mayordomo* was charged with caring for a saint's image during his or her year of service. Earlier in the century *mayordomos* supervised land allocated to the church, indicating that the system of individual *cargos* may have been predated by a *cofradía* system as characterized the Maya in colonial Chiapas (Wasserstrom 1983:241-246). Whitecotton records the presence of religious brotherhoods during the colonial period in the Valley of Oaxaca: "Indian *cofradías*...were responsible for staging various religious fiestas and providing supplies for them....Lands set aside for the maintenance of community *cofradías* were collectively owned and operated. They were supervised by *mayordomos*, a general term for supervisors of collective land in the Colonial period" (1977:216).

6. Thus, in the *velas* as in other spheres of life, the gender division of labor predominated. Women decorated and cooked, while men carried out the so-called "heavy" work of erecting the tent and provided the financing.

7. Covarrubias's (1947:370) colorful description took the following form:

> The girls climbed on the church, the bells tolled rapidly, firecrackers exploded, the ragamuffins took positions, the flute and drum played an exciting 'war' theme, and fruits of all sorts—mangoes, bananas, large pineapples—and toys began to fly down from the roof. The women delighted in hurling the heavy pineapples into the crowd, which fell back as the pineapples hit....Bowl after bowl of fruit was emptied over the crowd; coconuts and pineapples added a touch of danger to the sport. The excitement lasted until the last *xicalpextle* [gourd] of fruit and toys were emptied. Then everybody went home, some with bruises and bumps, but proud of their prizes, not because of their intrinsic value, but because they were captured dangerously.

8. For brief descriptions of the social role of Isthmus *muxes* see Chiñas 1985; Collins-Cook 1986.

9. This is no longer always completely true today. The Directive Board of Vela Guidxi sought to limit to one adult son the number of free admissions for those who paid dues and to charge families 200 pesos for each additional son. This proposal led to complaints that "the *vela* is becoming a business" instead of a celebration of solidarity among its members.

10. There was some logic to holding the *velas* in April (*labrada de cera*) and May, for this was the period when the males returned with money from their seasonal labor migrations.

11. Despite the demise of the formal ceremonial, a *mayordomo* still is charged with caring for the chapel of San Marcos. Aided by donations provided by members of Vela Primavera, neighbors, and others who contribute, the *mayordomo* oversees the decoration of the chapel and contracts a professional prayer-sayer to say prayers on Viernes Santo, the holy day of San Marcos.

12. In 1981 the approximate exchange rate was 25 pesos to one U.S. dollar.

13. The Directive Board also makes money from beer sales. The board purchases beer at wholesale prices from the Corona or Carta Blanca distributors in Juchitán and sells it to associates by the carton inside the tent and to the public outside the tent at retail prices. Quantities can be considerable. In 1981, the associates of one *vela* purchased 800 cartons of beer for sale to its members. Beer distribution is big business in the Isthmus, and those who control the agencies are powerful political figures well-entrenched in the regional PRI hierarchy. In Juchitán they frequently have been the targets of political protests led by the COCEI. For these and other reasons, a study of the economic, political, and cultural role of the Mexican beer industry is sorely needed.

14. The object of this campaign was to eliminate illiteracy, but researchers such as Pozas and Pozas (1971:97) and Friedlander (1975:68) have claimed that it also involved an effort to "detribilize" rural populations by instilling in them the values of nationalism, wage-labor relations, and consumerism. Plans called for an army of school teachers willing to live in rural communities, educate the population, and promote social and economic changes sanctioned by the government (Churchill 1987:60).

15. By taking advantage of the possibilities of steady employment that accompanied regional economic development, many people became bricklayers (52 among the 1316 censused male occupations) or taxi drivers (74). They relegated farming to secondary

occupation if they practiced it at all. The employment figures are incomplete because they leave out those locally-born men and women who live and work in other communities, regions of Oaxaca, and other states (frequently because no position was available for them within commuting distance of Espinal), and because no account is taken of professional women, of whom there are a substantial number but who are almost invariably listed, regardless of their economic activity, as "housewife" (Churchill 1987:69-71).

16. The Santiago Laollaga *vela* system differs slightly from those in other areas of the Isthmus in that all *velas* and most of the activities sponsored by the *mayordomo, capitanes,* and *capitanas* are compressed into a 10 to 11 day period in July. Whereas the cost of *vela* sponsorship has risen drastically over the last few years, it remains within the range of most of the peasants who predominate in this community, despite the national economic crisis. The *mayordomo* for 1987, a naval officer stationed in Salina Cruz, spent 3.8 million pesos and recovered approximately 1.8 million from the *mesas de co-operación,* leaving him responsible for the remaining 2 million. For 1988, the respective figures for the mayordomía were expenses of 10 million pesos with an income of 5.3 million pesos.

REFERENCES

Binford, Leigh
    1983   "Agricultural Crises, State Intervention and the Development of Classes in the Isthmus of Tehuantepec, Oaxaca, Mexico." Ph.D. dissertation, University of Connecticut.
    1985   "Agrarian Conflict and Land Tenure in the Southern Isthmus of Tehuantepec." *Journal of Latin American Studies,* 17 (Part 2):177-200.
Binford, Leigh and Scott Cook
    1987   "Toward a Marxist Rethinking of Third World Rural Industrialization." In *Economic Processes and Political Conflicts: Contributions to Modern Political Economy.* Richard England, editor, pp. 61-85. New York: Praeger.
Campbell, Howard
    1989   "The COCEI: Class and Politicized Ethnicity in the Isthmus of Tehuantepec." Unpublished manuscript.
Chiñas, Beverly
    1973   *The Isthmus Zapotecs: Women's Roles in Cultural Context.* New York: Holt, Rinehart, Winston.
    1985   "Isthmus Zapotec 'Berdaches'." *Newsletter of the Anthropological Research Group on Homosexuality,* 7(2):1-4.
Churchill, Nancy Ellen
    1987   "Knock on Any Door: Social Differentiation and Political Process in a Community in Southern Oaxaca." Master's thesis, University of Connecticut.
Collins Cook, Della
    1986   "Isthmus Zapotec Muxé: Social and Biological Dimensionsof a Third Gender Role." Paper presented at the Annual Meeting of the American Anthropological Association, Philadelphia, PA.
Cook, Scott and Leigh Binford
    1986   "Petty Commodity Production, Capital Accumulation and Peasant Differentiation: Lenin vs. Chayanov in Rural Mexico." *Review of Radical Political Economy* 18(4): 1-31.
    1990   *Obliging Need.* Austin: University of Texas Press.
Covarrubias, Miguel
    1947   *Mexico South: The Isthmus of Tehuantepec.* New York: Alfred A. Knopf.

DeWalt, Billie
  1975   "Changes in the Cargo Systems of Mesoamerica." *Anthropological Quarterly* 48:87-
         105.
Friedlander, Judith
  1975   *Being Indian in Hueyapan.* New York: St. Martin's.
Nader, Laura
  1969   "The Zapotec of Oaxaca." In *Handbook of Middle American Indians*, Robert
         Wauchope, general editor. *Volume 7: Ethnology: Part I*, Evon Vogt, editor, pp. 329-
         359.   Austin: University of Texas Press.
Pozas, Ricardo and Isabel H. de Pozas
  1971   *Los Indios en las Clases Sociales de México.* Mexico: Siglo Veintiuno.
Royce, Anya Peterson
  1975   *Prestigo y Afiliación en una Comunidad Urbana: Juchitán, Oaxaca.* Mexico:
         Instituto Nacional Indigenista.
Rubin, Jeffrey
  1987   "State Policies, Leftist Opposition and Municipal Elections: The Case of the COCEI
         in Juchitán." In *Electoral Patterns and Perspectives in Mexico.* Arturo Alvarado,
         editor, pp. 127-160. San Diego: Center for U.S.-Mexican Studies, Monograph Series,
         No. 22.
Sanderson, Stephen
  1986   *The Transformation of Mexican Agriculture.* Princeton, NJ: Princeton.
Smith, Waldemar
  1977   *The Fiesta System and Economic Change.* New York: Columbia University Press.
Wasserstrom, Robert
  1983   *Class and Society in Central Chiapas.* Berkeley: California.
Whitecotton, Joseph W.
  1977   *The Zapotecs: Princes, Priests, and Peasants.* Norman: University of Oklahoma
         Press.

Part III.
Political Conflict and Local Religion

Sanctity and Resistance in Closed Corporate Indigenous Communities: Coffee Money, Violence, and Ritual Organization in Chatino Communities of Oaxaca

James B. Greenberg
University of Arizona

INTRODUCTION

Fascination with the civil-religious hierarchies of closed corporate indigenous communities has been a staple of Mesoamerican anthropology for over 50 years.[1] In part, this emphasis stems from the recognition that these hierarchies, which organize age-grades, do for indigenous communities "what kinship does for African societies, or what social class does for *ladino* society" (Nash 1958:68). These civil-religious hierarchies consist of ladders of offices in which civil officials handle the communities' administrative affairs, and religious officeholders, *mayordomos*, hold fiestas and rituals dedicated to particular saints. Each ladder has several rungs or levels of offices of increasing power and prestige. Men serve alternately in civil and religious offices, until they reach the highest levels, such as *presidente* or *alcalde*. They then become village elders. Service is a family enterprise in which women play important roles, particularly in the rituals and fiestas sponsored by officeholders. Although it is men who hold formal office, these hierarchies also provide status for women. Because service often calls for officeholders to pay out-of-pocket any expenses connected with their office, the primary focus of these studies has been on their ritual and economic aspects, rather than on their political dimensions. The few descriptions of their political aspects that do exist usually emphasize their internal structure rather than their relationship to the state.

This essay explores the changing historical relationship of indigenous communities to the state and, by detailing conflicts in Chatino communities, examines the role that civil-religious hierarchies have played in this connection. Although this work focuses on the Chatino, much of it applies to closed corporate indigenous communities in Mesoamerica. These are indigenous communities which have retained communal land tenure and in which participation in their civil-religious hierarchies defines village membership, and hence use-rights on communal lands (Wolf 1955, 1957, 1986). In examining the linkages between indigenous communities and the wider society, I employ Richard Adams' concept of domains of power as it is especially useful for describing asymmetrical relationships. Adams proposes that, although players may interact with and influence one another, the stronger players are able to exert greater mastery and control over the environment of the weaker ones (Adams 1975:84). As applied to indigenous communities, Adams' concept outlines the dilemma faced by town officials. As constitutionally elected officials they not only must uphold and enforce state laws, but often are called upon by the state to carry out actions that may go against the interest of the community. Refusal to do so may end in a fine, imprisonment, or removal from office. Yet if they concede to such pressures, they risk social ostracism, possibly in their own communities. In answer to such pressures, indigenous communities have developed defensive mechanisms. Although not always effective, these mechanisms mediate the influence of outside power holders on community members' lives. Some of these mechanisms, such as fiesta systems with their economic consequences, are well known and have been the subject of long debate (Greenberg 1981). Others, such as consensus formation or the use of sanctity in the informal exercise of power by village elders, have received only scant attention (see Beltrán 1973; Dow 1974). Here I focus on these lesser known strategies, exploring how Chatino village elders use their informal authority in the politics of consensus to galvanize opposition to unfavorable actions by formal authorities, and to the often fickle politics of patronage in patron/client relations that power holders at local, state, and national levels use to exploit indigenous communities.

THE STATE AND THE PROBLEM OF ETHNIC DIVERSITY

To understand the political aspects of civil-religious hierarchies, we must examine their roots. Historically, the closed corporate community is—to use Wolf's phrase—a "child of the conquest" (1957:8). The Spanish used a strategy of indirect rule to govern the people they conquered. Spanish colonial policy was explicitly segregationist and discouraged Spanish settlement in native communities. Much like South Africa's current system of apartheid, the Spaniards treated indigenous communities as "home lands" in which indigenous communities legally were discrete political units, known as *republicas de Indios* (Indian republics). In theory, each Indian republic was a self-governing and self-supporting unit. Each had its own land base, and its own town government. Administratively and politically, however, these political units were subordinated to Spanish towns. By defining each community as an independent unit, and by dealing with each ruler individually, colonial policy undermined the alliances between communities which had integrated pre-Hispanic states. Effectively, this policy isolated indigenous communities from direct access to power and permitted local colonial authorities to continue to exploit them with little interference from higher levels of government.

By endowing each Indian republic with its own land base for subsistence, the Crown also opened what it defined as "unoccupied" lands for Spanish colonists. These policies, and similar ones passed by liberal governments after independence, created a political ecology in which indigenous "homelands" were surrounded by large private estates. Even though indigenous communities had served as labor pools for the surrounding capitalist enterprises, the tendency of private estates to expand at the expense of indigenous communities was a constant cause of friction between them.

Initially, the Spanish imposed a Castillian *municipio* (municipal) system of government over the pre-Hispanic political system, thus effectively limiting the power of the native nobility to the local level. In the early stages of its evolution, native noblemen held the highest offices in the town government. The native ruler was given the title of governor. Nobles served as *alcaldes* (judges) for minor crimes and civil suits, and as *regidores* (councilmen) who passed local ordinances. The town government often included a number of lesser posts assigned to commoners through a system of rotation.

Just as the Spanish adapted the Castillian *municipio* system to serve as a colonial instrument of control, indigenous communities soon began to modify these structures to fit the needs of the community. For example, in adapting the Spanish civil-religious system to the organization of their villages, the Chatino used a principal of dual organization. They divided offices evenly between two *barrios* (neighborhoods or sections) either by allotting each *barrio* an even number, or by alternating who would fill an office between the *barrios*. In addition to dividing power equally, they took care to fit the Spanish system to the demands of village kin groups. Thus, lineage membership is now considered in the naming of officials. No two persons from the same household or house compound can serve simultaneously. Concern about the number of people from any one of the maximal lineages or clans allowed to serve at one time is also a factor in the choice of officeholders.

Although indirect rule was a historical necessity in the early colonial period, the Spanish state ceaselessly worked to undermine the limited sovereignty of local indigenous communities. In fact, the state's approach to indigenous communities has oscillated historically between two poles, indirect rule and centralism. When its control has been weak, the state has relied on indirect rule; when it has been stronger, it has tried to extend direct forms of control into indigenous communities. As the power of colonial bureaucracy grew during the sixteenth century, the need to share power with native nobility diminished steadily, and the privileges granted them decreased. As Whitecotton notes,

> By the end of the Spanish colonial period, the Indian *cabildo* had taken a form that was neither distinctively Spanish nor like the government of pre-conquest times. Instead, it represented an adaptation of Spanish town government to local conditions—conditions that made holding of political offices less a right than a duty designed to preserve and protect a local Indian community of peasants. In this system, prestige became synonymous not with wealth and power but with their antithesis—poverty and service (1977:191).

In the closed corporate indigenous villages that emerged during the colonial period, and which took their classic egalitarian form in the nineteenth century (Chance and Taylor 1986; Wasserstrom 1983), service in civil and religious offices came to define the boundaries of membership in indigenous communities. As only natives who served the community as officeholders had access to communal lands, these offices became one of the principal mechanisms through which indigenous villages defended their lands against Spanish encroachment. In these egalitarian villages, officeholders often had to pay any costs their posts incurred.

Dow (1974) has argued that the fiesta system organized a redistributive system of exchange within the community. As Wolf (1955, 1957) argues, the costs of such service inhibited the ability of individuals to engage in those capitalistic forms of investment which would increase social inequality. Moreover, Harris (1964) notes that since these expenditures often called for cash to purchase goods in Spanish dominated market systems, these offices also served to pump goods and labor into the market, and ultimately into the hands of Spanish merchants.

With independence, the state's official stance toward indigenous communities changed. Constitutional reforms granted indigenous people "full citizenship" before the law. The Indian republics which had for so long segregated indigenous communities from the rest of society were abolished. Because indigenous people were now equal citizens of the new Republic, paternalistic colonial laws for the protection of indigenous communities were repealed. "Non-Indians were no longer forbidden to reside in Indian communities, and the special Indian courts such as the *Juzgado de Indios* were disbanded" (Taylor 1979:146).

After independence, because the political hold over indigenous communities in Oaxaca was comparatively weak, the state government moved toward a more centralized form of administration. In 1826, the political divisions of Oaxaca were reorganized into 26 *departmentos*, later called districts. These new centralized districts were administered by *jefes politicos* (district chiefs) who were named by the governor of the state and answered only to him. The *jefe politico* ruled on political matters. Elected civil officials had to meet the *jefe politico's* approval and any actions taken by local governments required his endorsement.

Between 1856 and 1859, liberals espousing a philosophy of growth and progress passed a series of reform laws which also profoundly affected closed corporate indigenous communities. These liberal reform laws were aimed against corporate properties, particularly those of the church, the largest landholder in Mexico. As an outcome, the property held by *cofradías*, the religious brotherhoods which sponsored religious fiestas in indigenous communities, came under attack and was alienated. In its place, a system of individual sponsorship by *mayordomos* was instituted (Chance and Taylor

1985:17-20). Moreover, because the state felt that corporate property was one of the major obstacles to Mexico becoming a modern industrial nation, the communal lands of indigenous communities also came under attack. During the Porfiriato (1880-1910), these laws were cynically applied to form haciendas and plantations on communal lands taken from thousands of indigenous and peasant communities.

LEGAL STATUS OF INDIGENOUS COMMUNITIES IN MEXICO

The current legal standing of indigenous communities, and their subordination to the political apparatus of the Mexican state, is a product of this complex history. The status of indigenous communities is quite distinct from those in the United States. Although there are no reservations, indigenous communities often form *agencias* (townships subordinate to a *municipio*) or *municipios*. Often these contain a mixture of private property and ancestral lands held either as communal lands or as *ejidos*. The latter were created as part of Mexico's land reform program which is administered by the Department of Agrarian Affairs and Colonization (DAAC). DAAC oversees land reform, has jurisdiction over boundary squabbles between communities, and validates titles to private, communal, or *ejido* lands. In theory, all indigenous Mexicans today have the same rights, duties, and privileges enjoyed by any citizen of the nation. In practice, however, such equality is seldom the case.

POLITICS OF PATRONAGE

In Oaxaca, nonindigenous elites not only control the state government, but dominate indigenous communities. The key to their power lies in the political organization of the state government's territorial units. Although Oaxaca has some fifteen indigenous ethnic groups and the largest indigenous population of any state in Mexico, these ethnic groups have been gerrymandered among the state's political divisions—districts, *municipios*, and *agencias*—in such a way as to effectively deny indigenous people full representation and access to power.

The state of Oaxaca is divided into thirty districts, each with a district capital. The district government almost always is controlled by *mestizos*, that is, by Mexicans, who consider themselves culturally non-"Indian." Each district consists of a number of *municipios*, which may be indigenous or nonindigenous. *Municipios*, in turn, are often further divided into *agencias*. The government of the *agencia* is subordinate to that of its *municipio*. The political gerrymandering of Chatino communities presents a typical case.

There are some 30,000 Chatino spread among some 23 Chatino villages (see Map 6.1). Politically, Chatino communities are divided between the districts of Juquila and Sola de Vega, whose district capitals—of the same names—are dominated by *mestizos*. In the district of Juquila, for example, *mestizos* manipulate 17 of the 21 Chatino villages directly. Of these, four are *municipios* in which a resident *mestizo* core controls the local government. Thirteen are

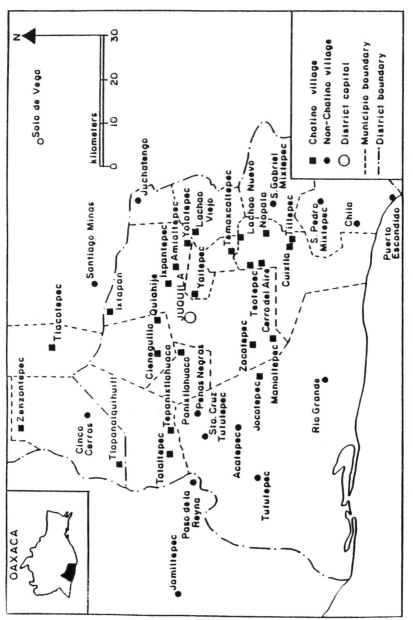

MAP 6.1. THE DISTRIBUTION OF CHATINO COMMUNITIES

agencias subordinated administratively to these *mestizo*-controlled *municipios*. In the remaining four Chatino villages which are *municipios*, *mestizo* manipulation takes a more indirect form.

In formal terms, *agencia* status means that the municipal *presidente* (mayor) must confirm the civil officials elected by the community, and they must report to him. So even though the *presidente* of an *agencia* may be indigenous, and may exercise a modicum of authority within it, he is nonetheless accountable to the *presidente* of the *municipio*. Even in the few Chatino communities which have the status of "free" *municipio*, the influence of nonindigenous elites is sharply felt. The adjective "free" refers to Article 115 of the Federal Constitution of 1917 which provides that free *municipios* will be administered by a directly elected government, "without intermediary authority between them and the government of the state" (Perez 1968:21). The Chatino community of Santiago Yaitepec, for example, is a "free" *municipio*. As a "free" *municipio*, the state constitution requires Yaitepec's *ayuntamiento* (town government) to have a republican form of government with executive, legislative, and judicial branches elected by popular vote. However, even in *municipios* where indigenous individuals hold elected offices, the civil officials are legally accountable to the *mestizo* authorities. Serious violation of state or federal law would lead to the removal of indigenous authorities from office, or to the demotion of their community's status to that of an *agencia* of a *municipio* in which *mestizos* are politically predominant.

Often, to guarantee the *agencia's* "smooth" administration, the *presidente* of the *municipio* names a nonindigenous individual as the *agencia's* secretary. Even in "free" indigenous *municipios*, since few people are capable of preparing the legal documents required of local government, their secretaries are usually *mestizos* from the district capital. The secretary's task is to make sure that legal formalities are followed, at least on paper. Secretaries also see to it that on all significant questions—the administration of justice, the collection of taxes—the *municipio* is the *agencia's* judge and arbitrator. This arrangement, which tightly links *agencias* to their *municipio*, erects sizable barriers that often short circuit direct communication between the *agencia* and state and federal levels of government.

The close ties the district capital has with its "free" indigenous *municipio* creates another closed circuit which often prevents direct communication between indigenous *municipios* and the state government. Between the district and the federal government is yet another buffer, the government of the state, further isolating indigenous communities from contact with Mexico City. This chain of closed circuits, moreover, coincides with another class of intermediaries, the system of markets (Smith 1977). The close association between economic and political intermediaries is no accident. Frequently, they are the same. Their close connection supplies each higher link in this chain with the fiscal, political, and jural control over its satellites required to exact surplus for commerce.

PATRONAGE FOR INDIGENOUS PEOPLE AND COMMUNITIES

The hierarchical structure of political units not only creates sets of administrative barriers which hinder the direct access of indigenous communities to power holders, but also helps to sustain *mestizo* elites in a dominant position because such barriers can be overcome only through patronage. For the Chatino, patronage means forming ties with *mestizos,* as no indigenous person has either the economic leverage or the political ties needed to be an effective patron. When a favor is needed, the Chatino commonly turn to local *mestizos*—merchants or coffee buyers, large landowners, public officials—who act as brokers in relations with the wider society. Usually, favors are predicated on personal ties with the broker, such as ties of *compadrazgo* (ritual kinship). In Yaitepec, these ties are commonly made with *mestizos* residing in Juquila, the district capital and principal market town of the region.

In Juquila there are two rival political factions representing cliques surrounding competing coffee buyers. A small group of coffee buyers, merchants, and large coffee plantation owners heads one faction. This faction controls the local chapter of the Party of the Institutional Revolution (PRI) which has ruled Mexico since the 1930s. The other faction is formed around a competing set of coffee buyers and peasant coffee growers. This faction controls the village's communal land organization. As an opposition party, this faction has had a number of political faces over the years. Until the village banished the priest who headed this faction for many years, its political face was the Party of the Authentic Mexican Revolution (PARM) a right wing conservative party. Currently, it presents itself as another right wing party, the National Action Party (PAN). Because both factions are organized around a core of coffee buyers, each faction has commercial and political networks which extend outward from the local community to wealthy buyer/exporters, with powerful political connections at the state and national levels.

Because considerable sums are at stake, especially in the competition to buy the coffee harvest, the rivalry between these two factions is intense and sometimes bloody. The factions often act like *mafias*, with bribes and assassinations as common occurrences. Since political and economic power rests on their client's loyalty, both sides spend a great deal of time watching who consorts with whom. Both parties compete for clients through the medium of ritual kinship. *Compadrazgo*, in this setting, is a way of formalizing the patron/client relationship. Coffee buyers, for example, give loyal clients credit in their stores and better prices on their harvest. In return, patrons expect clients will show their loyalty by giving them preferential consideration.

Even if patronage is rewarding for some individuals, it is not especially rewarding for indigenous communities. Both factions have used their influence to take advantage of Chatino communities. Under the PRI factions' direction, Juquila took a large tract of land from Yaitepec in a boundary dispute. This same bloc of property holders and businessmen has unwaveringly backed the owners of the plantation, La Constancia, against Yaitepec's attempts to reclaim its communal lands. The local PRI leaders have grown rich by using their influence to gain lumber leases from Chatino communities. The leadership of PARM/PAN has been no better. The priest, for example, who headed the local PARM organization, milked the community when they built the new church. Acting as contractor, he overcharged them for labor, materials, and transportation, depleted their funds, and left the church unfinished.

Although Juquila's factions compete for individual clients in Yaitepec and surrounding Chatino villages, the PRI and PAN are seen as *mestizo*-dominated institutions exploiting the dependent communities. Even though PRI and PAN compete for votes for candidates for state and federal offices, they do not play a meaningful role in the election of officeholders in predominantly Chatino communities.

SUB ROSA GOVERNMENT AND THE POLITICS OF RESISTANCE

The politics of patronage, however, are only half of village politics. The other half is the politics of consensus in which participation in the civil-religious hierarchy plays a major role. Typically, mass demonstrations or land invasions are expressions of this latter political process. Although elites try to mold consensus through their patronage, the undercurrents of consensus often run counter to them. Patronage and consensus are basically contrasting *modi operandi* in village politics. Under these conditions, patronage is the political arm of the capitalist relations of production. In contrast, the politics of consensus are the local populace's response to the often blatant forms of exploitation.

Although *mestizo* elites force indigenous authorities to comply with state and federal laws, and through skillful manipulation often coerce them into actions which favor *mestizo* interests, Chatino villages remain political entities in their own right. The Chatino remain citizens of a village first, a nation second. Despite state and federal constitutions which dictate the form that local government will take, indigenous notions of law and justice as well as their own principles of organization have not been entirely stifled. The constitutionally mandated posts have been reorganized by age-grades into ladders of civil and religious offices. Men alternate service in ranked religious posts (which sponsor fiestas for the saints) with civil offices of increasing prestige and power. Upon finishing this ladder, men become village elders and members of a committee of elders. The committee of elders, even though it has no constitutional status, has veto power over the community's civil government. Because the state cannot easily co-opt or manipulate such informal forms of organization, the elders often act effectively to oppose the state.

Authority in indigenous communities, as Beltrán has noted (1973:178-214), is based on a complementary duality of formal and informal power. Thus, Yaitepec's age-grades define a sub rosa government in which village elders use consensus to wield informal power in the community. Although the constitutional authorities may hold the secular reins of formal power, the elders have acquired informal political power during their careers in its civil hierarchy, and through service to the community's saints have gained an almost sacred status. Informally, the village elders play an important role in elections. No official, for example, can be elected or appointed without the elders' consensus and consent. Although they hold no office, the elders can overrule the constitutional authorities. They may even force officials to resign if they believe their conduct is detrimental to the community's interests. The age-grade system internal to the established civil and religious structures gives increasing political and moral power to each higher level of officials, ultimately sanctifying the sub rosa structure of authority embodied in the village elders. Because this hidden infrastructure of authority is not accessible to bureaucratic manipulation of the state, the indigenous community is able to resist, although not always successfully, pressures from *mestizo* dominated political and economic institutions. Any success, however, that the indigenous community has in opposing the wider society lies not in its formal political strength, but rather in the trouble the state system has (based as it is on bureaucratic control and patronage) in controlling a sub rosa power which is exerted informally (Dow 1973:16). Because the elders exercise power informally using consensus, they are not easily controlled by outside interests. In this context, the politics of consensus is a defensive check on the easily dominated constitutional government of the community.

THE POLITICS OF CONSENSUS IN CHATINO VILLAGES

In Chatino villages the major factional divisions are not by political parties. Instead, they follow lines of *barrio* residence and kinship. In Yaitepec, the opening of communal lands to coffee as a cash crop in the early 1950s transformed the system of land tenure and turned communal lands into *de facto* private parcels.

Coffee created a land market which led to the concentration of coffee land ownership in a few hands. This change produced deep divisions in the community, engendering blood feuds which divided the community along *barrio* and kinship lines, and gave rise to unprecedented levels of violence (Greenberg 1989). The homicide rate, which had averaged 120 per 100,000 from 1930 to 1949, jumped to 480 per 100,000 in the 1950s, 440 in the 1960s, and 511 in the 1970s (see Greenberg 1981:69, 179-182; Greenberg 1989). Even though these factional divisions and feuds led to carnage, and despite the deep factional divisions that existed within the community, consensus could be reached when communal interests are at stake. The history of Yaitepec's boundary disputes and its struggles to recover communal lands from a plantation may be used to illustrate the politics of consensus.

Yaitepec's boundary problems with the villages of Juquila, Yolotepec, and Temaxcaltepec date back to 1863, when the *jefe politico* of the district of Juquila issued new land titles. The new titles cut away large tracts of land from the area Yaitepec felt were its primordial boundaries. It is doubtful that Yaitepec's authorities grasped the purpose of the title at the time, but when they finally realized its effect, an attempt was made to alter the 1863 document to agree more closely with Yaitepec's claims. By 1926, the date of the notarized copy, the title had been altered to reflect the boundary conflicts with Temaxcaltepec and Yolotepec, but not those with Juquila. This oversight very likely occurred because the municipal secretary who made the changes probably came from Juquila. Since 1935, Yaitepec has repeatedly petitioned the Department of Agrarian Affairs and Colonization (DAAC) for clarification of its boundaries with other *municipios* and for the restitution of its lands held by the coffee plantation, La Constancia. Because DAAC's secretaries generally came from Juquila, the land dispute between Yaitepec and Juquila was rarely mentioned in these petitions. So in 1970, when DAAC finished its investigations of boundary disputes, this conflict was not mentioned in their report, and Juquila was issued a presidential decree giving its people clear title to the disputed lands.

The dispute with La Constancia is rooted in a lease. In 1899, Father Valencia,[2] a priest from Juquila, taking advantage of the indigenous authorities' simple faith, leased more than 1,000 hectares of communal lands from Yaitepec to establish a coffee plantation. Since the Reform Laws of 1857 had deprived the church and clergy of rights to own property, the lease was a way to evade this legal issue. The terms of the lease specified that the priest was to pay Yaitepec 60 pesos annually. Father Valencia, however, was no common parish priest. He was a businessman with five children. When he died around 1918, his sons inherited the coffee plantation. When land reform, long promised by the revolution, began in earnest during the Cárdenas administration (1934 to 1940), Yaitepec petitioned for the restitution of the plantation lands. The Valencia brothers (sons of Father Valencia) responded to this threat by harvesting the cornfields that the indigenous members of Yaitepec had planted along the boundaries of the plantation. When the indigenous people from Yaitepec went to complain, the Valencias fired shots at them. In 1940, to keep their property within the size limits allowed under the agrarian reform laws, the family divided the estate's 1,181 hectares into five smaller coffee *fincas*.

Despite the continual trouble with Yaitepec, the Valencias paid the annual rent for their lease until about 1970. In 1970, Yaitepec's communal land titles mysteriously disappeared. The following year, the Valencias refused to pay on the lease, claiming that their lands were private property and that they owed nothing on the land other than state property taxes.

THE POLITICS OF PATRONAGE VERSUS THE POLITICS OF CONSENSUS

In 1974, Yaitepec's land problems came to a head. The authorities in Juquila signed a 25 year lease with Etla S.A., giving the lumber company the rights to log a tract of land along the road to Yolotepec. Yaitepec's authorities were very perturbed by the agreement as they believed the timber was on Yaitepec's land. Although Yaitepec was tormented by factionalism and feuding, a threat to its communal lands was one issue that could unite the community. The villagers threatened violence if any of their trees were cut.

To prevent violence, a company agent agreed to meet Yaitepec's authorities so that they could show him the land boundaries in question. At this meeting the head of Yaitepec's Communal Lands Committee, Emiliano, showed the agent a map from 1862. The Etla representative was not impressed. Since their map had no notary marks, it would be worthless in court, he told them. Even though he wanted to cut the timber right then, because of the likelihood of violence, the agent promised he would delay logging on this tract long enough for the boundary dispute between Juquila and Yaitepec to be resolved. He told the villagers to take their case to the National Indian Institute (INI). The company would wait. But, the agent warned, if the dispute remained unsettled in five years, their lawyers would get the federal government to nationalize the land. The company would then obtain the lumber rights from the federal government and neither community would get anything.

Since INI was a government agency, Yaitepec's authorities viewed it with some suspicion. Experience had taught them to be wary of the state's *mestizo*-dominated institutions, but there was no other alternative. So Emiliano, heading a delegation, set out for Mexico City. There, Emiliano showed INI's lawyer the 1926 copy of the title. The original title, he explained, had been stolen by the Valencias in collusion with a former *presidente*. INI's lawyer told them their copy was worthless, and that according to information that DAAC had supplied to INI, there was no conflict between Juquila and Yaitepec. INI's opinion, moreover, not only favored Juquila, but also Yolotepec and Temaxcaltepec. The lawyer was pessimistic about Yaitepec's chances of winning their boundary disputes, but he encouraged them, saying that they might be successful in a fight for the Valencias' land.

When INI failed to champion fully Yaitepec's cause, Emiliano decided to seek aid from the National Confederation of Peasants (CNC). The CNC employs advocates to guide peasants through the DAAC's bureaucratic maze. An advocate told Emiliano they needed to obtain copies of their original titles and maps, and he would help them search DAAC's archives. DAAC was a bureaucratic nightmare. Officials had little time or patience for indigenous people. They had the indigenous people from Yaitepec fill out forms and file petitions, only to be told they had the wrong ones and needed to go to another office. Even with the CNC advocate's help, it took two weeks to obtain copies of the original 1863 land titles and maps. The titles, it should be noted, did not support Yaitepec's boundary claims, but they did support the claim against the Valencias' land. Finally, the advocate made an appointment to see the director of the Office of Communal Lands, an office within DAAC with jurisdiction over communal land disputes. The director reviewed Yaitepec's file. He told Emiliano that their file was complete and his office could proceed. It was his opinion that the titles did not support Yaitepec's dispute with Juquila. Because it was INI's opinion that the question of municipal boundaries should take precedence over conflicts with small landowners, the director scheduled a meeting in his office between representatives of Yaitepec, Yolotepec, and Temaxcaltepec for the following month. The director explained to Emiliano that if they could not settle the matter among themselves at that meeting, then DAAC would make the decision. As the delegation was leaving, the director took Emiliano aside and hinted that he would see what he could do to help them if they made it worth his while.

LAND DISPUTES AND THE POLITICS OF CONSENSUS

Upon their return, a council meeting was held, and Emiliano gave a full report to the *ayuntamiento*. Nearly every head of household in the village was present, and a lively debate followed over what should be done. It became evident that in 1970 Juquila had given the director of the Office of Communal Lands a bribe of 25,000 pesos (2,000 dollars) for a presidential resolution for Juquila's boundary conflicts. That decree gave Juquila the tract of land Yaitepec claimed. Emiliano reasoned that Yaitepec could do the same. All that was needed was money to bribe the director and "give force" to their claims. All agreed, and a collection was taken up. Contributions were meticulously recorded, and the sum of 15,000 pesos (1,200 dollars) was raised for the bribe.

The meeting had another very political aspect. By bringing back Yaitepec's titles and maps, Emiliano had extended his political influence in the community. As the ritual drinking proceeded, Emiliano became drunk and began to hurl accusations. He accused the municipal secretary of cheating the community. Worse yet, he charged that the secretary was still the head of the communal lands committee of one of the Chatino villages that Yaitepec claimed had taken its lands, a village in which he had previously served as secretary. With a stream of profanity, Emiliano accused the *presidente* of being in the pay of the Valencias, asserting that the *presidente* was their *compadre*, as well as suggesting that they had given him a piece of land on their plantation for services rendered. Drunk and abusive, Emiliano insisted that the *presidente* and secretary resign. Some of the more rational council members tried to mediate the conflict. They argued: "We should not fight among ourselves. How can we hope to win our battles with other communities if we fight among ourselves?" The affair, however, was not laid to rest. The next day the *presidente* and municipal secretary filed a complaint against Emiliano with the public prosecutor in Juquila, charging him with public defamation and threatening to kill the *presidente*.

However, before any action could be taken, Emiliano and the members of the Communal Lands Committee left for Mexico City to keep the appointment in the Office of Communal Lands. In Mexico, Emiliano went with the CNC solicitor to see the director of the Communal Lands Office. The solicitor, however, convinced Emiliano that it was unnecessary to bribe the director. Since the representatives from Temaxcaltepec and Yolotepec had failed to appear, the matter of their boundaries was turned over to a special studies unit for a decision. At a meeting, the CNC advocate and director evidently encouraged the village to invade the plantation. They told the villagers that if there were any problems with the public prosecutor in Juquila, they should come back to them. Since possession is nine-tenths of the law, one can only guess that the director and advocate calculated that if the indigenous people of Yaitepec invaded the plantation, administratively the matter would be easier to handle.

When Emiliano brought this account back to the *ayuntamiento*, a ferocious debate arose. The *presidente* and the municipal secretary opposed the invasion on firm legal grounds—no written permission had been given. Emiliano again accused the *presidente* and secretary of being traitors to the *pueblo*. Since the *regidores*, *alcaldes*, and the other members of the council opposed the *presidente*, they finally decided to put the question in God's hands. The decision was clearly a vote of no confidence in the *presidente* and secretary. It was a vote to bypass their authority and make the decision by community consensus. The council asked the village elders to go to Juquila and invite the priest to say five special masses.

The next day, the masses were well attended. The *presidente* and secretary, however, were noticeably absent. In this setting, the special masses not only measured the consensus of the community (both in terms of attendance and donations to pay for them), but also gave such consensus sanctity. After the mass, the donations were counted publicly on the church plaza by the elders who declared "there is force now." The money was taken to the priest, who tried in vain to convince them not to invade the plantation. After the priest left, a public meeting was held in the church plaza. Emiliano argued: "There is force in the *pueblo* now. Don't be afraid to enter! Our patron saint, Santiago, will give us his sword!" Again he called for the resignation of the *presidente* and secretary. After some debate, the men of the village voted to oust the *presidente* and secretary, and to invade the plantation the following morning.

From the reports given me, the villagers had cut the fences and were clearing the fields to plant corn when one of the Valencias emerged from the woods firing a pistol. He was gunned down. Frightened, the men returned to the village. Emiliano and the Communal Lands Committee set off for Mexico City to report the incident to the director of the Communal Lands Office and to the CNC advocate.

MESTIZO REPRISALS AND THE POLITICS OF PATRONAGE

Matters went from bad to worse. In Mexico City, the director of the Communal Lands Division gave Emiliano written permission to occupy the plantation's lands. Upon his return, the villagers again decided to invade the plantation. In the interim, however, the Valencias had gotten an injunction prohibiting the villagers from taking possession of their lands until the case was settled in court. When the second invasion occurred, the Valencias called in the state police who made arrests and opened fire on the villagers, wounding many as they fled.

In a patent effort to deprive the movement against their lands of its leadership, the Valencias accused Emiliano and the other members of the Communal Lands Committee of the "assassination" of their brother. The charges, however, were never proven. In the aftermath of this slaying, because the priest had gone to say masses in Yaitepec, the PRI in Juquila blamed him for the invasion as well. To prove that he had tried to prevent it, the priest used his influence in Juquila's Communal Lands Office to persuade them to refuse to rent communal land to the people of Yaitepec. Since almost half of Yaitepec families needed to rent lands from Juquila, this act of reprisal was especially cruel. In reaction to the second invasion, an attempt was made to gain greater political control over Yaitepec by demoting it from an independent *municipio* to an *agencia* of Juquila. However, when things simmered down, the pressure to degrade Yaitepec's status dissipated.

After the second invasion, the consensus in the village seemed to vanish. Although Emiliano continued to have considerable support, many blamed him for what happened.

FACTIONALISM IN YAITEPEC

After the ouster of the ex-*presidente*, Emiliano set himself up in Yaitepec as a *cacique* (a political boss). He expropriated the *presidente's* official seal. This gave him veto power over the town council, since he could refuse to stamp any document that he did not like. However, unlike *mestizo caciques*, who have extensive social and economic webs that link them to powerful patrons at the state and national level, Emiliano's base of power lay solely in Yaitepec. As long as things went well, this was sufficient. However, when they began to go badly, Emiliano had no one to turn to for help or protection.

Emiliano's seizure of the official seal did not sit well with the new *presidente*, who bore an old grudge against him because Emiliano had bought a piece of land which the *presidente* felt by rights of inheritance should have been his. Trouble soon followed. The new *presidente* accused Emiliano of being a *cacique*, and blamed him for Yaitepec's troubles with Juquila, the Valencias, and the state police. He incited an angry mob from one of the community's neighborhoods to attack Emiliano's house. They would have killed him had they found him, but Emiliano was not there. In self-defense, Emiliano armed a small army of his sons and supporters and threatened to kill the *presidente*.

BLOOD FEUDS

Not long after, one of Emiliano's sons was killed during the fiesta of Santa Cruz. In the month that followed a slaughter ensued: two or three men from the Barrio Abajo were killed. Although women are seldom murdered, blood feuds often continue until all male members of a family are dead. Thus, to protect his other son, Emiliano fled the village with his family. Since all of his property was in Yaitepec, life in exile was difficult. So when he thought the trouble was over, Emiliano moved back to Yaitepec. He was lighting a candle at the gate to his house to protect it when he was shot and killed. His other son returned to the village to avenge his father and brother. With some fifteen followers, they went on a killing spree, terrorizing the village so that people hid in their houses. As each murder created new enemies, Emiliano's son's own friends finally betrayed and slew him and to mock his brave heart, they cut it out and stuffed it in his mouth.

Although the passions which led to the tragic death of Emiliano and his sons were wrapped in local issues, their deaths were not merely the result of a local blood feud. Their murders were driven by conflicts and social processes which went far beyond the village. In this context, factionalism and blood feuds serve as mechanisms of social control to undermine the effectiveness of consentual politics. Emiliano and his family, like the other casualties of blood feuds, were victims not merely of their enemies, but of a much bigger game, a class struggle, of whose rules they were hardly aware.

With Emiliano's death in 1978, Yaitepec's struggle to recover its communal lands from La Constancia appeared to have failed. Some villagers had been shot by police; some leaders had gone to prison. Others, like Emiliano, had been killed in blood feuds. The movement was an apparent failure not only within the community, but legally as well. Don Florencio Valencia's son, Alfonso, who was serving as a member of the executive board of DAAC in Mexico City during the administration of president Luis Echeverria, unbeknownst to the village pushed a presidential resolution through DAAC which defined La Constancia as private property and excluded it from Yaitepec's communal lands (Cruz Lorenzo 1987:36).

NEW LEADERSHIP CONTINUES THE RESISTANCE

Although the Valencias had obtained this resolution in 1975, the community did not learn of it until 1979. When they did, private planning sessions began in the house of Juan Peralta Vásquez, the senior member of the committee of village elders. These gatherings led to meetings in other homes. As consensus began to build, larger *barrio*-level meetings took place to discuss the options. Finally, a general assembly was held in 1981. The prevailing argument put forward was that their communal lands could not be defended by using legal means; that unless

> they invaded the plantation and recovered their lands, they would lose them. The village *presidente* was vehemently opposed to force, fearing a repeat of earlier experiences. The assembly's response, however, was that they were determined to reclaim their lands, with or without his help, and if he did not lend his support, they would declare him a *persona non grata* in the village. Hoping to blunt the Valencia's anger and prevent acts of retaliation, the assembly voted to respect the areas the Valencias actually had under cultivation, about 20 percent of the *finca*. In addition, they would offer them the right to continue working these "communal" lands as members of the community. Seeing the depth of the community's support for the invasion, the *presidente* directed that the plan be implemented the following day, March 2, 1981 (Cruz Lorenzo 1987:38-39).

The next morning the *pueblo* invaded the plantation. Separating into bands of 10 to 20 persons, each led by a village elder, the groups moved across the plantation. The village elders allotted two pieces of land to each household: one to plant 300 to 500 coffee trees, and another to plant four *maquilas* of corn for subsistence. Since the elders were well-acquainted with the personal circumstances of each household, if a large family needed a little more land for subsistence, they assigned them more. Following their decision to respect the areas worked by the Valencias, the elders divided 80 percent of the finca's 1181 hectares among the village's 310 households. In less than 15 days they had sown corn on almost all their subsistence land. By June the villagers had planted more than 500,000 coffee trees (Cruz Lorenzo 1987:40).

ACTS OF RETALIATION

The Valencias were quick to retaliate. They lodged a complaint with the public prosecutor in Juquila, went to DAAC in Mexico City, and denounced the invasion. In July, the Valencias had a villager who was weeding his cornfield jailed for trespassing. When the indigenous members of Yaitepec marched *en masse* to Juquila to protest the arrest, he was set free. Still seeking to dislodge the villagers from the plantation, the Valencias let their cattle loose in the waist high cornfields. In October, still determined to evict the peasants, the Valencias had Juan Peralta Vásquez arrested, and charged the village elder with leading the conspiracy to deprive them of their private property.

Yaitepec's reaction to Juan's arrest caught Juquila's authorities off guard. The entire village marched on Juquila. Hoping to prevent the police from using force, the villagers entered Juquila led by children carrying a Mexican flag (a sign that the march was peaceful). Women followed, and armed with *machetes* in case of trouble, the men brought up the rear. The procession burst into the *palacio municipal* (city hall), took the district judge and public prosecutor hostage, and announced that they would not leave until Juan Peralta Vásquez was set free (Cruz Lorenzo 1987:40-43).

Predictably, the authorities in Juquila transmitted a plea to the state for help. The next afternoon, 200 state police arrived. All through the day, the police attempted to intimidate the villagers into leaving the town hall. In actuality, however, there was little they could do. If they attacked, they risked being hacked up. Even if their assault succeeded, if any of the indigenous women or children were killed or injured, this episode, could turn easily into a national and even international issue. It was a standoff. About midnight, a commission from Oaxaca arrived to negotiate. The commission, however, was headed by the Secretary of State and Alfonso Valencia, now the rector of the Universidad Autónoma de Benito Juárez de Oaxaca. Not surprisingly, rather than deal with the land question, the commission turned its attention to the occupation of the town hall. Finally, a deal for the release of Juan Peralta Vásquez was struck. The commission would put up the money for his bail if the villagers would leave the *palacio municipal*. Although no resolution was reached over the status of the land, acts of retaliation and repression ceased (Cruz Lorenzo, 1987:44-45).

CONCLUSION

Because many of the important forces which shape closed corporate indigenous communities lie outside the local arena, their internal politics cannot be understood without examining the domains of power which enclose them. Because such communities have been denied access to the real domains of political and economic power in the wider society, they have evolved a set of strategies to defend their lands from private parties. One of these strategies has been that of closure. By limiting access to communal lands to members of the community in good standing, and forbidding the sale of land to outsiders, the possibility of their becoming a free and alienable commodity is sharply reduced.

The politics of consensus is another strategy indigenous communities have used to protect their interests. Because outsiders often use the formal structures of the state to exploit indigenous communities, resistance to such attempts often requires the politics of consensus, thus making the communities appear leaderless. The politics of consensus, however, is not leaderless. Rather, its leaders are village elders. Because these elders hold no office, they cannot be manipulated readily by outside power holders. Yet, because they have earned a kind of sacred trust through their past service in civil and religious offices, they are able to exert enormous influence on decision-making processes within the community.

The village elders not only wield informal power, but they represent an enormous reservoir of experience. As they have held all level of civil posts, they have a firm understanding of the problems the village's constitutionally elected officials must face in dealing with the state and other outsiders. Where the elected officials change from year to year, the elders—though death may alter their numbers—are a more stable body. Because of their cumulative wisdom, their advice is often sought in dealing with ticklish problems.

Because the committee of elders is a fairly stable body, they learn from the past. Yaitepec's struggle to recover its communal lands from La Constancia illustrates their ability. The first attempts to take the plantation by force were an utter fiasco. The community was unprepared for acts of retaliation or the connivances of patronage, but they learned valuable lessons from them. The successful invasion was much better organized, as were the actions to defend the community from the acts of retaliation that followed.

Yaitepec's struggle for its communal lands illustrates the delicate state of the politics of consensus. Consensus is constantly negotiated and the unity it promises is under constant attack. Because outside elites often use patronage to manipulate the communities, factional divisions constantly are created in the community. The conflict between Emiliano and the *presidente* who was a *compadre* of the Valencias is a good example of how such factions emerge. Moreover, as Emiliano's case shows, the politics of consensus are not merely a defense against outsiders, but can be directed at homegrown political bosses.

When the politics of consensus in indigenous communities—as in Yaitepec—succeed, persistence rather than great strength is usually the key. Historically, defense of communal land in closed corporate communities has been the basis of this persistence. Because indigenous people have been denied access to power and wealth in the wider society, their lives literally have depended on their communal lands. Because these lands were, as one Chatino writer puts it, "given by the gods to a community, not to individuals" (Cruz Lorenzo 1987:31-32), such lands are not simply so much property, they are sacred. Thus, even though Yaitepec was racked with internal feuds when this struggle began, the threat to its communal lands was the cause that could unite the people of Yaitepec and keep them united.

NOTES

1. For examples of this focus see: Tax 1937; Carmara 1952; Wolf 1955, 1957, 1986; Nash 1958; Carrasco 1963; Harris 1964; Cancian 1965, 1967; Dow 1974; DeWalt 1975; Smith 1977; Wasserstrom 1983; Farriss 1984; Chance and Taylor 1985.

2. With the exception of historical personages, all names mentioned are pseudonyms.

REFERENCES

Adams, Richard N.
  1975   *Energy and Structure: A Theory of Social Power.* Austin and London: University of Texas Press.
Beltrán, Gonzalo Aguirre
  1973   *Regiones de refugio: el desarrollo de la comunidad y el proceso dominical en mestizo America.* México: Instituto Nacional Indigenista, Serie de Antropología Social, No. 17.
Camara, Fernando
  1952   "Religious and Political Organization." In *Heritage of Conquest.* Sol Tax editor, pp. 142-173. Glencoe, Illinois.: The Free Press.
Cancian, Frank
  1965   *Economics and Prestige in a Maya Community: The Religious Cargo System in Zinacantan.* Stanford: Stanford University Press.
  1967   "Political and Religious Organizations." In *The Handbook of Middle American Indians,* Robert Wauchope, editor. *Volume 6: Social Anthropology,* Manning Nash, editor, pp. 283-298. Austin: University of Texas Press.
Carrasco, Pedro
  1963   "The Civil-Religious Hierarchy in Mesoamerican Communities: Pre-Hispanic Background and Colonial Development." *American Anthropologist* 63:483-497.
Chance, John K. and William B. Taylor
  1985   "Cofradías and Cargos: An Historical Perspective on the Mesoamerican Civil-Religious Hierarchy." *American Ethnologist.* 12:1-26.
Cruz Lorenzo, Tómas
  1987   "De porque las flores nunca se doblegan con el aguacero." *El Medio Milenio.* Oaxaca, México: No. 1, April, pp.28-49.
DeWalt, Billie R.
  1975   "Changes in the Cargo Systems of Mesoamerica." *Anthropological Quarterly* 43:87-105.
Dow, James
  1974   *Santos y sobrevivencia: funciones de la religión en una comunidad Otomí,* México: Instituto Nacional Indigenista, Secretaría de Educación Pública.
Farriss, Nancy
  1984   *Maya Society under Colonial Rule: The Collective Enterprise of Survival.* Princeton: Princeton University Press.
Greenberg, James B.
  1981   *Santiago's Sword: Chatino Peasant Economics and Religion.* Berkeley and Los Angeles: University of California Press.
  1989   *Blood Ties: Life and Violence in Rural Mexico.* University of Arizona Press.
Harris, Marvin
  1964   *Patterns of Race in the Americas.* New York: Walker.
Nash, Manning
  1958   "Political Relations in Guatemala." *Social and Economic Studies* 7:65-75.
Perez, Jimenez Gustavo
  1968   *La institución del municipio libre en Oaxaca: protuario de legislación organica municipal.* México.
Smith, Carol A.
  1977   "How Marketing Systems Affect Economic Opportunities in Agrarian Societies." In *Peasant Livelihood: Studies in Economic Anthropology.* Rhoda Halperin and James Dow, editors, pp. 117-146. New York: St. Martin's Press.
Smith, Waldemar R.
  1977   *The Fiesta System and Economic Change.* New York: Columbia University Press.

Taylor, William B.
   1979   *Drinking, Homicide, and Rebellion in Colonial Mexican Villages.*   Stanford: Stanford University Press.
Tax, Sol
   1937   "The Municipio of the Western Highlands of Guatemala."   *American Anthropologist* 39:423-444.
Wasserstrom, Robert
   1983   *Class and Society in Central Chiapas.*   Berkeley and Los Angeles: University of California Press.
Whitecotton, Joseph
   1977   *The Zapotecs: Princes, Priests, and Peasants.*   Norman: University of Oklahoma Press.
Wolf, Eric R.
   1955   "Types of Latin-American Peasantry: A Preliminary Discussion." *American Anthropologist* 57:452-471.
   1957   "Closed Corporate Peasant Communities in Mesoamerica and Java." *Southwestern Journal of Anthropology* 13:1-18.
   1986   "The Vicissitudes of the Closed Corporate Peasant Community." *American Ethnologist* 13:325-329.

CHAPTER SEVEN

Appropriating the Enemy: Highland Maya Religious Organization and Community Survival

Duncan M. Earle
Texas A & M University

No student of Mesoamerican indigenous societies can fail to note the importance of religious organizations in indigenous community life. A major focus of many of these organizations, be they community-wide or focused on some smaller subdivision, is periodic festivities and related activities in veneration of local saints. This fiesta system is maintained by a ranked group of status-seeking individuals who, during their period of service or *cargo*, fulfill religious obligations, expend time, energy, and money in preparation for and facilitation of votive, public festivities. The system often is formally integrated with the traditional civil authority system, creating what has been called a civil-religious hierarchy or *cargo* system at the municipality level. In the fiesta system, prevalent until recently in most highland Maya communities, eligibility for a public civil office depends upon participation in the religious hierarchy, such that ascending status seekers must move periodically between the two authority subsystems, eventually retiring at the top as community elders. Recent research has demonstrated that civil and religious systems were not always so explicitly integrated (Wasserstrom 1983; Chance and Taylor 1985). The trend is a return to greater separation between religious institutions and secular authority, as the "traditional" integrated system breaks down in the face of religious, political, and socioeconomic change. However, as I wish to demonstrate here, highland Maya community religious organizations, based on the colonial *cofradía* (religious brotherhood) model introduced by Spanish friars, have always played a central role in the political dynamics of the community, both internally and in relation to the larger sociopolitical system, regardless of their formal relationship to civil authorities.   Furthermore, the evolution of the *cofradía* system of saint veneration appears to reflect an active indigenous response to the evolving political conditions that have threatened the survival of coherent indigenous communities over the centuries, and which continue to threaten them today. Both historical and contemporary data from a variety of highland communities support this view, as we shall see below.

The origin and sociopolitical function of Maya religious organizations remains controversial.   Earlier ethnographies emphasized their internally integrative and economic leveling aspects; some even viewed them as "survivals," remnants of pre-Hispanic organizations underlying "folk" interpretations of Catholicism.   From this perspective, ancient notions of communitarian egalitarianism survive embedded within socially hermetic, economically marginal corporate communities.   More recently, this view has been countered by those who see *cofradía*-like religious institutions simply as vehicles of church and state oppression and economic exploitation of the powerless and largely deculturated survivors of the chaos of conquest (Harris 1964; Wasserstrom 1980).   From this perspective, indigenous religious themes expressed in these public rituals reveal a "symbolism of subordination" toward the external exploitative system (Warren 1978), or movements of religious revitalization based on an idealized vision of Catholicism (Wasserstrom 1983; Bricker 1981).   Folk survivalism and ideological self-infliction models both suffer from a failure to appreciate the importance of religious institutions as effective means of political resistance to community dissolution and cultural extinction arising out of the experience of conquest.   The appropriation and transformation of Catholic religious sodalities reflect neither spiritual conversion to the beliefs of the enemy nor slavish, politically naive maintenance of tradition, but rather a dynamic response to the destabilizing social and political changes brought about by the conquest, especially those changes which destroyed or undermined previous political structures.   With elites dissolved or corrupted, military resistance futile in the face of reduction into municipalities, and an acute need for autonomous organization at the community level, *cofradías* were community institutions enjoying both legitimization within the colonial system and some autonomy from it.   This historical situation gave rise to the successful appropriation of alien institutions for novel political goals.   History provides a basis for understanding the fiesta systems that operate today in Highland Maya villages of Chiapas, Mexico, and Guatemala, as people continue to fight for cultural and community survival by marshaling familiar institutions and symbols of community and ethnic identity.

In the aftermath of the conquest of Middle America, Spanish civil authority over indigenous communities was based largely upon explicit force and corporal sanctions, with little emphasis given to legitimacy.   The chaotic early years of colonization demonstrated how corrupt, unstable and, ultimately, illegitimate civil authorities were, even in the eyes of their own clergy and the more honest agents of the crown.[1]   Friars well before and after the great defender of indigenous peoples, Las Casas, complained bitterly about the immoral, abusive, illegal treatment of indigenous people by colonists and self-interested Crown authorities. By contrast, effective indigenous authorities sought legitimization through the indigenous religious system, and relied on religion as a basis of social sanction and institutionalized religious service as a central validating mechanism to underwrite authority. Clearly, authority sanctified by religion has its origins in pre-Hispanic practices, but it takes on novel dimensions as a result of the conditions imposed by Spanish domination. With the decline of the pre-Hispanic elite class and the external control of indigenous civil authorities who relayed the increasing tributary and labor demands made on populations now undermined by European diseases, some alternative social structure had to be found to ameliorate the damage and soften the blow to the weakest community members, as well as to provide an institution for resistance to cultural anomie and economic enslavement for the social whole, and a way to legitimize indigenous authorities committed to those goals. I believe the *cofradía* and similar ranked religious sodalities became popular and widespread in indigenous communities of Mesoamerica at the end of the sixteenth century because they were able to fulfill these needs, and that some version of the fiesta system continues to persist in many indigenous communities today for similar reasons. That is, through the process of religious sanctification associated with saint veneration and festivities, indigenous leaders "purchase" legitimized authority over those less economically capable in the community, and employ their authority to improve the ability of the community to survive as a unit embedded within an alien and hostile social, economic, and political system over which they have no control.

Farriss' historical research on the Yucatec Maya (1984) and Dow's study of an Otomí fiesta system (1973, 1977) provide examples of how religious organizations serve to help indigenous communities economically and politically. When outside forces seek to extract maximum profit from their asymmetric power relationship and to prevent explicitly economic activities independent of external control, fiesta expenditures become economic competition with external demands. Typically this economic recycling occurs as the more prosperous members of the community are motivated to produce surpluses in order to enter into an exchange relationship with a "saint," a local deity usually represented by a wooden or stone image, housed and cared for like a person of status. They view their expenditures as the cost of maintaining, honoring, and entertaining a protective spiritual being, in exchange for which they receive social status, religious sanctification, and the promise of power and authority upon completion of their service. At the same time, they redistribute food and other goods within their community, giving away to the less prosperous community members (in the name of the saint) resources that otherwise might be carried off or not produced at all. In colonial times, *cofradías* maintained a fund to aid the destitute, and many communities maintained land and animals as *cofradía* capital. Due to later reforms, however, capital often had to be amassed nearly in the moment in which it was to be spent, usually through a social network built on money lent as advances on labor sold to nonindigenous ranches and plantations. Once thought to level economic differences, this system of cargos appears to be internally redistributive, often in the interest of legitimizing inequality rather than eliminating it. This is so even as the religion promotes an ethic of group solidarity and equality, in what might be termed a dialectic of commonality and hierarchy, contrasting and complementarily distributed elements found within many dimensions of highland Maya community social structure and ritual practices.[2] In this system status and authority are not acquired from capital accumulation for personal economic investment (as in the nonindigenous world), but as the result of accumulation of capital and resources for social investment in one's community via the fiesta system. Inequalities in productive potential are translated into status inequalities, ones that are blessed by the saint in exchange for proper "care and feeding". This inhibits the process of external appropriation of resources, as people are motivated to produce, distribute, and consume them locally, and also slows class divisions within the community through partial leveling and the periodic ritual reiteration of religiously based ethnic solidarity, symbolized in the public honoring of the saint.

Viewed in this way, the fiesta system resembles neither a relic nor a static collective delusion, but appears as a viable adaptation to the colonial and later postcolonial sociopolitical and economic environments. The appropriation of Catholic religious practices to serve the community political economy cannot be seen as just a desperate reaction to the trauma of colonization, or a blind embrace of the colonizers, but as a politically astute, adaptively beneficial response to the loss of power beyond the community. In the historic and ethnographic examples that follow, I will explore the Chiapas highland Maya fiesta system with these issues in mind, in an effort to demonstrate the particular way in which the traditional religious system of periodic communitarian festivities affects the political landscape. Historically, I intend to show evidence of the economic dimension of saint worship and briefly explore the institutions' political and economic relationships with the local clergy, the Crown, and Spanish colonists. Then I will move to ethnographic examples of the fiesta system in Chiapas, Mexico. I will offer an interpretation of the forces behind the recent conversion of one large and very traditional Tzotzil municipality from Catholicism to an obscure competitor, Mexican Orthodox, and give reasons for the reappearance of a *cargo* system in a rainforest colony that had abandoned the fiesta system, placing them both in the context of the political threats to indigenous community survival. In the cases examined, highland Maya religious organizations take on roles in active response to the evolving sociopolitical and economic conditions of the larger world within which Maya communities are embedded.

AN HISTORICAL OUTLINE OF MAYA FIESTA ORGANIZATIONS

The abrupt changes brought about by Spanish conquest severely limited the political possibilities for the surviving indigenous populations. The ebb and flow of alliance states and militarized empires, dependent upon supracommunity systems of organization, was replaced with the politically circumscribed indigenous township or *municipio*, and indigenous authority rarely operated beyond the boundaries of the community thus formed. The efficaciousness of this "divide and conquer" approach to colonial and postcolonial control of indigenous political ambitions is especially evident in any examination of Maya uprisings, where lack of intercommunity solidarity frequently weakened potentially successful rebellions.[3] Another technique for controlling and limiting Maya political autonomy, especially in Chiapas, has been the pervasive, if inconsistent, interference in local civil government, through illegal expropriation of municipal funds and through the manipulation of its officials.   Time and again in the history of Maya communities, and especially during depressions and periods of political change, the indigenous civil authorities were placed in a position of facilitating a degree of exploitation of their own people that violated civil law itself (Wasserstrom 1983; MacLeod 1973). It was therefore to the great advantage of the Maya to invest some organization outside of the direct grasp of civil authorities with communitarian power.

To understand the origins of the *cofradía*, the principal form of communitarian religious organization in the colonial period and the historical antecedent to most current fiesta systems, one must position it within the events and conditions of the end of the sixteenth century and the beginnings of the seventeenth. In the initial restructuring of indigenous society, it was the Crown's intention to preserve indigenous nobility, or *caciques*, in a form of indirect rule, for ideological, economic, and political reasons (MacLeod 1973:136-138).   There was a desire to preserve legitimate local rulers, independent of the colonists, who were more easily controlled than the "uniformly suppressed race" over which they ruled (MacLeod 1973:136). However, the system was rarely a success. *Encomenderos* and corrupt officials often removed legitimate nobles and replaced them with more pliant natives. Even when they survived efforts at external manipulation, indigenous elites suffered from being caught between the demands of Crown authorities and dwindling resources. Responsible for collecting tribute, as well as organizing labor for church and municipal construction, their demands and personal exemptions did not endear them to the commoners. They were frequently at odds with the competing authorities of the civil system, or *cabildo*, which was introduced at varying points during the sixteenth century. In Yucatan, where conquest was later, slower, and less disruptive of indigenous society, the nobility was able to coexist with elected civil and religious officials, and by the seventeenth century they had merged into a single system, preserving a degree of continuity of ascribed social stratification (Farriss 1984:232-236). However, in Chiapas, we see a pattern closer to the Central Mexico and Andean trend, of elites either taking advantage of their privileges by removing themselves from their communities of origin, especially after suffering a loss of legitimacy over corruption or privilege or power struggles with nonelite indigenous officials, or alternatively attempting to preserve their authority at the expense of their wealth, as tribute demands failed to keep current with the downward demographic trend associated with pandemics and other disruptions of the latter half of the sixteenth century. By this point, those nobles who remained among their people, as MacLeod describes it, "all had sunk to the same level of poverty" (1973:141).

As economic depression compounded the chaos of disease, tribute demands and the undermining of local authority structures and extractive pressures on the surviving natives increased from all quarters. The Church, and especially the monastic orders, began promoting the establishment of local saint cults, or *cofradías*. As other sources of Church revenue declined, local clerics saw this new institution as a means to guarantee continued financial support for their services, based on a fund taxed progressively from the community that was beyond the reach of secular authority. This was essential, for by this point the civil municipal funds, or *caja de comunidad*, had become threatened with unbridled pillage at the hands of colonial authorities, themselves dismayed with the decline in head tax and other revenues since mid century. Farriss, who draws parallels between the early *caja* organization and *cofradías*, says of indigenous Yucatan, "Much of the community's public revenues were generated and allocated under their aegis, but unlike the *cajas de comunidad* they remained virtually immune from royal officials" (1984:266). In Chiapas, MacLeod finds the indigenous response to clergy efforts to found *cofradía* usually quite enthusiastic, so much so they often founded new ones without waiting for ecclesiastic authorization (1983:69).

The reasons for the popularity of the *cofradía* seem clear. In exchange for maintaining the priest, an ally after all against the rapaciousness of secular colonists, the indigenous community was allowed to maintain an autonomous organization with power to tax, an inviolate treasury, and the ability to reappropriate local authority and redistribute local goods and services, all clothed in the protective garb of Catholicism. Furthermore, as *cofradías* quickly extended their authority beyond religious matters, their isolation from corruption, their charitable activities (helping the indigent, sometimes even with tribute payments), and their devotional service to the saints, those icons of the community's well-being, all provided a moral basis for legitimacy. As lineage ceased to define access to authority, *cofradía* service became the prerequisite to achieving principal or "elder" status, a status that continued to be coterminous with authority up until the twentieth century in most Chiapas Maya communities. The indigenous communities had regained control of themselves.

Soon after their establishment, the redistributive economic impact of the *cofradía* came to the attention of the colonial authorities and high church officials, who were quick to complain. Some complaints were directed at heterodox religious practices, but most focused on lost revenues, as "too much of the surplus capital remained at the local level, as much by way of redistributions and exchanges within the indigenous society, as by way of payment to the low-level, local clergy" (MacLeod 1983:69). How much the actual feasting improved the nutritional condition of the poorest community members is hard to establish, but it had a significant impact, apart from the valuable social bonding that surrounded ritual meals. Farriss describes how *cofradías* in Yucatan contributed to the economic needs of those incapable of self-maintenance, and this function of providing a security net against agricultural or other economic failure no doubt contributed to the popularity of the institution in Chiapas and Guatemala.

The *cofradía* also had a symbolic impact on the community, one which translated into a political contribution to the health of the community parallel with the economic one. The saint cult became an expression of a viable social unit, with the saint as the symbolic embodiment of that social group—frequently a group based on the postconquest face-to-face community. Periodic ritualized reiteration of ethnic identity helped to socially unify and define the group, something of especially great value when a group is under acculturative and exploitative pressures.[4] The common veneration of that which embodies the community as a spiritual and physical entity created a bond of social force sufficient to delineate the community as a sociopolitical one, just as the saint's area of spiritual domain was delineated by its community of followers. Those who best attended the saints, were considered to have best attended the community, and their attentions were compensated by the promise of eventual community authority, as elders or *principales*.[5] Further, as a social force to counteract natural fissioning tendencies of the community into neighborhoods, kin groups, or even individual households (tendencies that could be exploited by outsiders), *cofradías* served to sanctify and reward those who overcame kin interests for the sake of the larger group, and to ostracize those who resisted service. Thus the saint symbolized the bounded domain of a social and political unit, marking a boundary against smaller and larger interests and unifying the group.

The creation of a financial competitor with the compromised *cabildo* also served to exploit the conflictive relationship that existed between the Church and the colonists, a conflict abetted by Spain. The Crown was dismayed with the depopulation of Hispaniola, and feared the rest of the colonies would follow suit, thus killing off the only scarce resource over which the Crown had some control, and their most powerful means of controlling the colonists. Should all natives perish and be replaced by slaves who were exempt from the Spanish laws governing labor allocation, the colonists could move swiftly toward independence. Thus the Crown vigorously backed the complaints of priests such as Las Casas, proclaimed the "New Laws" of 1542 to restrict *encomendero* rights and increase the protection of their politically pivotal "subjects," and generally encouraged the clergy to report abuses. The Crown quickly appreciated the value of protecting the natives through progressive laws and clerical watchdogs, especially once European diseases had made them a truly scarce commodity. Even when financial concerns replaced the original missionary zeal of the church, the interdependent relationship between *cofradías* and local clergy served to keep them buffered against external manipulation. Only with the decline in power of the church, first with the Bourbon reforms and later with independence, did the *cofradía* system experience serious changes.

Prior to these changes, many *cofradías* had come to maintain a fund of capital (similar to the *caja de comunidad*), and frequently invested it in some profitable enterprise, such as cattle raising or the cultivation of communal land. With the advent of administrative changes at the end of the colonial period and at independence, *cofradía* land and capital were lost in highland Chiapas, although some *cofradía* holdings survived into the twentieth century in Guatemala.[6] During this period, responsibility for financing festivities shifted to individuals, initiating what is now called the *cargo* system. While I have yet to find conclusive data on this issue, I suspect the shift to individual *cargos* was an adaptation to the plundering of the collective wealth of *cofradías*, for clearly the wealth quickly amassed through a complex network of prestations and debts would be far more difficult to expropriate than the *cofradía caja*, since the network is invisible until called upon. For Chiapas, this fits well with the available historical data.

At about the same time that *cargos* began to replace *cajas*, the indigenous civil authorities ceased to be held personally responsible for the tribute debts of the community they represented, and indigenous officials were no longer imprisoned for failure to pay their township's debts. With no need to keep *cofradía* and *cabildo* formally separate, their links became stronger and more institutionalized, evolving into the civil-religious hierarchy noted by ethnographers of this century, and in a process that may have been quite similar to that discussed by Chance and Taylor for Oaxaca and Central Mexico (1985). It should be noted, however, that informal links between religious and civil authorities at times did exist. Wasserstrom (1977:64) notes an early case (1580s) of such links in Chiapas, for example. The widespread institutional melding of the two organizations is at least in part a response to the decline of the power of the church and the removal of the central political obstacle to unification, the external control of the civil authorities. However, contemporary evidence suggests that the covert system of authority, based on passing through formal positions sanctified by the religious system to become an elder or *principal*, has its roots in the *cofradía*, and that religious legitimization has always played a central role in the political structure of the Maya community.

COFRADÍAS AND POLITICAL POWER

Dow has noted in his study of the sierra Otomí the importance of saint-venerating religious corporate groups as mechanisms that stimulate the production, redistribution, and consumption of goods locally, preventing their appropriation by agents of "colonialistic exploitation" external to the indigenous community (Dow 1977:225). He has also described a central political mechanism of the *cofradía* system, one that would not necessarily be evident to scholars attending the historical record. Even before the time when most *cofradías* became personal *cargos*, the public responsibility for community funds and for the maintenance and veneration of a religious image that functions as a symbolic condensation of the community transformed the *cofrade* (*cofradía* member) into a legitimized candidate for leadership. He is a candidate because it is upon retirement from the system, as a *principal* or *pasado* (elder) that political power is acquired. "The political structure of religious corporate groups is based on the formal acquisition and informal exercise of authority...In the Otomí religious corporate groups the formal system of ritual offices is a framework for acquiring authority (Dow 1977:222)." The political weight of former ritual officeholders has been noted in the ethnographic literature for the Maya, but its informal nature, as "power behind the throne" of civil offices, makes it easy to miss.[7] Such covert power is even more difficult to evince in the ethnohistorical record. However, the need for religious service as a prerequisite to political authority may help to explain the eighteenth-century amalgamation of the civil system into the religious hierarchy in many areas of Mesoamerica and, ultimately, why *cofradías* and other derivative religious corporate groups arose as political organizations.

Denied participation in the larger political system, the religious arena (and the informal, personal nature of the power of the elders) appears to be the only redoubt of uncorrupted authority for these indigenous communities.

The previous interpretation of the initial popularity of the *cofradía* is derived in part from what we know about Mayan and other Mesoamerican communities in the ethnographic present. While the details of this organization and the names of the saints or spiritual entities venerated may have changed, the *cofradía* and analogous, community-level corporate groups modeled after the *cofradía* continue to focus around annual feasting and community-level ceremonialism, and to be managed by community elders. This politico-religious system has existed primarily at the township or *municipio* level, although smaller subcommunities and even extended households have also sponsored fiestas, for the township has been the primary unit of ethnic identity, at least until recently.[8]   Even in cases involving separate groups which have been brought together to form a township, and where they maintain territorial dress and ceremonial distinctions, their differences have been integrated into and to some degree subsumed under a larger, more inclusive religious system coterminous with the township as a legal entity delineated by nonindigenous authorities. This integration is no doubt largely because the *municipio* remained the unit of both external control and collective resistance. From the time of the *caciques* in the sixteenth century, the central struggle for power between legitimized indigenous leaders and those who operated for the interests of the dominant sector was carried out at the municipal level, barring those few cases of multivillage rebellions.[9] Tribute demands, forced production and consumption of goods, church taxes, debt peonage and other labor extraction arrangements, forced military recruitment, and many other humiliating and traumatizing experiences were shared with the legal community, and the people's success or failure at survival was usually manifest at the municipal level. Survival was a collective enterprise, symbolized in the well-being of the saints of the township, and organized by those who cared for them. One of the more impressive cases of resistance to both external forces of destruction and to internal decomposition is San Juan Chamula.

CHAMULAS IN THE WORLD OF THE ENEMY

San Juan Chamula is the largest and most populous municipality in the State of Chiapas, Mexico. One of the most populous Maya townships in southern Mexico (with over 100,000 inhabitants), it also has the most elaborate festival system of all the Tzotzil, Tzeltal, Tojolabal or Chol communities in the state. More than twenty public ritual events take place annually in the municipal square. The largest, *k'in tahimoltik* or "Carnival," involves over 2000 official positions, each with as much as two years of *cargo* service. Two months of increasingly intense ritual activity culminates in five days of frenetic celebrations, comprising perhaps the largest and most elaborate festival in Chiapas (Gossen 1986). Technically not a *cofradía* celebration, "The Festival of Games" reflects a Chamula appropriation of the Christian pre-lenten carnival to express sociopolitical and symbolic themes associated with world view, indigenous identity and ethnic conflict. The organizational forms such as the main *cargo* positions, however, follow those of other *cofradía* ceremonials in the community as well as those of neighboring Zinacantan, with whom Chamulas exchange official delegations for their major fiestas. Indeed, *k'in tahimoltik* may be viewed as the ceremonial of the *cofradía* to the solar deity, a deity fused together with Jesus by the Chamulas and embodied in the elements of the lance-tipped flag poles carried by the leading *cargo* officials in their processions around the village center. With the other more typical *cofradía* celebrations, Chamula exhibits the "full-blown" religious hierarchy (there are actually three subhierarchies, one for each section or *barrio*, and they are ritually integrated and ranked), and the system is closely linked to the civil authorities, forming a "classic" example of the civil-religious hierarchy. Gossen, analyzing Chamula's *k'in tahimoltik*, sees it as a ritual statement of the themes central to Chamula ways of viewing the world, that of the Chamulas themselves and also that of the outside, the "enemy":

> It is a folk commentary in the mode of macroanalysis, a reenactment and appraisal of centuries of ethnic conflict that Chamulas have seen and survived as a people. It shows clearly that they are aware of where they have stood in these centuries of conflict as tribute-paying victims, not beneficiaries, of the larger world's interventions in their affairs. The festival sheds some light not only on why Chamula has assumed a defensive posture toward the world at large, but also on how they have coped with the threat of intervention. They do so by keeping a fanatically centralized political and religious organization that systematically purges unwanted foreign presence and militantly discourages intra-community factionalism (Gossen 1986:248).

The history of the relationships between the religious hierarchy and the powerful elders it produced on one hand and the civil authorities in charge of the Chamula *cabildo* (town council) on the other is complex, and there are times when they are more closely linked than others, but with the fall of Díaz and the end of forced labor recruitment in 1910-11, the Chamula elders appeared to have wrested control over the process of selecting the municipal officers (Rus and Wasserstrom 1980:473). Those selected had to have served at least one religious *cargo* and usually more, and the municipality in turn was involved in the approval of new religious *cargo* holders (Pozas 1959). This insular civil-religious hierarchy, like many others in the area at the time, still had to cope with the considerable power of the *ladino* municipal secretary, who had replaced the Church as the local agent of control over the Chamulas after the Cuzcat revolt of 1867-1870 (Pozas 1959; Kohler 1982; Aguirre Beltran 1967).

During the Cardenas period, the state authorities sought to "modernize" relationships with the highland Chiapas Tzotzil and Tzeltal communities, in part to secure their political hold on areas where the Mexican Revolution proffered few benefits for the indigenous peasantry (Rus and Wasserstrom 1980). One technique was to begin to appoint younger, Spanish-speaking Chamulas to municipal positions, beginning with scribes (replacing the hated *ladino* secretaries) and by 1940 including the municipal president's office. The elders prevailed until finally one of the government candidates agreed to serve in an expensive religious cargo, and was put on the waiting list (Rus and Wasserstrom 1980:474). Rus and Wasserstrom see this state action as a cooption of Chamula authority, for these new scribes, school teachers trained by the National Indianist Institute, became agents of community development which they monopolized on the basis of their special relationships with the state, and they eventually evolved into *caciques* or political bosses legitimized by their religious cargos (see also Kohler 1982).

In a pattern historically parallel to the original *caciques* or noble class, these worldly brokers both exploited their position (their knowledge of Spanish, the *ladino* political system and their connections within it) for personal gain and expended a portion of that wealth in an effort to purchase, through the support of the *cargo* system, legitimacy within the community. They also served to control and therefore inhibit the penetration of development efforts that were impossible for the Chamulas to control. In some ways they replaced the powerful *secretarios*, although their support for traditional religious practices and their shared Chamula culture made them less alien, despite some abuses. In some respects they resembled authorities in earlier centuries, compelled to capitulate to external exploitative interests in order to retain some measure of indigenous autonomous authority. The labor conditions for Chamulas, while inferior to those for most nonindigenous laborers (especially on the coastal coffee plantations), became far better than at any time prior to 1910. The rise to power of the worldly bilingual school teachers in the Chiapas Highland communities cannot be viewed only from the outside, as an imposed plan to subvert indigenous communities by elements of the state. It also arose as a response to the perceived need for cultural and political brokerage, by indigenous people increasingly aware of regional and national issues. Subsequent events in Chamula's recent history tend to support the idea that, far from losing control of their municipal *cabildo*, the ultimate outcome has been a further strengthening of community autonomy and political independence.

The gain has not been without political conflicts and costs. By the late 1960s, a small group of Protestants appeared in Chamula. Many converted with the assistance of a semi-"ladinoized" enemy of the Chamula elites and American missionaries, who up to that point had been largely unsuccessful in their Chamula conversion efforts. By 1969, there were some 120 converts, who began to refuse to pay municipal taxes related to the financing of "pagan" religious ceremonies and the maintenance of the church.[10] By 1973, an opposition party was formed in Chamula. Affiliated with the National Action Party (PAN), a generally conservative competitor with the official party, disgruntled Protestants affiliated themselves with the new group.[11] An internal rebellion ensued, sparked by Panista accusations of electoral fraud and financial corruption in 1974. The Chamula authorities responded by expelling over 2,000 of them, and eventually established a policy of expelling all Protestants and "new" or reform Catholics. By 1983, estimates of displaced indigenous protestants were as high as 7,000. The majority of them were Chamulas. Many resided in *barrios* surrounding the town of San Cristobal de Las Casas, the local seat of *ladino* power. Clearly, the leaders of both the status quo and the opposition utilized religious affiliation to bolster their respective political identities.

From a national perspective, the actions of the Chamula leaders were illegal, violating the constitutional right to freedom of religion, and the exiled converts let this be known in protest marches through the streets of San

Cristobal, and with delegations sent to the state and national authorities. However, from a Chamula perspective, preservation of the political system necessitates the expulsion of non-believers, for political affiliation at all levels is traditionally inseparable from religion. *Paraje* (hamlet) leaders adjudicated neighborhood conflicts not significant enough to be referred to the center, with the help of spiritual sanctions against those who rejected a negotiated settlement. Social behavior was regulated by the integration of spiritual and secular power, and converts were seen, even on a local level, as serious liabilities to the *paraje*, even when there was general agreement about Chamula center corruption. One such informant explained how the Protestants' lack of respect for San Juan not only made them scofflaws, but angered the patron saint such that the whole community might suffer drought or other misfortune as a result. Chamulas viewed their authorities, local or municipal, as both backed by and responsible to their deities, who in turn legitimized them in the eyes of the township. Religious conversion therefore was viewed as politically seditious, not just religiously disrespectful, and this sedition had dangerous spiritual as well as political consequences.

This view of Chamula's actions was not, of course, shared by the Mexican official party, or anyone else beyond the township. But the affiliation of the Protestants with the opposition PAN and the reform Catholics made it nearly impossible for the PRI to pay much attention to their complaints about their lost lands. In fact, when vocal Protestant leader Miguel Kashlan was kidnapped and murdered by apparent allies of the Chamula leadership in 1982, no one investigated the case, because to do so would have only further antagonized the state and national authorities (Gossen n.d.:12). Local Chamula interests, while utterly distinct from those of the PRI, coincided with them regarding the exiles. The land has remained under municipal control.

Despite the extreme shortage of land, most homes and fields abandoned by converts remain untouched, awaiting the return of the errant Chamulas to "the way of San Juan." The political advantages of this policy are clear. Expropriation of land would give strength to the claim that the motive for expulsion was material, or a political effort at rewarding loyal Chamulas with their exiled neighbors' land. It would also contradict the typically Chamula view that religious conversion, like party affiliation or political revolt, is a temporary social schism which, like all forms of abandonment and rejection of Chamula, is followed by return. Moreover, this approach to land reflects usufruct notions deeply held by many Maya groups. In this view, land cannot be sold or employed as capital for the purpose of leaving the community. Departure signifies forfeiture of land rights, and land inalienability rules serve as a powerful social mechanism to keep young people from abandoning their community (Siverts 1969).

The regional diocese of the Catholic church joined in the protest against Chamula in order to advance its own political and religious agendas, which included the suppression of "pagan" practices and beliefs, and the cultivation of a local indigenous "reform" Catholic constituency in the Chiapas Highlands. Because the protest was against government inaction regarding repatriating Protestant Chamulas, it was also an opportunity for criticism of the PRI, which brought the diocese into alignment with the national church, which was and remains a vocal opponent of the federal government's policies.

In the indigenous regions of the Highlands, the Catholic church has made missionary inroads in areas of intracommunity political conflict.   One example of this specifically involves Chamula.   Fierce conflicts have arisen in the last 20 years between the outlying Chamula hamlets technically inside the municipality of San Cristobal, and the Chamula center over the latter's right to collect taxes.   Many of these communities developed strong affiliations with the Catholic church through the *catequista* (catechist) movement, and had broken from Chamula traditional religion (and political affiliation) with church encouragement and assistance.   Further, the priests visiting Chamula became more and more insistent upon catechism classes before performing baptisms and other religious services, raising the ire of most Chamulas.   One priest was expelled in 1974, another threatened with immolation ten years later.   Meanwhile, the church continued to rail against the sins of "Indian paganism," and especially in the context of the Chamula expulsions and their "drunken" celebrations.   This did not endear them to the Chamula leaders, and made for serious strains between two parties that have had to cooperate for centuries.

Nationally, relations between the church and the PRI deteriorated in the 1980s.   PAN was nationally identified with the church and was making political inroads in the north of Mexico.   Meanwhile in the state of Chiapas, the Bishop became a vocal opponent of the government over official treatment of the Guatemalan refugees pouring into the state after 1981.   With over 150,000 refugees in Chiapas by 1983, reports of governmental aid agency incompetence and corruption, not to mention political ambivalence, were widespread.   Much aid never arrived and many refugees suffered.   In the face of this human and political crisis, the diocese' complaints gained the attention of the nation and the world, at a time when Mexico was in the throws of a severe economic crisis and its leaders fearful that Central American political upheavals would spill over into Chiapas, the resource-richest and income-poorest state of the republic.[12]

In 1985, after consultation with hamlet leaders, the municipal leaders of Chamula decided to end their affiliation with the Catholic church and convert their whole community to an affiliate of the Mexican Orthodox Church.   The reasons for this conversion extend far beyond the ones often offered up by Chamulas as well as by their critics: less expensive religious services carried out by the Mexican Orthodox Bishop (a former Catholic priest residing in the state capital) and the absence of any requirement for catechism classes before baptism.   In addition to these politically popular community issues, the *cabildo* apparently decided to "publicly" divorce itself from Catholicism as a part of its "foreign policy" efforts regarding Protestant "repatriation."   The Catholic church had become an unpopular affiliation from the standpoint of the Chamula government's modus vivendi with the PRI, and a threat to Chamula sovereignty over its constituents, especially residents of communities beyond the municipal limits.   Obviously unreceptive to Protestant churches, the *cabildo* leaders did not wish to swear off all outside church contacts, for clergy have always served a role in their life rituals and a switch to Chamula priests would be difficult.   Moreover, conversion to another version of Christianity served outside political concerns as well, for it would be harder for people to discredit their religiosity as "degenerating" into "paganism" with a cleric at the spiritual helm. The Mexican Orthodox church, an obscure sect that has sometimes taken the place of Roman Catholicism during various conflictive periods in Mexico's past, fit in with Chamula center's political needs very nicely.[13] This move, moreover, seemed to solidify their allegiance to the PRI at a time of great political insecurity for the official party, and it all but destroyed any efforts by the exiles to regain their lands without returning to the politico-religious fold. The unsolved murder of Kashlan exemplifies the current futility of the rebel Chamula cause. Unlike the Chamula Protestants, the municipal "conversion" had little impact on people's daily religious practices or their fundamental religious beliefs. Religious affiliation is ultimately revealed again to be fundamentally a political relationship, and at some distance from issues of theology and faith.

The Chamula case appears to suggest that the political cost of effective external brokerage and internal cohesion is corruption, the creation of a now sanctified microcosm of the Mexican national political panorama. But however supportive of the *cargo* system the *caciques* have been, the corrupt manner in which they have operated in the *cabildo* has not gone unnoticed by the average Chamula, and periodic demonstrations of the limits of Chamula center power remind the leadership of their dispensability. For example, when in 1983 the municipal president allowed one of his Chamula center friends to plant corn on one of the three sacred mountaintop shrines in the center, leaders from the *parajes* of San Sebastian (the section of Chamula to which the shrine pertains) rushed to the *cabildo* and nearly threw him bodily from the second story balcony. Many such instances demonstrate the participatory inclination of Chamulas in township politics, and suggest that there are limits to what they will abide in terms of abuse of power. Finally, perhaps sensing relative security against external threats, the community rose up in 1985 and removed the *cacique* -supported president, replacing him with a literate Chamula widely considered as honest and fair. Several attempts were made by supporters of the old regime in 1986 and 1987 to remove the reformer, with the apparent backing of local *ladinos,* unhappy with the interruption of their "special relationship" of patronage. But the vast majority of the Chamulas defended the new president, and the Chiapas governor and state legislators decided to back them as well, seeing the advantage in agreeing with so many loyal voters. Their representatives spoke to the community representatives amassed in the township center in August 1987 in support of the popular president, to the cheers of thousands of Chamulas and over the complaints of the Chamula PRI agent and followers of the *caciques.* For the time being, at least, popular power has won out.

Mexican Orthodox, energetic proponents of a tradition derived from the Catholic *cofradía* organization of circa 1700, militant followers of San Juan (their founder deity) and Jesus (the sun god), Chamulas have reestablished popular control over their municipality to a degree virtually unheard of in the rest of Mexico, without a shot fired, and without sacrificing their ethnic identity in the process of reasserting their political autonomy.

RELIGION AS A POLITICAL SYSTEM

Both Redfield's (1956) analysis of Yucatan Maya communities and Aguirre Beltran's of Chiapas (1967) sought to explain the strength of traditional indigenous institutions in terms of their isolation from the urban centers of change. Numerous anthropologists have noted, however, that the most militantly traditional Maya communities in Chiapas are close to the main center of nonindigenous power, influence, and markets—San Cristobal, while more isolated communities have often been more vulnerable to acculturation. Wasserstrom has taken pains to demonstrate that Chamulas and Zinacantecos, residing close by the colonial capital, have been deeply involved in the economy of the state, as workers, artisans, producers of maize, and so on (Wasserstrom 1983). Against the notion that indigenous people, by their marginality, are caught in the "precapitalist" refuge regions, he argues persuasively that they have always been part of the larger capitalist system, but in a dominated, subordinate position. Some anthropologists, however, follow Harris' view that their dependent position condemns their community organizations to functioning as forms of self-exploitation, and even view their traditional religious system as a colonialist ideological weapon (Warren 1978, and see Favre 1973:360-372). Against this view of indigenous passivity and submission, the historical and ethnographic data suggest that these indigenous communities actively engaged in efforts to counter colonialism, a kind of "anticapitalist" posture in terms of resource extraction and an anticolonial struggle for control and authority over community affairs. Wasserstrom's historical analysis is filled with efforts by community leaders to reassert their authority, especially through religious organizations, and the "Tzeltal Rebellion" of 1712 can best be understood within this political, not simply religious, revitalization perspective.

The active struggle to establish, on one hand, an anticapitalist system of redistribution and prestation and, on the other, an anticolonialist system of legitimate authority, becomes most developed where the threat is most proximate and continuous. This is no doubt why Chamula and Zinacantan have such powerful and resistant civil-religious hierarchies. The concept of appropriation and resistance also adds to our understanding of the economics of *cofradías*. They often function to level wealth and prevent accumulation, although as Cancian has pointed out, this may be an ideal that obscures the ritualized justification of wealth differentiation (Cancian 1965, 1973). The colonial conditions of institutionalized plunder no doubt has tended to perpetuate a negative view of wealth accumulation, unless that wealth is used for a communal social end. Dow and Farriss both suggest that periodic festivals serve to redistribute the surpluses accumulated by the most productive community members to those who might not survive without such assistance. Thus they partially compensate economic inequality, but not for an egalitarian end—quite the opposite. Dow argues that successful producers are best rewarded in exploitative market systems by swiftly exchanging surpluses for authority, purchasing power with social service. If there is no profit in investing them in a hostile external system, and if accumulation creates envy, which can quickly translate into witchcraft or accusations of it, then social status and security may be best derived from investing in a saint that is, in turn, viewed as a spiritual caretaker of the community.

Thus the *cofradía* system may be seen as an adaptation to intracommunity economic inequality and extracommunity threats to indigenous resources, be they accumulated capital and goods, exploitable land, or labor. While it is clear that the basic integration of religious organization and community politics is very ancient, the "social contract" promoting community integration and solidarity took the form it did because of the harsh realities of colonialism, not despite them.

RELIGIOUS ORGANIZATION AND POLITICAL ENVIRONMENTS IN NUEVO SAN JUAN

If this view of the appropriation of religious *cargos* is of worth, a valuable test would be to remove the conditions of ethnic prejudice, economic asymmetry, poorly paid labor exploitation, and intracommunity wealth disparity, and examine the impact on the religious system. If the importance of the Chamula annual ceremonials derive from their semeiotic power to reiterate ethnic identity against the acculturative pressures of *ladinos* and internal agents of change, as well as from their ability to sanctify and thus legitimize wealth distinctions within a system where those distinctions, if left unauthorized, could lead to community conflicts and external cooption of authority, and where civil authority is difficult to control without religious sanction, what would occur to the *cargo* system if these factors ceased to exist? In the Chiapas highlands such conditions are rare, but one group of communities thrives in a social, economic, and physical environment radically distinct from the Chiapas highlands. It is in the study of these communities that the above question can be addressed.

Tzotzil and Tzeltal colonies established in the last 25 years in the tropical rainforest region of eastern Chiapas, formed on the basis of the Mexican *ejido* (agrarian reform) laws, are an extension of the demographic expansion of indigenous communities within the highlands, but colonizing an entirely different physical, sociopolitical and economic environment. Land-impoverished indigenous people were awarded, as legally recognized *ejidatarios*, 20 hectares of tropical land, far more than most "cold country" holdings. Moreover, it was soon established that this new tropical habitat, nestled up against the highland mountains of Chiapas and Mexico, supported coffee cultivation as well as corn. As with many frontiers, infrastructure was slow to develop, transport was and remains difficult, and labor has always been scarce, while land is relatively abundant. These conditions contrast sharply with Chamula, where land is entirely insufficient and available labor is superabundant.

I began to examine the *ejido* (agrarian reform community) of Nuevo San Juan Chamula as a part of a larger comparative project investigating a number of Chamula's numerous colonies.[14] The study was also appealing because this *ejido* is the oldest indigenous colony in the whole Santo Domingo river catchment of the southern Lacondon jungle. Although these Tzotzils began with great difficulties and suffered many hardships, they are now very prosperous, especially when coffee prices are good. For example, in 1979 the 65 *ejidatarios*, located in two distinct settlements separated by a large ridge, earned an average of over ten times the income of their highland relations from Chamula. They continue to speak Tzotzil, the women still dress in traditional wool clothes, raising a few bedraggled sheep and arranging their kitchens in the traditional way. The men have both traditional and Western clothes, as do many highland Chamulas if they can afford them, and they maintain subsistence plots of maize and beans as well as complex "kitchen gardens", in addition to their coffee plots. Their relations with the few nonindigenous *ejidos* are good, for they share the same concerns and goals, although the communities founded by the Chamulas, as well as those from Zinacantan and Tenejapa, tend to allow only settlers from their own respective ethnic group to become *ejido* members. In this sense they are "closed" and "corporate" communities.

One of the two *ejido* settlements is called Ojo de Agua, situated close to the Santo Domingo river. It is the site of the first settlement in the region, along with the neighboring ladinoized community, Santa Elena, which is located across the river and downstream about a kilometer. The *ejido* civil government operates on consensus, as do the *parajes* in Chamula, but it has civil offices that do proffer some status. With numerous offices stipulated in the laws of *ejido* formation, however, and only twenty *ejidatarios* in Ojo de Agua, nearly everyone participates formally as well as informally in the authority system. Wealth is not associated with civil or religious posts, but only with the variations in quality and quantity of the coffee plants and the number of able-bodied dependents.

Despite the initial antagonism some founding members of the *ejido* harbored over a tax dispute against the mother community, they immediately established a *cargo* system and a community cross, following a pattern typical of Chamula colonies in the Highlands. But soon the cross was abandoned, Catholic missionaries were well received in the *ejido*, and community support for the *cargo* and its saint declined. By 1979, only two men continued the *cargo* tradition, passing the saint back and forth between them from year to year. The local church became the domain of "reform", antitraditionalist Catholics, allied with missionaries who condemned the idol worship fostered by their ancestral brethren. By the early 1970s, the first Tzotzil-speaking Protestants began to arrive in Ojo de Agua, as well as to the other *ejido* settlement called Pacayal, and a number of Chamula colonists became followers of *riosh k'op* (literally "God speech," those affiliated with Pentacosts, Adventists, and other fundamentalist protestant sects) from both sides of the ridge. A small temple was established in Ojo de Agua, and the Adventists began to refuse to do collective community work (trail maintenance, bridge repair, schoolhouse repair, etc.) on Saturday, their Sabbath. The community *ejido* leader complained to me about this, but in as much as he was reform Catholic, two of his sons had become Protestants, and his wife's father was one of the two remaining traditionalists taking care of the old saint, there was little motivation to restrain the religious heterogeneity of the community.

Pacayal, a rambling settlement across the high ridge that bisects the *ejido*, also followed this pattern of *cargo* system decline and the rise of other religious groups, some of them spreading from a base in Ojo de Agua. Then the road came to Pacayal. Bypassing Ojo de Agua, the road connected Pacayal with Mexico and made it the "gateway to the jungle", as the network of *ejido* footpaths converged upon the last point accessible by truck. Soon came a regional secondary school for the southern jungle colonies, as well as the base camp for the road construction and maintenance crews, as plans were made to extend the road to the east. This was followed by a military post, responding to the new strategic importance of the settlement. In addition, the road allowed some *ejidatarios* to acquire and maintain trucks, and their location as a "jumping-off" place for new colonists provided them with work. A few of Pacayal's *ejidatarios* had been allotted land suitable for cattle raising and with transportation available, they were encouraged to raise them by Mexican development agencies, who offered cows and credit.[15] Suddenly the sleepy settlement was exposed to serious new forces and agents of change.

By 1975, the internal religious divisions were becoming coterminous with political cleavages within Pacayal. Facilitated by the road and regional school, religious groups became a base for inter-*ejido* groups with agendas that were in part political, and were viewed as such by Pacayal's elders, for they sought to promote their religion to the exclusion of others (and sought to have their members gain *ejido* offices in order to foment this) as well as to encourage national integration and a rejection of indigenous beliefs and identity (Earle 1986:557). Suddenly, and in contrast to Ojo de Agua, Pacayal's sense of community identity was threatened by external and internal forces.

During the same year, one of the oldest and wealthiest founding members of the settlement and a former chief authority in the *ejido* government, announced that he would take on the principle *cargo* of the Chamula ceremonial called *k'in tahimoltik*, or Carnival, a festival never before celebrated in the *ejido*. Within two years, the celebration of Carnival enjoyed the support and participation of the whole community (with the exception of those who went to Chamula for it.) Even colonists who claimed no traditional religious affiliation participated in it as a social event. The result, in a short space of time, was the total abandonment of other religions. According to numerous informants' testimony, this change was not by force. The involvement of present and past authorities in the *cargo* system relegitimized the old religion, and the participation by Pacayal religious "converts" in the festivities tended to make their own sects reject them (Earle 1986:558). Pacayal closed ranks around religious identity.

Detailed examination of the initial conversions, in Pacayal, Ojo de Agua, and San Juan Chamula, suggests that converts were motivated partly by political disputes with the community authorities, now a familiar pattern. Even in Ojo de Agua, religious affiliation can be best understood in the context of power struggles between community members (Earle 1986:558-559). But what of religious belief? How can people change their theological orientation with such ease and frequency? This was a question I asked repeatedly while in Nuevo San Juan, and the answer should not be too surprising at this point. Unless directly contradicted by known doctrine, most traditional beliefs about the spiritual and corporal world remained constant, regardless of religious affiliation. That is, the basic cultural "grammar" or logic about the nature of things remained intact, and distinctly Maya (Earle 1986:559; Earle 1984). What apparently caused the Pacayal community to close ranks and reject religious diversity has much to do with perceived threat to this basic shared fabric of cultural identity, and little to do with the formal tenants of a particular religious affiliation.

In another article I have gone into more detail regarding the way these threats are manifest in Pacayal, and why Carnival serves as a symbolically potent antidote for cultural and political insecurity (Earle 1986). The Ojo de Agua case suggests that the *cargo* system withers when civil authority is responsive, when the potential for wealth is evenly distributed among households, and when external threats to the community are minimal. The Pacayal case suggests renewed external pressures that contradict community identity and solidarity and threaten to undermine the ethnic basis of their collective "social contract" (a contract rather explicitly spelled out in their land-grant petition for a Chamulas-only *ejido*) give rise to a new case of appropriating the religious organization of the enemy. But this appropriation is not a slavish imitation of the mother community, as Pacayal is not in the same sociopolitical dynamic as Chamula. For Pacayal, Carnival has become "tradition" because it addresses the age-old Maya concern for collective identity in a hostile, nonindigenous world. Regardless of political conflicts with Chamula, *k'in tahimoltik*, the "Festival of Games," remains part of the communitarian ritual baggage that reinforces Chamulaness against cultural and political conquest, for its symbolic content specifically emphasizes this resistance. But it does not have the redistributing, leveling, or even the legitimizing functions, in an economic sense, that it sustains in Chamula, for food is abundant, while wealth differences are still small. This explains why the cost, in money and time, of the *cargos* is low, given the average income of the *ejidatarios*. The resuscitated ritual has been retailored to the circumstances, with an emphasis on political and ethnic issues that vastly overshadows concern for internal economic divisions, transforming the festival to fit Pacayal's needs. Chief among them is the legitimization and sanctification of authority, as the perception of threat increases.

ECONOMY AND RESISTANCE

Detailed economic studies of indigenous communities in Mesoamerica have brought into question Harris' claim that *cofradías* operate merely as institutions of economic extraction. While a variable percentage of funds generated for ceremonial expenditures do leave the community, as did the money paid to the local clerics when these religious sodalities were first formed, *cofradías* actually serve to resist the social transformations brought about by acculturation into a capitalist economy by preserving local systems of reciprocity, redistribution, and communitarian economic interdependence (Cook and Diskin 1976). The fiesta, like an enlarged household, functions to redistribute the resources unequally acquired in a compensatory fashion, as a farmer and seasonal wage earner might do for his or her family. The redistributed resources are either locally produced agricultural products, representing the food (and sometimes the drink) of the celebration, or wages that are exchanged for the ceremonial objects, such as candles, fireworks, incense, and other obligatory purchases and fees. In his review of *cofradía* economics, Greenberg notes that in a number of communities studied these expenditures are split about fifty-fifty between internal and imported products (1981:192). While no data is available on Chamula, it appears that considerably more of the expense is derived from external purchases (especially meat), although a calculation of the value of voluntary labor might bring it back into balance, as these ceremonials demand time and effort from a huge number of officeholding participants and kin. In Nuevo San Juan, as noted above, costs are lower and more resources are contributed locally (such as cattle, which are imported to Chamula), but then the colonists have far less need to average their "level of adversity" than most peasant farmers, given their uniformly high income (Greenberg 1981:191). While not always the case, food traditionally produced in the community has typically gone to the community in *cofradía* feasting, whereas a considerable amount of the cash derived from external wage income goes to purchases of goods not locally produced.

Harris argues that the rising demand for cash to finance fiesta expenditures finds indigenous people increasingly in a search for work outside the community, and thus becomes a capitalist "hook" to exploit indigenous labor (and helps to explain nonindigenous support for the fiesta system). But Harris fails to address what this differential exploitation of labor "purchases" for the community, in terms of an internal system of distribution and redistribution resistant to external appropriation, and in terms of mechanisms that maintain internal political self-governance, a system outsiders do not wish to destroy precisely because of the labor exploited. He also undervalues the importance of stimulating wealth for consumption as a way of attenuating the exploitation of local resources by outsiders, and of the development of intercommunity exchange systems that compete with the outside economy. In the case examined here, the coffee producing colonies serve as an alternative source of seasonal employment for land-scarce Chamulas, and communities like Pacayal purchase ceremonial goods in Chamula center, including cane liquor (Chamula wrested control of the production of most ceremonial liquor from *ladinos* in the late 1950s, after a period of intense conflict over control of "moonshine" production.) These economic relationships are reinforced through shared cultural identity epitomized by preparations for and participation in fiesta celebrations.

The value in resisting exploitation by creating socioeconomic interdependence and in fomenting an ideology of ethnic solidarity within the indigenous community (as well as between communities) may be difficult to measure, but it must be included in any cost-benefit analysis. The interdependence created by the partial leveling of income and the partial legitimization of income differences, the exchange of wealth for status and the complex systems of prestation and obligation—all of these *cofradía* related activities reflect part of a socioeconomic whole that, struggling against outside forces, encloses its corporate community in an economic system that both pays and withholds, both serves and resists. The thesis of conquest, and all it implies in terms of appropriating indigenous resources and the imposition of European ideology, encounters its antithesis in indigenous communities that devise "self-consumptive" systems of redistribution and promote ideological structures of egalitarianism and corporate closure. Within this dialectic, the appropriated *cofradía* institution may be better understood as a creative response to colonialism, rather than its slave.

The San Juan fiesta in Chamula, while important, takes second place to Carnival, with its saint impersonating solar warriors. As I have argued (Earle 1986), the significance of Carnival is associated symbolically with ethnic resistance to acculturation. In contrast to San Juan, a saint related to internal issues of land tenure and fertility, the three barrio *pashyon* players and their entourages address the history of conflict with the outside world (Bricker 1973, 1981; Gossen 1986), and their "play" serves as a public drama that teaches and reflects the importance of community solidarity and resistance to the chaos of cultural conquest (Earle 1986:563). Given Chamula's long history as a source of labor outside the community, the many conflicts that have arisen out of this form of exploitation, and the continued high number of Chamulas who work seasonally for wages in culturally alien areas of Chiapas, the prominence of the "Festival of Games" and the prestige of its *cargo* holders is understandable. Carnival is Chamula's central ritual of community resistance: "Chamula stages and wins a moral, military and ethnic battle that is not unlike its everyday battle with disruptive forces from within and with intrusive forces from without (Gossen 1986:247-248)."

The focus of Carnival on internal and external conflict, as I have said, makes it appropriate for the Pacayal colonists. While San Juan is also celebrated, it is of very little importance and does not have a formalized *cofradía* or any link with the secular authorities in Pacayal. Land is abundant, land rights are not in contention, and harvests always exceed subsistence needs. The threat in Pacayal is cultural and, therefore, explicitly political. The response asserts political authority, and therefore, appropriates this particular religious form.

CONCLUSION

The vitality of the Chamula municipal fiesta system is not typical. Few indigenous communities of Chiapas or Guatemala have been able to maintain the high degree of monolithic integration of religion, religious institutions, and civil government, although traditional religion still plays a significant role in the social and political structure of many of them. The relative power of Chamula, having adapted to the circumstances of the national political crisis, should not be seen as anomalous to some larger, natural and progressive trend away from traditional religious practices, but as an example of unusual success at resisting sociopolitical and cultural disintegration at the community level. Nuevo San Juan, flush with coffee wealth, also has come to actively defend its autonomy, as its members close ranks against the atomizing, isolating forces of capitalist penetration and nationalist hegemony. Chamula religious intolerance, much criticized by those who oppose Chamula's own hegemony, must be seen in light of the political implications of missionization for those who lack political power beyond their own community. When religion is the basis of legitimizing power and sanctions, conversion becomes sedition, a threat to the very basis of indigenous social and political order. It is a disturbing irony to witness the complaints of missionaries against Chamula's "tyranny", who would have the state continue to authorize their efforts at undermining local indigenous authority and at attempting to complete the process of conquest begun nearly five centuries ago. The appropriation of early instruments of spiritual conquest for collective resistance to cultural and political decline over the centuries demonstrates a sophisticated indigenous understanding of what religion means in political terms. The dialectic of conquest and resistance continues.

NOTES

1. Murdo MacLeod's 1973 study documents in some detail the particularly corrupt situation in the *cacao* producing Izalcos region, but also demonstrates how generalized the violations of Spanish law by officials were , occasioning frequent Crown audits, constant revelations of fiscal scandals, and nearly endless reports of abuses of the indigenous work force (1973:90-95, for example).

2. One other important aspect of ethnographic work by Vogt, Cancian, Gossen, Kohler and others has been the examination of these two, seemingly opposed elements in Tzotzil and Tzeltal public life, an ideology of egalitarianism and communalism and a strong emphasis on status and hierarchy. The contradiction between the need for solidarity based on an ideology of equity and inclusion on the one hand, and the need for an hierarchical system of social management and control on the other, is resolved by a religiously validated system that allows for social differentiation to be tolerated, even legitimized, provided those in the position of wealth redistribute a portion of it equally among the potentially envious remainder of the community. One might even characterize such a system as sanctified witchcraft insurance.

3. Both the Tzeltal uprising of 1712 and the Cuzcat or "Saint Rose" revolt of 1869 suffered from the lack of unity among the highland communities (Saint Lu 1981; Bricker 1981), although ultimately both efforts helped to lessen the degree of abuse experienced by the indigenous population of the Highland Chiapas region (Favre 1973).

4. Anthony Cohen (1985:268-270) discusses how the symbolic expressions of a community and the demarcation of its cultural boundaries by means of public rituals increase dramatically in importance when there is a perceived threat to that community. Myths depicting the founding of highland Maya communities in Chiapas and Guatemala frequently involve the patron saint, who demarcates the boundaries of the community and then settles in the church. One might argue that contemporary saint processions around the limits of the town center are a ritual reiteration of the boundaries of the community, both by its founder and its caretakers.

5. *Principal* is the most common term to denote an elder of the indigenous community who has passed through an accepted number of formal religious and civil positions, including some if not all of the most important ones, and has retired to a position of great authority. In Tzotzil, such a man is often called *pasaro,* from the Spanish *pasado,* or "passed", one who has passed through the status-bearing offices, and is a formal title of address. Their community authority appears analogous to that of a father in a nuclear family, for as caretakers of deities viewed as kin to the sun, "Our Father", they become venerated as community parents.

6. Brintnall documents the demise of the traditional religious system in Aguacatan, Guatemala, and includes a brief mention of the *cofradía* cattle holdings that were taken from them by the Catholic church only three decades ago. A more detailed description of a surviving example is provided by Hill and Monaghan for nearby Sacapulas (1987). A vestige of cattle raising persists in Chichicastenango, where the *cofradio* of Santo Tomas requires its incoming members to provide capital for the purchase of cattle (currently about 116 dollars U.S.) to be butchered and rendered by the members. Profits from the meat and tallow candles thus produced go to the maintenance of the saint, while the *cofradía* member receives his capital again upon leaving the organization after his 13 month "year" of service.

7. Ruth Bunzel, working in Chichicastenango, was never able to see the top *principal* of the township, nor would anyone point him out to her on the few occasions he was reported to be in town, despite her good rapport with the second ranked *principal* who served as spokesman for the town's five elders (1952:186). This, I believe, is a Quiché example of what Dow has described as "informal authority" possessed by past *cargo*holders, which maintains itself hidden from outsiders and therefore difficult to corrupt, control, or kill (Dow 1977).

8. Social units smaller than the municipality have frequently maintained some form or system of saint worship. *Guachibales,* family-based saint veneration celebrations were common in colonial times and the celebration of a neighborhood saint in rural Guatemala is common today, especially in areas where the municipal civil-religious system has largely disappeared. Zinacantan has recently experienced an upsurge in saint veneration at the *paraje* or hamlet level, while neighboring Chamula has actively suppressed competing saint church sites that might draw away from their center. Hill and Monaghan (1987) described how Sacapulas' system of *cofradías* reflects identity based on *parcialidades* derived from prehispanic land and social units called *chinamits.* But the weak level of integration in the Sacapulas case is due in large part to postconquest changes in population composition, which included groups that are still mostly unaware of their membership in a larger *municipio* (Hill and Monaghan 1987:144). As a rule, however, despite continuing maintenance of internal subdivisions (which in Chamula are expressed in terms of three *barrios,* divisions that are also traceable to preconquest groups), the municipality-wide *cofradía* continued to be the institution that defined community authority for the highland Maya as long as it still functioned.

9. The highland Maya rebellions never integrated all or most contiguous indigenous municipalities, and in Guatemala revolts rarely went beyond a single township (Bricker 1981). This contrasts with the Yucatan, where Mayas arose from much of the southern and eastern parts of the peninsula in the late nineteenth-century Caste War. This was facilitated, however, by the impact of large scale recruitment of Mayas from diverse communities for conflicts between liberal and conservative non-Indians shortly before the revolt, and the greater cultural and linguistic similarity between groups involved.

10. This material is largely from oral histories gathered by Gary Gossen, who has generously allowed me access to his rich data on the Protestant rebellion in Chamula (Gossen, n.d.).

11. This conversion process had a forceful political dimension, in that missionaries affiliated with the Summer Institute of Linguistics had been largely unsuccessful in making Chamula conversions prior to the political conflicts that arose between village leaders and a coalition of merchants, school teachers, and seasonal plantation workers. With the start of the conflict, Protestantism became a vehicle for opposition to Chamula authorities, especially after a failed electoral effort. Rus and Wasserstrom claim as many as 500 of the 800 families converted by 1976 had members involved in the movement for political reform (1979:170). Divisions between more political and more religious Protestants continues to this day.

12. Political tensions between the Church and the federal government were especially pronounced from 1982 through 1984, when the Chiapas diocese repeatedly criticized the actions of immigration officials and the official Mexican organization for refugee aid (COMAR) with regard to their treatment of Guatemalan refugees. In addition, there was official concern about church involvement in situations leading to clashes between state authorities and indigenous community members in the *municipios* of Simojovel, El Bosque and Bochil, mostly conflicts over land rights. It also appears the federal government feared that the Guatemalan refugee camps would become bases for guerilla operations, although there has never been any evidence of this. One right-wing paper went do far as to accuse the Bishop of Chiapas of training hoards of indigenous guerillas to bring the Central American conflict to Mexico. Such wild and unsubstantiated rumors reflect the degree of insecurity felt in Mexico City toward the political conditions in Chiapas, made all the more disquieting in the context of the national financial crisis and the decline in political popularity of the PRI.

13. My understanding of the historical role of the Mexican Orthodox church began with information provided by Jan Rus (personal communication).

14. This research began as part of a larger project directed by Dr. Gary Gossen and funded by the National Institute for Mental Health and the National Endowment for the Humanities, which focused on the Chamula diaspora.

15. By offering credit for cattle but not for coffee, the federal government failed to appreciate the dangers of cattle raising in a rainforest ecosystem, as well as ignoring the environmentally sound development model already in operation in the *ejido* based on unfertilized coffee.

REFERENCES

Aguirre Beltrán, Gonzalo
   1967   *Regiones de refugio: el desarrollo de la comunidad y el proceso dominical en mestizo América.* Instituto Nacional Indigenista, Serie de Antropología Social, No. 17. Mexico.
Bricker, Victoria
   1981   *The Indian Christ, the Indian King.* Austin: University of Texas Press.
Brintnall, Douglas
   1979   *Revolt against the Dead: The Modernization of a Mayan Community in the Highlands of Guatemala.* New York: Gordon & Breach.
Bunzel, Ruth
   1952   *Chichicastenango: A Guatemalan Village.* Seattle: University of Washington Press.
Cancian, Frank
   1965   *Economics and Prestige in a Maya Community.* Stanford: Stanford University Press.
   1973   *Change and Uncertainty in a Peasant Economy.* Stanford: Stanford University Press.
   1985   "Cofradías and Cargos: An Historical Perspective on the Mesoamerican Civil-Religious Hierarchy." *American Ethnologist* 12 (1):1-26.
Cook, Scott and Martin Diskin, editors.
   1976   *Markets in Oaxaca.* Austin: University of Texas Press.
Dow, James
   1973   "Saints and Survival: The Foundations of Religion in a Central Mexican Indian Society." Ph.D. dissertation, Brandeis University. Ann Arbor: University Microfilms.
   1977   "Religion in the Organization of a Mexican Peasant Economy." In *Peasant Livelihood: Studies in Economic Anthropology and Cultural Ecology.* Rhoda Halperin and James Dow, eds., pp. 215-226. New York: St. Martin's Press.
Earle, Duncan
   1986   "The Symbolism of Politics and the Politics of Symbolism." *América Indígena* 46(3):545-568.
   1984   "Cultural Logic and Ecology in Community Development: Failure and Success Cases Among the Highland Maya." Ph.D dissertation, SUNY Albany.
Farris, Nancy
   1984   *Maya Society Under Colonial Rule.* Princeton: Princeton University Press.
Favre, Henri
   1973   *Cambio y continuidad entre los mayas de México.* Mexico City: Siglo veintiuno.
Gossen, Gary
   1974   *Chamulas in the World of the Sun: Time and Space in Maya Oral Tradition.* Cambridge, MA: Harvard University Press.

1986 "The Chamula Festival of Games: Native Macroanalysis and Social Commentary in a Maya Carnival." In *Symbol and Meaning Beyond the Closed Community: Essays in Mesoamerican Ideas*. Gossen, editor, pp. 227-254. Albany, New York: Institute for Mesoamerican Studies.

n.d. "Vida y muerte de Miguel Kashlan: Héroe Chamula." MS.

Greenberg, James
1981 *Santiago's Sword: Chatino Peasant Religion and Economics*. Berkeley: University of California Press.

Harris, Marvin
1964 *Patterns of Race in the Americas*. New York: Walker & Co.

Hill, Robert and John Monaghan
1987 *Continuities in Highland Maya Social Organization: Ethnohistory in Sacapulas, Guatemala*. Philadelphia: University of Pennsylvania Press.

Kohler, Ulrich
1982 "Estructura y funcionamiento de la administración comunal en San Pedro Chalchihuitán." *América Indígena* 42(1):117-146.

MacLeod, Murdo
1973 *Spanish Central America: A Socioeconomic History, 1520-1720*. Berkeley: University of California Press.

1983 "The Social and Economic Roles of Indian Cofradías in Colonial Chiapas." *Mesoamerica* 5 (June):64-86.

Posas, Ricardo
1959 *Chamula, un pueblo indio de los altos de Chiapas*. Mexico City: Instituto Nacional Indigenista.

Redfield, Robert
1956 *Peasant Society and Culture*. Chicago: University of Chicago Press.

Rus, Jan, and Robert Wasserstrom
1980 "Civil-Religious Hierarchies in Central Chiapas, A Critical Perspective." *American Ethnology* 7(3):462-478.

Siverts, Henning
1969 "Ethnic Stability and Boundary Dynamics in Southern Mexico." In *Ethnic Groups and Boundaries*. Frederik Barth, editor, pp. 101-116. Boston: Little, Brown and Company.

Warren, Kay
1978 *The Symbolism of Subordination: Indian Identity in a Guatemalan Town*. Austin: University of Texas Press.

Wasserstrom, Robert
1977 "White Fathers and Red Souls: Indian-Ladino Relations in Highland Chiapas, 1528-1973." Ph.D. dissertation, Harvard University.

1983 *Class and Society in Central Chiapas*. Berkeley: University of California Press.

Part IV.
Missionaries, Institutionalized Churches, and Popular Religion

CHAPTER EIGHT

Mission Rivalry and Conflict in San Blas, Panama

James Howe
Massachusetts Institute of Technology

During the first quarter of the twentieth century, rival Catholic and Protestant missionaries competed for the souls of the San Blas Kuna of Panama in a struggle which in more recent years has been replicated throughout much of Latin America. The two representatives of these faiths among the Kuna–a Spanish Jesuit, Padre Leonardo Gassó, and a British lay missionary, Miss Anna Coope–could not in most respects have differed more strikingly, but they mirrored each other in courage, dedication, and the conviction that the other's religion was the work of Satan. They labored successively in the same communities, with many of the same converts, even occupying in turn the same building. Both left lengthy and vivid accounts of their work, written largely in the field (Gassó 1909, 1910a, 1910b, 1911a, 1911b, 1911-1914; Coope 1917). These frank and revealing memoirs, though by their nature biased and one-sided, can, when supplemented by other sources, offer a vivid picture of mission rivalry and the conflicts it provoked, conflicts as fierce between Catholic and Protestant as between Christian and Kuna traditionalist.

Beidelman has urged (1982:29-30) that the systematic study of missionization and its impact on the non-Western world most needs ethnographically informed case histories that give equal weight to missionizers and missionized. The brief account offered here ignores the longer span of church efforts in San Blas since Coope and Gassó's time, focusing more narrowly on the initial heroic period of pioneering individuals, first encounters, and active struggle. Situating regional and local events in the wider context of national politics, I try to make sense not just of missionization's overall impact, but of the way in which specific features of Catholic and Protestant practice articulated with particular aspects of indigenous culture. In the concluding sections of the paper I argue that most Kuna adherents accepted one church or another to maximize a key value in their own culture, namely advancement through learning, and that they used mission affiliation as a badge of identity in cultural clashes that were largely about mundane rather than spiritual issues. Concerning the effects of proselytization on consciousness, I suggest that missionary activities most marked the thinking, not of Kuna converts, but of the government officials who followed, thus setting the terms of the next phase of cultural struggle, in which missionaries themselves played only a peripheral part.

FIRST STAGES

When the government of Panama, newly independent from Colombia, took stock of its situation in 1903, it found itself without the resources to subdue and incorporate the San Blas Kuna. The Kuna, inhabiting several dozen villages along the San Blas Coast on the Caribbean side of the Isthmus (as well as a few more villages on rivers well inland), actively traded with outsiders, but they had not been missionized for several centuries, and both religiously and politically they remained largely independent. Given its lack of funds and military might, of necessity the Panamanian government began the task of pacification through missionary intermediaries.

Some Kuna villages were more open to outside influence and change than others, particularly two sister islands, Nargana and Nusatupu,[1] located only a few hundred yards apart in central-western San Blas (see MAP 8.1). In 1904 Nargana elected as its first chief a young man, Charlie Robinson, who had been fostered as a boy by a merchant/captain and educated in English on the Colombian island of San Andrés, after which he spent several years as a sailor to European and North American ports.[2] A first chief like Robinson shares power with secondary chiefs, other officers, and village men as a whole, but among all of them he has the greatest potential to set the tone and agenda of village politics (Howe 1986). Commerce, schooling, and change came first on Charlie Robinson's agenda, and during villagewide sacred gatherings, in which traditional chiefs sing to their followers about Kuna history and cosmology, Robinson told the bible stories he had learned abroad.[3] Soon after his election, he and several other pro-Panamanian, modernist leaders were invited to the city by the country's first president, Manuel Amador Guerrero, and during an interview in 1905, which was conducted in English (López n.d.), Robinson and the president arranged to establish scholarships for Kuna students.

In October of the following year, Robinson brought 17 Kuna boys to the city, where President Amador arranged to have them educated at government expense by the Christian brothers in a special annex to a school run by the order.[4] Despite difficulties getting through to the boys, the first group of twelve was baptized in October of 1907 (Gassó 1911-1914 V:59; VI:85),[5] and other cohorts followed them into the city in the next few years.

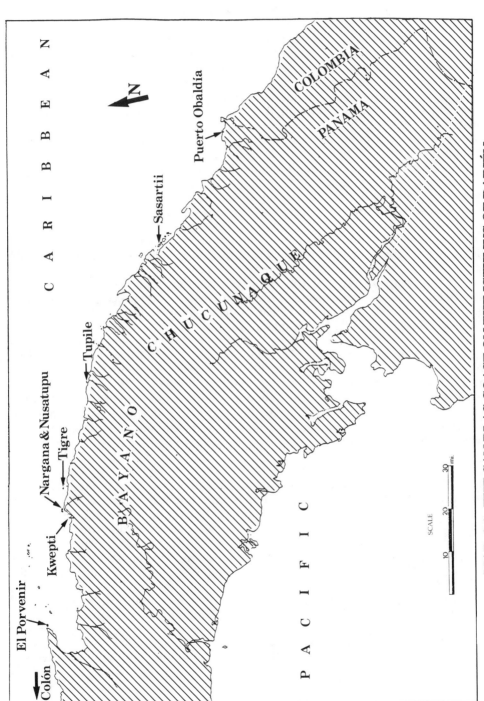

MAP 8.1. THE SAN BLAS COAST ON THE ISTHMUS OF DARIÉN

ENTER FATHER GASSO

In December of 1906, Father Leonardo Gassó, a Spanish Jesuit with considerable missionary experience among Quechuan speakers in Ecuador and the Tarahumara of Mexico, was passing through Panama and stopped for the night at the Bishop's residence (Gassó 1911-1914 II:205). Bishop Junguito, who had been looking for someone to send to San Blas, seized the opportunity presented by Gassó. Convincing him to alter his destination, the bishop squared the change with the Jesuit order (of which he was also a member), and arranged with his good friend, President Amador, for a monthly stipend in support of a mission to the Kuna to be run by Gassó.

After learning some of their language from Kuna in the city, Gassó set out for San Blas in mid-March. With considerable difficulty, he reached Nargana a week later, at the beginning of Holy Week. Initially rejected by Chief Henry Clay of Nusatupu (known to Gassó as Enrique Clair), he crossed to Nargana, where Charlie Robinson welcomed him warmly. Gassó threw himself into teaching prayers, celebrating mass, and observing Good Friday and Easter. Within a few days he had, by his own count, taught 70 boys, 12 girls, and 21 men a few prayers and songs, and in the process he had instilled proper respect towards himself and the chief. Opposition, however, soon began to show itself, in the form of mockers during a Good Friday procession, and until his Kuna improved, he found it difficult to communicate adequately with Chief Robinson (Gassó 1911-1914, Volumes II-V).

After only two weeks, Gassó took Robinson, his wife and child, and two especially devoted boys to the city. There, in a whirl of activities, President Amador communicated his support for the mission to Robinson; the Bishop baptized Robinson's child, with President Amador standing as godfather; Robinson and Gassó visited the Kuna boys in school; the two little Kuna helpers were baptized; the priest shepherded a friendly delegation from San Blas to the Presidential Palace; and he got the president to trade commercial favors for support of the mission with a secondary chief from Nusatupu (1911-1914, Volumes V-VII). Only at the end of seven weeks in the city did he return to the islands.

Thereafter, Gassó continued the pattern of periodic extended visits or *entradas* to Nargana, spending as much time away from the Kuna as with them.[6] During his longest absence of more than seven months, in 1907 to 1908, between his third and fourth *entradas*, Gassó and a young Kuna sacristan made an extended trip to Spain, where he toured the country soliciting support from the order and from pious laymen, collecting religious images for the mission, and having a Kuna grammar and catechism printed (1911-1914 vols. XVIII,XIX).

Within these first two years, Gassó gained a toehold on Nargana and gathered a core of followers, but he threw the community into turmoil, sending shock waves throughout the region and provoking antagonism and conflict. Direct and confrontational in everything he did, Gassó, like the Kuna, soon recognized the parallels between his institutions and theirs. Although willing to tolerate, even respect much in Kuna culture, he felt impelled to suppress the major rituals in Kuna religious life, at the same time that he sought individual conversions and the acceptance of Catholic Christianity throughout San Blas.

MISSIONARY METHODS

The fundamentals of Gassó's work among the Kuna were rote instruction in prayers and devotional texts, and catechization, i.e., systematic question and answer indoctrination in Catholic dogma. He offered some drilling in ABCs to the young boys who formed the largest and most enthusiastic group of catechists, but he denigrated the importance of schooling and literacy (1911-1914 VI:85; XV:64) to the extent that he tried to have his Kuna catechism printed in a script so unusual that his flock would not be able to transfer their new reading skills to newspapers, Protestant bibles, and other evil influences (XIX:186). In the long run this lack of commitment to education, by alienating potential supporters and adherents, proved a fatal mistake.

Gassó worked hard to baptize young children (108 by the first week of July 1907, 1911-1914 XIV:42), but with adults he feared backsliding, baptizing only committed and thoroughly catechized followers and dying people willing to make professions of faith (V:56; XIV:42; XVI:89,106). He also labored to get the Kuna to construct a combined residence/chapel on each island as a device to elicit and test their support and to familiarize potential converts with himself, as well as to fill the mission's building needs (IX:182-183; XII:15, passim).

Using an explicit top-down model (1911-1914 VI:85), Gassó struggled to convert a nucleus of village leaders, especially Charlie Robinson. With Robinson, relations were highly ambivalent. The chief felt torn between his identification with the mission and conformity to his followers' expectations. Gassó for his part, oscillated between effusive praise of "my great Carlos" and scorn for his Americanized modernist outlook (V:58; VI:86), and his authoritarian soul was offended by Robinson's inability as a democratically elected village chief (see Howe 1986) to command obedience. The priest also sought the support, or at least the acquiescence, of the whole village of Nargana, but failing that, he was willing to settle for a core group of supporters, and as opposition developed, he confronted it directly, even welcoming polarization of the community into pro and con factions (1909, 1911-1914 XXI:66-67).

A highly energetic and skillful political manipulator and broker, Gassó pressured local leaders with letters from the government and threats of supernatural punishment—"the curse of God will fall on you; sicknesses and misfortunes will come upon you; you will die in your infidelity and you will descend to be burnt" (1911-1914 VI:88; Canduela 1909)—along with such inducements as arms, commercial concessions, titles, and honors. Henry Clay was made a general, and Robinson was named Governor of the San Blas Coast (1910a, 1911-1914 XV:67). Resisting Robinson's desire to bring in Panamanian policemen to coerce opponents of the mission, which he realized would arouse too much enmity (IV:56), Gassó did get Nargana to build stocks for malefactors, and through his intervention the government armed Robinson and his followers to support them against threatened attacks from other islands. On the national scene, Gassó lobbied the government expertly, dealing directly with the President whenever possible, and at the end of his second year the legislature passed Law 59 of 1908, which largely conceded to the church the task of civilizing San Blas (XXII:181-182).

The administration backed Gassó and Robinson with the hope that they could bring the whole coast under national control. It rapidly became clear, however, that many Kuna villages opposed the mission, and in fact that no villages other than Nargana and its twin, Nusatupu, accepted Robinson's leadership. The great majority of the several dozen Kuna islands belonged to one of two confederacies, whose leaders, Cimral Colman and Inapakinya, began to deal with the government on their own behalf, ignoring Robinson's nominal governorship.

Although Gassó's ambitions extended to all of San Blas and he invoked government backing to quell opposition, he played a double game with the government. He labored to keep the Kuna isolated from the modern world, which he loathed (IV:56; V:21; X:206), emulating his ideal, the Jesuit mission settlements of the colonial period. He repeatedly yearned for a *quinta de español* (see IV:16, XIII:16), by which he meant a few local non-Indian secular authorities, but otherwise he struggled to exclude outside influences other than Christianity.

Gassó's ambivalence encompassed Kuna culture itself. At his most accepting, he praised Kuna morality and customs repeatedly (see Volume X). "It is certain they lack for nothing, except to know and love Christ and preserve his law, and as for the rest they enjoy more than anyone" (1911-1914 X:26). At the other extreme, he could not restrain himself, even in his published journal, from anti-"Indian" epithets and enraged outbursts. "How will I explain what a gentile village of those people is like? Saying that it is like a cageful of crazies" (IV:236). He soon felt compelled to suppress two key institutions, the sacred gathering and the *chicha* or puberty ceremony. Above all, he could not abide the Kuna sense of superiority to outsiders, which was all too much like his own pride.

STRUGGLE AND CONFLICT

Gassó, as brave as he was pugnacious, went out into the streets each afternoon "to visit the sick and conquer the stubborn" (1911-1914 XVI:89), which led to many antagonistic encounters with the stubborn, notably at the hammocks of the sick and dying, where he attempted to leave Christian images in place of the small wooden figures used in Kuna curing (see Gassó 1909:208). In one instance, when a patient let him place an image of the Sacred Heart in his hammock, Gassó ended up in a virtual tug-of-war with the patient's mother, who wanted to take the image out (1911-1914 XVI:90,106). In another encounter (XV:65), when a sick old woman refused baptism, Gassó declared that she would die and go to hell; two days later, when she did die, he went to her hammock, and cross in hand, he preached to the mourners around the corpse, pointing out that all who had refused baptism had died. The mourners did not heed him, he wrote, but later in the day several men confronted Gassó and warned him off. In a struggle against drinking (see below), Gassó confronted not only Kuna at puberty ceremonies or *chichas* (puberty ceremonies) which occurred every few weeks, but also black sailors off of trading vessels, who as "ambassadors of hell" (XXI:17) represented for him the horrors of Protestant modernism. On more than one occasion, he narrowly escaped violence against himself.

Gassó's presence also provoked fierce opposition from other coastal villages, as well as from Kuna in the Bayano and Chucunaque River Valleys across the cordillera. At the beginning of his second *entrada* in June 1907, a party from the nearby island of Tigre partially destroyed his house (1911-1914 VI:88), and rumors of more serious impending attacks circulated. In October of 1908, just after Gassó left at the end of his fifth *entrada*, flotillas of canoes approaching Nargana threatened to burn the church building and kill Robinson, thus preventing Gassó's return; the Nargana people, united by the threat of fire (a severe danger to the whole village), drove the would-be invaders off (XXII:81; 1909:210). On other occasions, outsiders made peaceful visits to Nargana, to attend *chichas* or regional sacred gatherings, during which they would whip up sentiment against the priest (XVI, XXI:67).

Within Nargana, support and opposition waxed and waned week by week, and with them Gassó's mood as recorded in his diaries. Almost invariably, he would return from a trip to find things in disarray, with opponents in the ascendant and his followers in retreat, forcing him to redouble his efforts. From the beginning, Gassó identified as his particular enemies a number of senior male ritualists, notably a man named Portete (1911-1914 IV:236, VI:88), as well as old women as a class. Over time, as he found himself unable to bear the noise of carousing, conflict grew between Gassó and participants in both *chichas* (XII:15; XVI:87), some of which involve several days of drinking, and small private drinking parties including black sailors and Kuna men. In 1908, he managed to have imposed a prohibition on rum selling (XVII:135), though as soon as 1910 visitors to the island reported its renewed availability (*Diario de Panamá* 8/17-20/10). Later, as the priest and traditional Kuna recognized the equivalence between the Kuna sacred gathering (Howe 1986) and Gassó's prayer services, he increasingly insisted that converts abandon the former in favor of the latter, structuring conflict as competition between the two ritual forms.

With the death of his enemy Portete in 1908 (1911-1914 XIX:259,279), the occasion of frank rejoicing on Gassó's part, enmity flowed most strongly between the priest and Portete's son Smit, a secondary chief and a leader of the traditional group centered on the sacred gathering (XX,XXII). At the end of his fifth *entrada* in October of that year, Gassó went to Smit's home to complain that he had lured away some of Gassó's young followers, capping an acrimonious exchange with the statement that God punished all who were against the mission, most notably Smit's father Portete. At this, Smit leapt up howling, and, according to Gassó, a hostile crowd of Smit's partisans came pouring out of the gathering house. While Gassó preached on their damnation, he noticed a would-be assailant creeping up with a knife, but by turning and facing the man directly, he escaped attack (1909:208-209; 1911-1914 XXII:136). Despite this incident, by the end of the month he felt he had established some ascendancy over Nargana and consolidated his support, probably in large part because a number of conservatives had permanently abandoned the island. Opposition continued, but a narrowly averted attack on

Nargana just after his departure (mentioned above) probably increased village unity and a sense of opposition to the rest of San Blas (1909:210; 1911-1914:XXII).

CATHOLIC MISSIONS AND GOVERNMENT POLICY

Along with Gassó's success in beating down Kuna opposition, the fate of his mission depended on government support, which was weaker than it might have seemed, and on national politics.   Panama's independence from Colombia in 1903 followed by only a year the end of a fierce civil conflict, known as the War of a Thousand Days, between anticlerical Liberals and more orthodox Catholic Conservatives.   The new nation's adherence to orthodox Christianity was tepid and ambivalent, and many leaders, especially in the Liberal party, were Masons and anticlericalists.[7]   Although the 1904 constitution promised official support for missionization, the measure was conceded as consolation for recognizing Catholicism only as the majority, not the official or sole religion of Panama (Rojas y Arieta 1929:242; Mega 1958:297). Government backing for Gassó depended on a personal relationship between the country's first President, Manuel Amador Guerrero, and Bishop Junguito, on the Conservative Party's tenuous control of the government, and on the perception that Gassó was an effective proxy for national interests in San Blas.

Already, by 1908, an official publication voiced disappointment in the practical results of the mission, and subsequent statements expressed disillusion with the ability of the appointed governor, Charlie Robinson, to deliver San Blas, as well as with missionization itself.[8]

The missions established with civilizing goals on the part of the government, which sustains them, have not given, nor probably will give, the slightest result, if one excepts the fact that some number of Indians give themselves to receive a baptism whose significance will gain many souls for heaven, but which benefits the Republic of Panama very little (Memorias de Gobierno y Justicia 1912:103, in Herrera 1984:97).

With the elevation in 1910 of a Liberal and Mason, Carlos Mendoza, as President, the government turned the Kuna boys boarded with the Christian Brothers over to secular teachers, and within a few months, closed down the special boarding school altogether. (Chief Robinson and others continued to seek scholarships, however, and over the next 15 years a number of Kuna youths, the majority from Nargana and Nusatupu, were educated in secular and religious schools.) After the death of Bishop Junguito in 1911, Catholic influence declined further, and with the 1912 election as President of the preeminent Liberal of the era, Belisario Porras, the Liberal dominated legislature soon enacted measures drastically reducing Catholic influence and the ties between church and state (Rojas y Arieta 1929:242-243; Mega 1958:298). Among other things, financial support for Catholic missions was terminated.

FROM CATHOLIC TO PROTESTANT

Well before the loss of government funds, trouble had appeared on the horizon for Gassó. In late 1909, a nondenominational British Protestant missionary, Anna Coope, made an abortive attempt to enter San Blas. Gassó's equal in fortitude and devotion to a cause, Coope felt that God, by giving her a homely nose and thus preventing her from marrying, had chosen her for His purposes (Coope 1917:2-5). Arriving in Panama from previous mission work in the United States, the West Indies, and Venezuela, she secured an invitation to open a school from a chief of the Kuna village of Tupile, entering San Blas on the same launch on which Gassó happened to be returning to Nargana. Although forcibly ejected from Tupile, she did learn of discontent with Gassó and of possible interest from Charlie Robinson in her school (Coope 1917:79-98; Gassó 1911a). After an arduous return trip, during which she and Gassó had a heated verbal confrontation (Coope 1917:93-98), Coope decided to cut her losses, at least for the moment, and left the country.

During this period, Gassó seemed to be consolidating his beachhead in San Blas. In May of 1909 (a few months before Coope), he succeeded in visiting Tupile, and despite strong opposition by visitors from another island, he gained provisional acceptance; a few days later, however, raiders from several neighboring islands invaded Tupile and removed the religious images Gassó had left there.[9] The government responded by sending a small shipment of arms to Robinson (Gassó 1910b:153) and by setting up a police post in the newly created border town of Puerto Obaldía at the east end of San Blas (Puig 1948:225-226).

On Nusatupu, Chief Henry Clay stalled Gassó on building a church, until Clay was replaced in early 1909 by another chief named Soo or Sho. The latter, thoroughly alarmed by Coope's sally into San Blas, made a deal with Gassó for monopoly rights to missionization in return for keeping out other foreigners (Gassó 1911a). Soo, however, showed more interest in schools than in the church (despite heavy pressure by the missionary, it was not completed until January 1911), which influenced a reluctant Gassó to bring in another priest to teach school (1911a, 1911-1914:88,109-110).

On Nargana proper, Gassó's fiercest opponent, Smit, died during 1909 (IV:236) and the missionary got the village to abandon completely their "cultos," i.e., the sacred village gatherings (Fernandez 1911). He constructed two buildings with zinc walls, and in 1910 Robinson had the village reorganized on a grid plan. A number of boys from other islands boarded with Gassó (sixteen in all, according to Puig, 1948:152), and several more priests and brothers joined the mission, for a total of eight between 1907 and 1912 (Erice 1961:68).

As late as September 1910, Gassó apparently anticipated the rapid conversion of all the Kuna (Fernandez 1911). In fact, however, other islands rebuffed him decisively, and things began to come apart on Nargana and Nusatupu. At the time of Coope's visit in 1909, Robinson communicated a waning commitment to the priest and was induced to continue his support only with a monthly stipend of fifteen dollars (Gassó 1911a). Many individuals continued to hold out against conversion, and others fled Nargana for unmissionized villages a few miles to the East (López n.d.). Even among those who stayed, several young men schooled by the mission abandoned Christianity (1911-1914:VI,85), and Gassó's dictatorial manner and inattention to schooling inspired dissatisfaction among converts.

In ill health, discouraged by Kuna intransigence, and with his government support at an end, Gassó left San Blas in late 1911 or 1912, never to return (Misioneros Hijos 1939:114; Falla n.d.26,28). Catholic missionaries continued to visit Nargana, but the Jesuit order shifted most of the resources previously dedicated to the Kuna to its Asian missions (Misioneros Hijos 1939:114).

Coope returned to Panama in August 1912. Rather than attempt another direct assault, she waited in Colón. In January 1913, she buttonholed Charlie Robinson while he was visiting the city, securing an invitation to establish a mission school on Nargana. By the end of February she was on the island, with the school underway.[10] Soo, the first chief of Nusatupu, wrote diatribes against her to President Porras (3/09/13, 3/12/13) while Gassó's primary successor, Father Benito Pérez, petitioned the government for a new partnership (Porras Archives: Pérez to B.Porras 1/29/13) and tried to incite the Kuna of Cimral Colman's confederacy against Coope (Pérez to Colman 3/02/13), both efforts unsuccessful. The Christian Brother who was still running a small school on Nargana left within a few months, and in July a sympathetic government official on tour of the region encouraged Coope to take over the principal Catholic mission building.[11]

THE PROTESTANT MISSION

Coope opened her school the day after her arrival. She actively wooed her students, using a good deal of music and physical activities in her teaching, and the Kuna were eager to learn. Although a broad segment of the population attended in the initial weeks, adults soon dropped out in favor of children (Dietrick 1925:15). On Sunday nights she led prayer and hymn services for all ages, and by day taught school, mostly in English. Girls were encouraged to attend, to the extent that at one point Coope closed the school to pressure parents who were keeping their daughters home (Dietrick 1925:15), but she paid special attention to educating and converting young boys (Coope 1917:112-119,132-148). Over the next few years a handful of boys were sent abroad to mission schools, first to the United States and then to Venezuela.

Opposition to Coope, which persisted strongly for some months on Nusatupu and neighboring communities, flowed fiercely from more distant islands and, on 2 November, Robinson sent an urgent appeal for help against an imminent attack by a canoe flotilla from hostile villages (Porras Archives: Robinson to Arcia 11/02/13). The lack of a vessel prevented the government from responding (Porras to Arcia 11/08/13), and Robinson was forced to deal with the threat himself, apparently by neutralizing the first canoe-load of attackers with his superior weaponry.[12]

Like Gassó, Coope worked hard at converting and controlling Charlie Robinson, who was almost as ambivalent as he had been with the priest, feeling torn between the missionary and social pressure from fellow Kuna (Dietrick 1925:15). To avoid tense situations or the necessity of taking sides or making a decision, Robinson often fled to his work camp on distant offshore islands.

Many of the families who had put their children in the Catholic school soon switched them to Coope's, and although a few of Gassó's converts like Chief Soo of Nusatupu refused to change, she won over most of the many Nargana Kuna interested in education. Where Gassó had stressed hierarchy and obedience, Coope won favor with her democratic and egalitarian outlook, and though just as strong willed and single-minded as her predecessor, both her book and informant memories a half-century later suggest a much warmer and more good-humored presence. According to one informant,[13] she tolerated the Kuna sacred gathering, which Gassó had opposed so ardently, perhaps because her much more superficial involvement in Kuna culture did not alert her to the competition the gathering offered, and in general she was willing, at least for the short run, to put up with a great deal of native custom. Most of all, she offered schooling, which is what the Kuna of Nargana wanted.

The indigenous Kuna religion seemed to arouse Coope's ire much less than Catholicism. To demonstrate her conquest of the Catholic mission, she not only took over its building, she also had religious images thrown in the water, except for one, which she "kept...to use as an object lesson." She had boys recite the 115th Psalm ("They have mouths, but they speak not...) while she touched the appropriate parts of the statue, and "when we had finished I laid the image down and stepped on it, asking: 'Can it feel, can it help us, can it hurt me, can it get up?'" (1917:118).

Coope was joined by an American missionary, Martha Purdy, who worked with her on Nargana for half a year, until a priest passing through Nusatupu arranged to reestablish a school there. Coope and Purdy temporarily abandoned Nargana to set up their own school on Nusatupu. When the priest returned he found himself forestalled, and Coope was able to return to Nargana, leaving Purdy on the other island. By 1916, the Nargana school had an average daily attendance of 90 students, the Nusatupu school 40 (Coope 1917:124-129).

An ardent prohibitionist with strong ties to the Women's Christian Temperance Union, during her first two years Coope was preoccupied with the issue of alcohol. The effect of Gassó's earlier crackdown had disappeared, and a number of little stores sold rum freely, among them one run by Charlie Robinson's brother Alfred, whom Coope was sure merely fronted for the chief himself (1917:120-123). After working on Robinson over a period of months, she got him to impose partial prohibition—rum selling ceased, and puberty ceremonies were few and short (Coope 1917:120-125). By the end of 1914, however, pressure was growing again for a large puberty ceremony, pressure that Coope countered in long earnest conversations with Robinson. On 14 November, during a severe illness, Robinson was converted to Protestant Christianity; he had himself carried downstairs on his sickbed to supervise the destruction of the *chicha* brewing pots, imposing complete prohibition on Nargana. The ban provoked a reaction against his leadership by a pro-*chicha* faction, which continued to sponsor puberty ceremonies across the water on Nusatupu (Coope 1917:149-155). During the three months of Robinson's convalescence, "he learned lessons of obedience," and although clearly Coope meant obedience to God, her own influence over the chief consolidated along with His.

THE IMPOSITION OF SECULAR CONTROL

Coope, however, had Nargana to herself for only two years. In early 1915, the government created a new administrative unit, the Circunscripción de San Blas, and in late March President Belisario Porras toured the archipelago with an entourage of dignitaries (Anonymous 1916), installing an intendente or governor at a new headquarters called El Porvenir at the western end of the region. Porras spoke with Coope, and he arranged to have government schools and police detachments installed on Nargana, Nusatupu, and two other receptive villages. In a contemporary letter (Coope to Jeffrey 5/26/15, in Keeler 1956:156), she wrote that Robinson and the Indians rejected the offer of schools; her memoirs (1917:155-161), however, have it that Robinson overrode objections and gained local assent in a dramatic village meeting. In any case, the schools were in session by mid-1916.

In her memoirs (1917:161), published shortly after the schools arrived, Coope mentions them with seeming approval, but conflict soon developed with her own work. As early as January of 1917, a report on examination results in government schools complained that attendance was lower on Nargana and Nusatupu because many families sent their children to the English-language schools.[14]

Until that point, the Panamanian government had at least tolerated Coope. Enrique Hurtado, the official who suggested in 1913 that she take over the Catholic mission building, and who filled the role of intendente from 1915 to 1917, had an unusually relaxed attitude towards English-speakers and Protestantism,[15] and very likely higher members of the administration accepted his view that, at least in the absence of secular control, her mission helped civilize the Kuna. By Coope's own account (1917:99-101; Keeler 1956:152-153,161),[16] she secured the acquiescence of Presidents Mendoza and Porras by confronting them at the Presidential palace. On one occasion, she complained to the British consul, who apparently pressured Porras (Keeler 1956:157), and she had an active group of supporters in the Canal Zone, probably including the American Minister of the time, an evangelical Christian. Hurtado was succeeded as intendente in 1917 by a time serving nonentity, which probably gave Coope some breathing space, but in late 1918, when the nonentity was succeeded in turn by a fiercely intolerant nationalist named Vaglio (Coope referred to him as "the old Dago"),[17] the situation changed radically.

Before Vaglio's arrival, Robinson apparently had continued to enjoy the trust of the government, but a domestic challenge to his leadership, as well as to the mission, had already appeared in the form of young Kuna graduates of urban schools, most of them fervently nationalist and modernist as well as Catholic. Foremost among them was a young man named Claudio Iglesias, who while training to be a carpenter had lived in a Catholic hospice in Panama City (Puig 1948:188-190; López n.d.). Claudio's brother, Lonny or Alcibiades, Coope's most important convert, was one of the boys Coope sent abroad for schooling, but after an unhappy experience, he returned to public school on Nargana and threw in his lot with his Catholic brother (Coope 1917:132-36; Iglesias & Vandervelde 1977; Vandervelde & Iglesias 1983). With Claudio's return to Nargana in 1917, Robinson and his gringophile supporters increasingly came in conflict with the young turks, who, allied with government teachers and police, began agitating to suppress indigenous custom. Claudio and two other literate men soon were salaried as "indigenous policemen."

Conflict between Claudio's group and the policemen on one side, and Coope, Robinson, and conservative and moderate Nargana people on the other, came to a head in late 1918 and early 1919 (see Keeler 1956: 158-159). On December 25, 1918, the teacher of the Nargana school organized an evening of student skits, recitations, and a Panamanian folkloric dance. Many conservative Kuna, like Coope, viewed the dancing as immoral. During the performance a fierce argument broke out, and the next day remarks by one man led to his arrest. On the 28th, Robinson and a large group of supporters, armed with staves and bayonets, threatened a teacher, defied government authority, and unsuccessfully tried to free the prisoner. The intendente intervened personally to put down the uprising, after which both Robinson and his modernist opponents pressed their cases to the government in letters and delegations.

The intendente threw all his support to the modernists, condemning Robinson as a "rebel" and "absolutist," and in April he sent an order closing down Coope and Purdy's schools. Coope was forced to sign a contract agreeing to teach evening bible classes only in Spanish and to give up other teaching altogether, and on 12 April President Porras decreed that the government should take over from Coope the mission building originally erected by Gassó. (She soon had another one constructed, financed by outside contributions.)

In early May, President Porras prohibited young girls from wearing to school the nose rings and bead limb bindings that formed essential parts of women's dress, a ban that Coope and Robinson claimed to support, but which aroused adamant opposition among conservatives and moderates. Through May and June, girls continued to wear the ornaments at home and at mission services, but not in school, and feelings against both the prohibitions and compulsory public schooling grew rapidly. Both Robinson and Coope favored the elimination of nose rings, but only gradually and voluntarily (Coope to Jeffrey 6/19, in Keeler 1956:158). Many Nargana conservatives and moderates adamantly defended traditional dress, and like Robinson himself, they strongly preferred schooling in English.

After an unsuccessful mission by Robinson's group to President Porras to persuade him to go more slowly in changing Nargana, policemen tried on 29 June to arrest three agitators, sparking off a new uprising. Holed up, arms in hand, the police sent an urgent message for reinforcements from Porvenir, which arrived that evening. Even so, it took them several days to reestablish control. The administration drew up a list of fines on 19 of the rebels, prominent among them Robinson's brother Alfred, and although his own participation could not be proved, Robinson was held responsible for payment of the fines.[18]

Thereafter, the police and intendente worked assiduously to support the young Catholic radicals and to suppress Coope and Robinson. In about 1920,

Claudio and his followers formed a social and political club as their base, and the police soon began forcing villagers to attend obligatory weekly dances at the club. In April 1921, when the administration compelled women on Nargana to abandon native dress completely, many inhabitants once again fled to unpacified islands to the East, but Robinson apparently kept quiet, and thereafter the modernists and police held the upper hand. (A few days after the ban on native dress, when police pursued a woman fleeing the policy to the nearby island of Kwepti or Río Azúcar, Claudio Iglesias was killed during a melee in the dark.)

From about 1921 on, the police actively suppressed the Protestant missionaries, to the point of severely punishing anyone who met with them or supplied their needs.[19] Purdy smuggled one of her prize students out of Nusatupu in 1922 and sent him off to school in the States, for which the police filed a complaint against her (Keeler 1956:164-165). Coope herself was expelled from Nargana in the same year but managed to gain an interview with President Porras, who gave her permission to return in January of 1923 (Vandervelde & Iglesias 1983:31-36; Keeler 1956:161).

In late February 1925, the Kuna of the confederacy led by Cimral Colman revolted against Panama. (The other confederacy remained neutral.) During the revolt, Charlie Robinson, along with 72 others, signed a petition written down by Coope, in which they protested police tyranny and called for American intervention.[20] The rebels, however, identified Robinson with the pro-Panamanian modernists, and when their forces came to Nargana, he first hid in Coope's wardrobe, pistol in hand, and then fled to the city (Erice 1975:372-375). When the American minister came out to San Blas on a warship and successfully negotiated a treaty between the Kuna and the Panamanian government, the British consul evacuated Coope from Nargana.[21] Her mission building was sold to the government, and after an unsuccessful attempt to return, she left San Blas forever.

Panama reestablished control of Nargana (though little of the rest of San Blas) immediately after the revolt, but except for occasional visits, missionaries left it alone until 1928, when the government entrusted to Franciscan nuns the region's public schooling. In September of that year, when a new and much larger Catholic mission was inaugurated, a reconverted Charlie Robinson welcomed and supported it (Misioneros Hijos 1939:116-117). In the early 1930s, the Kuna of the confederacy that had revolted reestablished ties with the government, leading to recognition of the San Blas coast as an indigenous reserve.

Foreign Protestants were by then excluded by law. Soon after the Kuna revolution, however, Coope had encountered in the city her ex-student, Alcibiades Iglesias, brother of the slain radical Catholic modernist Claudio Iglesias. Coope persuaded Alcibiades to go to the U.S. for Protestant schooling, and in 1932, he returned to San Blas with a North American wife (Iglesias & Vandervelde 1977; Vandervelde & Iglesias 1983). He ran an independent native Protestant mission and school (with covert outside support) until 1955, when relaxed laws allowed him to affiliate with the Southern Baptists (Holloman 1969:347-348, 379-383). During the 1950s, both Protestants and Catholics made numerous converts on several islands (though backsliding, token allegiance, and syncretism with Kuna religion are the norm rather than the exception), and in the late 1950s and early 1960s, followers of the two faiths passed through a period of renewed competition and conflict (see Howe 1986:237-249,271-272)–all of which lies outside the scope of this paper.

MISSIONS AND CULTURAL ARTICULATION

It was not inevitable that the integration of the Kuna into Panama should begin with religion. Both Gassó and Coope appreciated that commerce and missions offered alternative paths, and both saw the coasting merchants who traded with the Kuna as competitors and sometime antagonists. Given that the Kuna were already selling coconuts and other local products, given that merchants were prevented from controlling or exploiting their trading partners, and given that the Kuna all agreed on the value of trade, it is regrettable that they could not have been brought closer to national society through that medium rather than through religious proselytization. Whatever the long-term effects of attempts to convert the Kuna, in the short run, by provoking latent divisions and stirring communities and individuals up against each other, the missions imported conflict and dissent along with the gospel.

Understanding and analysis of Kuna missionization should begin at the national level, with consideration not only of laws regarding indigenous peoples but also, as Herrera (1984) and Falla (n.d.) indicate, of particular parties, policies, administrations, and even individual politicians. Government initiatives and support got Gassó into San Blas and helped keep him there; loss of that support drove him out again. The tolerance or indifference of the Liberal government between 1913 and 1918 gave Coope the opening she needed, while the subsequent growth of nationalist intolerance hampered and then ended her work.

Within that wider context, events on the local scene were determined in large part by the interaction or articulation of indigenous and mission cultures (Comaroff 1985; Bowden 1981; Axtell 1985). In addition to the balance of power between the two sides and the political resources available to them, the way in which specific features of mission ideology and practice articulated with specific features of their Kuna counterparts most encouraged certain outcomes and discouraged others. And since Gassó, Coope, and the handful of coworkers they brought with them represented mission cultures to the Kuna, the process of cultural articulation depended on the personal quirks and idiosyncrasies of those individuals as well as the commonalities of Catholic and Protestant Christianity.[22]

Significant results flowed even from the articulation with Kuna socialization patterns of such seemingly secondary factors as Gassó and Coope's shared affection for young boys (and a common missionary policy of shaping as yet unformed minds). Kuna boys, up to the age of 13 or 14, enjoyed considerable independence and free time; except for regular fishing and occasional agricultural work, they were free to run around in groups, playing, and raising hell. Both missionaries employed the boys extensively, Gassó as sacristans, boarders, and the core of his prayer groups, Coope as school pupils and prime converts. In the long run, Protestant missionization achieved its goals in San Blas largely through what a handful of these boys, notably Alcibiades Iglesias, did in later life. Neither missionary, however, managed to deal effectively with the boys' restlessness or rebelliousness, and each was traumatically rejected by close disciples.

A more fundamental aspect of Kuna culture, the love of vocal music, was exploited by the missionaries in different ways, Gassó through devotional chants, Coope through gospel songs. Gassó also tapped into Kuna interest in memorizing texts. Traditionally, ambitious Kuna men gain prestige and supernatural power by learning curing chants, myths, and other esoteric knowledge; with Gassó, of course, they memorized prayers, devotional exercises, and the catechism, showing a surprising zeal for rote learning, a zeal whose roots Gassó apparently did not recognize.

The interest in magically powerful texts forms part of an intense Kuna concern with the spirit world, encompassing worries about the anger of the primary deity, Great Father, who may punish the Kuna or even end the world, as well as fear of the more immediate harm inflicted by malevolent spirits. Coope, about whose preaching little is known, apparently did not exploit these concerns to any extent. Gassó, however, was already on the same wave length as the Kuna. He readily and repeatedly threatened supernatural punishment for thwarting him, punishment whose reality he never doubted, and he interpreted events favorable to the mission, even the gruesome death of his enemy Portete, as divine support. Promising health and economic benefits as well as protection, he was firmly convinced that converts caught more turtles than "gentiles" or apostates (1911-1914 IX:162), and that the crosses and icons he substituted for the carved wooden figures used in Kuna medicine cured as well as saved; inevitably, encounters at patients' hammock-side and elsewhere turned into contests between Catholic and Kuna magic. His promises and threats produced results, especially the threats, which won him grudging entrance into Nusatupu (VI:88; VII:133).

These contests also followed from Gassó's highly developed sense of the Kuna as beings who were simultaneously radically different from himself (especially in that he was saved and they damned) and equivalent, in that aspects of their culture paralleled his own. Coope, with a superficial universalism and tolerance, insisted only on eradicating sin, by which she mostly meant drink. Gassó, with his appreciation of Kuna alterity, ended up in a life-and-death struggle with those aspects of Kuna practice that mirrored his own, curing through religious images, and even more so, the Kuna sacred gathering.

Coope and Gassó, like the faiths that formed them, differed radically in many ways. Gassó emphasized oral learning, especially catechism; Coope written scripture. Gassó venerated images; Coope destroyed them. Gassó insisted on adherence to dogma, Coope personal conversion. Gassó engaged himself more deeply with Kuna culture, but Coope apparently stayed in the field for much longer periods.

In other respects, some of them surprising, the two converged on common positions. Liquor was never an issue of theological importance to Gassó, but first through irritation with carousers, and then through his identification of drinking with his enemies, namely, Protestant sailors and Kuna traditionalists, he ended up working as fiercely as Coope for prohibition.

Catholics baptize people as infants, evangelical Protestants only with conversion, but because Gassó worried about the effects of baptizing future apostates, ultimately he was almost as demanding as Coope, insisting on evidence of a lasting and firm conversion except from little children and dying people (1911-1914 V:56; XIV:42; XVI:89,106). Their working methods were similar as well: both assiduously cultivated contacts in the government to gain support or toleration, both publicized their missions with books written while still in the field, and both developed personal support groups in Panama and overseas.

The difference which remained a difference, the difference which made a difference, concerned education. The Catholic church as an institution has frequently used schools as vehicles for religious conversion and socialization, but since Gassó as an individual strongly preferred *oral* instruction, his commitment to schooling was at best halfhearted. He distrusted literacy, because it could open up unwanted influences, and he loathed the modern ideology that glorified schools. Coope, on the other hand, embraced that ideology, and she saw literacy as a tool facilitating personal contact with scripture, the core of her religious practice.

Schooling, about which the Kuna cared most, gave Coope the decisive advantage. The value in Kuna culture of apprenticeship in esoteric knowledge as a path to prestige and influence carried over to the new form of learning, making the Kuna (then and now) enthusiastic proponents of schooling.[23] Some individuals, of course, chose between the missions for other reasons, and some even stuck with their choice. But many chose on the basis of which one offered the best educational prospects, changing allegiance opportunistically as circumstances altered.

Charlie Robinson, first Catholic, then Protestant, then Catholic again, was a prime example of such opportunism, despite his basic leanings towards Anglophone culture and Protestantism. So was the Iglesias family, which provided the prime converts to both faiths: Alcibiades entered a Protestant school while Claudio was in a Catholic one. As the Protestant mission ran into trouble, Alcibiades switched to public schools and the Catholic faction. After the revolution, he reverted again to Protestantism. His father, though identified with one side or another, stayed a traditional curer throughout. Whatever mission came and went, Kuna faith lay in schooling.

RELIGION AND THE POLITICS OF CHANGE

When the Kuna *did* decide in some more lasting way between the two faiths, they typically appropriated them as symbols of positions on cultural and political issues, positions in which religion itself was relatively unimportant except as a badge of identity and orientation. From 1907 through 1915 there were many shifts and swings in support for the missions, but by the late teens and early twenties, the period of perhaps maximum struggle and turmoil, Nargana and Nusatupu had sorted themselves out into two more or less distinct camps, Catholic and Protestant. (The irony here of course is that by this time one mission had been gone for more than five years and the other was on its way to being suppressed.)

The two faiths, as they were presented to Nargana, came wrapped in cultural/linguistic/political packages, one anglophone, the other Hispanic, and this wrapping ultimately mattered more than the theological contents within. It is not irrelevant that for several hundred years the Kuna had been playing Spanish- and English-speaking powers off against each other, with a marked preference on the part of most Kuna for things English and North American. More important, however, was the current relationship to encompassing national powers, which in the context of early twentieth-century Panama implied a choice between a weak state and a much greater power enclaved within the territory of that state. Catholicism implied identification with national culture and with the sovereignty and authority of Panama; Protestantism was associated with the culture and might of the United States in the Canal Zone, which many Kuna saw as more powerful, but less apt to intrude in and control their lives.

By the end of the decade 1910 to 1920, identification as Protestant or Catholic had come to signal two different stances on the degree, rate, and direction of social change. The Catholics, whose dominant core members consisted of young men and boys back from the city, pushed for a complete and almost instantaneous transformation, in which national culture would entirely replace Kuna. The Protestants favored change, but of a considerably more gradual and partial nature, and with traits borrowed from both Panama and the United States. If the Catholics were radicals, the Protestants were moderates. (On Nargana and Nusatupu, the conservatives and reactionaries who disliked both positions had fled, thrown in their lot with the moderates, or were keeping their heads down.)[24]

In both instances, major discrepancies are apparent between the political and cultural stances of the opposed factions and those of the two missionaries, discrepancies so major that Coope undoubtedly was very uneasy and Gassó, had he known, would have been horrified. Gassó and the radical modernists differed on the following issues:

(1) The radicals opposed North American influence and advanced the cause of the Panamanian state. Gassó hated the United States, in part because of the Protestant liberalism with which he associated it, in part because of Spain's recent military defeat in the Spanish-American War, and he worked with the Panamanian government, exploiting and invoking state power as needed. But (unlike later Catholic missionaries) he never transferred his political loyalties from his native country to Panama, and his goal was to prevent rather than promote the political integration of San Blas into the national polity (an extreme version of the common missionary ambivalence about civilization, see Beidelman 1982:27).

(2) The Catholic radicals pushed Panamanian culture, with the liberal and commercial outlook then dominant; above all, they pushed modernism. Gassó loathed modernism, liberalism, and commercialism, all of which he saw as essentially Protestant and anti-Catholic.

(3) The radicals insisted on suppressing Kuna culture entirely rather than accommodating it to national culture. Gassó was ambivalent on the value of Kuna practice, but he leaned towards preservation: he wrote that if the Kuna would accept Jesus, learn their catechism, and drop a few nasty practices, they would be much better off than city dwellers.

(4) The radicals and their police allies directed their efforts obsessively towards suppressing the traditional costume of Kuna women, in particular gold nose rings and the beads with which women wrapped their limbs. Gassó, for his part, cared so little about this issue that in order to gain acceptance for a second missionary he had a Brother trained in goldworking.

(5) Finally, for reasons discussed elsewhere (Howe 1988), the Catholics imposed social dancing to the music of windup victrolas as a cornerstone of their social change program. Gassó, at the opposite extreme, had not only confronted sailors throwing parties to the music of accordions and phonographs, but he saw American "mone" and gramophones as the essence of modern decadence.

The contradictions and discrepancies between Coope's position and the Protestants' were not so glaring—as one might expect, given that she was still present and Gassó was long-gone—but they were real enough:

(1) Protestantism was used as a banner for resistance to state control. Coope, though hardly a Panamanian patriot or supporter, subscribed firmly to the doctrine of "Render unto Caesar." Both Coope and Protestantism were widely identified as North American, and although the mistake is understandable, given her backing in the Canal Zone and her enthusiasm for things American, she never gave up her British citizenship, and her national loyalties were more complex and ambiguous than those of her Kuna adherents.

(2) The moderates made their stand in defending beads and nose rings, and the administration and young turks saw Coope as pro-nose ring, or at least soft on the issue. In fact, though she seems to have been tolerant of native dress in general, she strongly disliked the custom of piercing infant noses, and she differed from the government on the question only in that she opposed using coercion to eliminate nose rings.

(3) The Protestant moderates included many defenders of traditional puberty ceremonies, which included heavy, prolonged drinking. Coope's opposition to drink and the lengths to which she would go to suppress it were by 1915 only too apparent to everyone on Nargana. The moderates, however, were willing to ignore or cover over this difference, precisely because the general cultural associations of Protestantism were so much more important to them than either Coope or the faith itself.

As noted earlier, the struggle between the two parties on Nargana was decided by state coercion, with the suppression of Robinson and Coope in favor of the Catholic radical modernists. In the period between 1920 and 1925, despite the dominance of the supposed Catholics, priests returned for only short visits. Missions were on hold, and Catholicism and Protestantism continued largely as symbols of political and cultural orientation. Conflict between the Kuna and the government came to a head in these years throughout San Blas, but it was secular conflict, pitting Kuna moderates and conservatives against Panamanian police and administrators. The two sides fought over culture, that is, over the replacement of Kuna customs by Panamanian, but the customs—dancing, drinking, dress, sanitation, modesty, education—had little to do with Christian faith, and the struggle must be understood in terms of *secular* ideology (Howe 1988).

The most important effect of mission rivalry up to 1920 on the later secular struggles was to establish in the minds of police and bureaucrats that the contest was not just between civilization and savagery, but in part between Panamanian and North American culture. There were other reasons why this viewpoint took hold, notably the huge North American presence in Panama, but it was the struggles between an English-speaking Protestant and Spanish-speaking Catholics that first planted the notion in the official mind that the issue was Hispanic versus anglophone culture.

Anthropologists, following in Weber's tracks, have for some time concerned themselves with the impact of missionization on the consciousness and practice of indigenous peoples and other ethnicities. Kay Warren (1978), for instance, shows that conversion of traditional Guatamalan folk Catholics to a more orthodox variety of Catholicism transformed their understanding of the nature of "Indian"/*ladino* relations. Sheldon Annis (1987), similarly, finds that the social and economic orientations of Protestant converts in another Guatamalan town differ significantly from those of Catholics. In two of the most acute studies of Christianity's impact on the Third World, Jean and John Comaroff show that missionization can transform indigenous consciousness even in cases like that of the Kuna, when conversion fails and missionaries depart (Jean Comaroff 1985, Comaroff & Comaroff 1986). In early twentieth-century San Blas, however, what is most striking is the way in which Kuna converts appropriated missions for their own purposes, and the degree to which mission rivalry affected the consciousness, not of the Kuna, but of the administrators and police sent to pacify them. Elmer Miller (1970) argues that proselytization can transform consciousness in ways that missionaries neither desire nor expect—in the case of the Toba of Argentina they inadvertently promoted a secularized, disenchanted world-view. Early missionization of the Kuna, in addition to sending the wrong message, also hit the wrong target.

NOTES

Acknowledgements: I appreciate the helpful comments of Mac Chapin, Jean Jackson, Lynn Stephen, and the discussants and participants of the symposium in which the papers in this volume were presented. I am also grateful to William Merrill for bibliographic suggestions.

1. Gassó called Nusatupu Corazón de Jesús, the name most generally used today; for simplicity, I use Nusatupu throughout this paper. He called the other island San José de Narganá.

2. E. López n.d.; Gassó 1911-1914 II: 204-205; Puig 1948:143-149; Moore 1983:100-101.

3. Samuel Morris: interview.

4. Puig 1948:173-178; Gassó 1911-1914 II:204-205; E. López n.d.; anonymous account in E. López MS.

5. Gassó's diary was published in installments between 1911 and 1914. It is cited here by volume number within the diary (*not* volume number of the journal), and by page number within each diary volume. Given the nature of serial publication in this journal, the same page numbers appear in different volumes of the journal. The date, 1911-1914, is referenced once at the beginning of each paragraph.

6. First *entrada*, 26 March to 7 April 1907; second *entrada*, 30 May to 18 July 1907; third *entrada*, 14 September to 4 October 1907; fourth *entrada*, 17 June to 3 July 1908; fifth *entrada*, late August to 26 October 1908.

7. Ariza 1964:7; Rojas y Arieta 1929:233,248.

8. Memorias de Gobierno y Justicia de 1908, in Herrera 1984:94; Memorias 1910, in Puig 1948:224-227, also in Herrera 1984:89-90; Memorias 1912:103, in Herrera 1984:97.

9. Gassó 1910a; Memorias de Gobierno y Justicia 1910:315-316, in Herrera 1984:90-91; Gassó 1910b:153.

10. The sources on Coope's mission include: her own memoirs (1917), which only cover her work through 1916; two inspirational books about her student, Alcibiades Iglesias (Vandervelde & Iglesias 1983; Iglesias & Vandervelde 1977); a contemporary magazine article (Dietrick 1925); letters by Coope published by Keeler (1956); documents from the archives of the Intendencia El Porvenir; a memorandum based on an interview with her in 1925 and an ethnographic sketch of the Kuna written either by her or based on information from her, both in the records of the Canal Company (file 80A-15), United States National Archives; various documents in the State Department records (file 819.00), also in the National Archives; a manuscript written by a visitor to San Blas (Markham MS); the field notes of the explorer Richard O. Marsh; and documents in the Belisario Porras archives, University of Panama.

11. Coope 1917:116-117; Hurtado to Secretaria de Gobierno y Justicia 8/15/13.

12. Coope 1917:163-164; Coope to Jeffrey 11/01/13,11/05/13, in Keeler 1956:154,162.

13. Samuel Morris: interview.

14. Report to the Inspector of Public Instruction, 1/16/17, archives of the Intendencia.

15. He later became an agent for the United Fruit Company in San Blas.

16. See also Coope's letters in Keeler (1956:152,153,161).

17. Coope to Jeffrey 6/19, in Keeler 1956:159.

18. The narrative of events on Nargana, 1918-1919, is based largely on documents, too numerous to be individually cited in this paper, from the archives of Porvenir, primarily correspondence between the Intendencia and the Nargana police and the Intendencia and higher authorities, supplemented by the Memorias de Gobierno y Justicia for 1920.

19. Sources on Coope's suppression include a letter written by a Panama Railroad employee (William Markham to Porras 2/08/24), the explorer Richard Marsh's diary (1/20/25), and Vandervelde and Iglesias (1928:31-37), and Purdy and Coope's own correspondence (in Keeler 1956:157,164).

20. Files of the United States Legation to Panama, 1925, U.S. National Archives.

21. Records of the Department of State Relating to the Internal Affairs of the State of Panama, 1910-1929, 819.00/1154-1180, United States National Archives.

22. Gassó's methods in Panama, for instance, and even the way in which he abruptly departed when the tide turned against him, repeated patterns already evident in his earlier work in Mexico (Ocampo 1966).

23. A desire for schooling is a common motivation for conversion in much of the world and by no means limited to San Blas. Many Kuna from other villages fiercely opposed schools: I would argue that they differed from proponents of schooling, not in the value placed on education or in the shared perception of equivalence between indigenous and modern forms of learning, but in the threat to Kuna culture they (correctly) perceived in mission and government indoctrination.

24. The two primary stances concerning religion, national affiliation, and social change taken elsewhere in San Blas echoed in a peculiar way the positions of the moderates and radicals on Nargana. The leaders of the confederacy headed by Cimral Colman generally favored slow, careful change. Pagan and vehemently antimissionary (though open to a little syncretism), less opposed to American influence than Panamanian, they feared the government schools, but let a few leaders' children go away for education—one island even set up a private school in 1918, staffed by ex-students of Coope. In sum, despite their fierce

opposition to both factions on Nargana, they resembled the moderates in their anglophone bias, gradualism, and interest in schools.

The reactionary position of the other confederacy led by Inapakinya of Sasartii categorically rejected schools, missions, and foreign innovation. Paradoxically, Christianized narratives and Latin American popular history had largely replaced Kuna myths in their religion, and although they doggedly stuck with Colombia up to 1919, thereafter they supported the Panamanian government against Colman's group. Thus they ended up as a kind of distorted Levi-Straussian mirror-image of the Nargana radicals at the opposite end of the political spectrum.

REFERENCES

Annis, Sheldon
 1987   *God and Production in a Guatemalan Town*. Austin: University of Texas Press.
Anonymous
 1916   *Excursión á la Costa de San Blas en Panamá*. Publicaciones del "Boletin" de la Real Sociedad Geográfica. Madrid.
Ariza S., Fr. Alberto E.
 1964   *Los Domínicos en Panamá*. Bogotá: Cooperativa Nacional de Artes Gráficas.
Axtell, James
 1985   *The Invasion Within: The Contest of Cultures in Colonial North America*. Oxford: Oxford University Press.
Beidelman, T.O.
 1982   *Colonial Evangelism: A Sociohistorical Study of an East African Mission at the Grassroots*. Bloomington: Indiana University Press.
Bowden, Henry Warner
 1981   *American Indians and Christian Missions: Studies in Cultural Conflict*. Chicago: University of Chicago Press.
Canduela, H. Macario
 1909   Ministerios apostólicos entre los karibes; Carta del H. Macario Canduela al P. Socio. Panama, 2o de Agosto de 1908. *Cartas Edificantes de la Asistencia de España*, Año 1908:198-202. Burgos, Spain.
Comaroff, Jean
 1985   *Body of Power, Spirit of Resistance: the Culture and History of a South African People*. Chicago: University of Chicago Press.
Comaroff, Jean, and John Comaroff
 1986   "Christianity and Colonialism in South Africa." *American Ethnologist* 13:1-22.
Coope, Anna
 1917   *Anna Coope: Sky Pilot of the Kuna Indians*. New York: American Tract Society.
Dietrick, Jackie
 1925   "For Twelve Years a Saver of San Blas Souls." *Panama Times*, May 9, 16, 23, 30.
Erice, P. Jesús,
 1961   "Primera etapa de la civilización de San Blas." *Lotería* 65:67-68. Panamá.
 1975   "Historia de la revolución de los indios kunas de San Blas." *Estudios Centroamericanos* 30:283-304,362-388.
Falla, P. Ricardo,
 n.d.   *Historia Kuna, historia rebelde: la articulación del archipielago kuna a la nación panameña*. El indio panameño no.4. Panamá: Centro de Capacitación Social. [approximate publication date 1976 or 1977].

Fernandez, P. Jesús María
    1911   "Panamá, Noticias de la misión de los caribes; Carta del P. Jesús Ma. Fernández al P. Juan Ma. Restrepo; Colón, Septiembre 11 de 1910." *Cartas Edificantes de la Asistencia de España*, Año 1910:285-289. Burgos, Spain. (reprinted In *Lotería* no.66:97-100, Panamá, 1961.)

Gassó, P. Leonardo, S.J.
    1909   "Ministerios apostólicos entre los karibes; Carta de Padre Leonardo Gassó al P.Cesáreo Ibero. Panama, 7 de Noviembre de 1908." *Cartas Edificantes de la Asistencia de España,* Año 1908:204-211. Burgos, Spain.

    1910a "Fundación de un pueblo cristiano entre los caribes; Carta del P.Leonardo Gassó al R.P. Antonio Iñesta. Panama, 28 de Mayo de 1909." *Cartas Edificantes de la Asistencia de España,* Año 1909:319-338. Burgos, Spain. (reprinted In *Lotería* 63:79-95, Panamá, 1961.)

    1910b "Informe sobre la catequización de los indios karibes de la Costa de San Blas y del Rio Bayano, en la República de Panamá." *Las Misiones Católicas* XVIII:152-153,163-165. Barcelona.

    1911a "Viaje á la isla de San José, y entrevista con los caribes de la isla del sagrado corazón; carta del P. Gassó al P. Alos. Panama, 3 de Enero de 1910." *Cartas Edificantes de la Asistencia de España,* Año 1910:282-290. Burgos, Spain. (reprinted In *Lotería* 65:75-82, Panamá, 1961).

    1911b "Funciones religiosas y bautizo de catecúmenos entre los caribes; conversaciones á la hora de la muerte; carta del P.Gassó al P.Cesáreo Ibero. Panama, 14 de Septiembre de 1910." *Cartas Edificantes de la Asistencia de España,* Año 1910:289-296. Burgos, Spain. (reprinted In *Lotería* 67:70-75, Panamá, 1961).

    1911-1914 "La Misión de San José de Nargana entre los Karibes (República de Panamá)." *Las Misiones Católicas* XIX-XXII. Barcelona [intermittent serial publication].

Gurruchaga, H. Leonardo
    1909   "Ministerios apostólicos entre los karibes; Carta del H. Coadjutor, Leonardo Gurruchaga, al H. Portero del Colegio de Belén. Panama, 30 de Octubre de 1908." *Cartas Edificantes de la Asistencia de España,* Año 1908:202-204. Burgos, Spain.

Herrera, Francisco
    1984   "La revolución de Tule: antecedentes y nuevos aportes." B.A. thesis, University of Panama.

Holloman, Regina
    1969   *Developmental Change in San Blas.* Ph.D. dissertation, Northwestern University. Ann Arbor: University Microfilms.

Howe, James
    1986   *The Kuna Gathering: Contemporary Village Politics in Panama.* Austin: University of Texas Press. Latin American Monographs No.67.

    1988   "An Ideological Triangle: the Struggle over San Blas Kuna Culture, 1915-1925." Presented at the conference, "Nation State and Indian in Latin America," April 30, 1988, Austin, Texas.

Iglesias, Marvel, and Marjorie Vandervelde
    1977   *Beauty is a Ring in my Nose?* [no publisher].

Keeler, Clyde
    1956   *Land of the Moon-Children.* Athens: University of Georgia Press.

López, Estanislao
    n.d.   [miscellaneous undated manuscripts, lists and chronologies of historical events in San Blas, private archive, Panama]. MS.

Markham, William
    MS   [untitled account of a visit to San Blas in May 1923]. Tioga Point Museum.

Mega, Pedro
    1958   *Compendio biográfico de los iltmos. y excmos. monseñores, obispos, y arzobispos de Panamá.* Panama: Ministerio de Educación.

Miller, Elmer
   1970   The Christian Missionary, Agent of Secularization. *Anthropological Quarterly.* 43:14-22.
Misioneros Hijos del Corazón de Maria
   1939   *Memoria del Vicariato Apostólico del Darién, Panama,* R. de P. Panama: Imprenta Acción Católica.
Moore, Alexander
   1983   "Lore and Life: Cuna Indian Pageants, Exorcism, and Diplomacy in the Twentieth Century." *Ethnohistory* 30:93-106.
Ocampo, Manuel
   1966   *Historia de la Misión de la Tarahumara (1900-1965).* Mexico: Editorial Jus.
Puig, P. Manuel Maria
   1948   *Los indios cunas de San Blas: su origen, tradición, costumbres, organización social, cultura y religión.* Panama: [no publisher].
Rojas y Arrieta, P. Guillermo
   1929   *History of the Bishops of Panama.* Panamá: Imprenta de la Academia.
Vandervelde, Marjorie, and Marvel Iglesias
   1983   *Nacido primitivo.* Emmetsburg (Iowa): Velde Press.
Warren, Kay
   1978   *The Symbolism of Subordination: Indian Identity in a Guatemalan Town.* Austin: University of Texas Press.

CHAPTER NINE

Shamans Reconsidered: The Emberá (Chocó) in Darién, Panama

Stephanie Kane

Shamans are specialists who employ a set of traditional ritual practices in order to effect changes between everyday and other worlds. These ritual practices are extraordinary not only because they penetrate that which is unseen by ordinary persons, but because they consist of techniques that are ancient in origin and global in extent. The complex of symbols which anthropologists have come to recognize as shamanic, such as those found in carvings of spirit familiars and song patterns, probably arrived on the American continent with the first travellers crossing the land bridge from Siberia 40,000 years ago (Brodzky et al. 1977). Unlike other practices with archaic beginnings, however, shamanism continues to be a vital part of everyday life among the Emberá Indians of Darién, Panama.[1]

In its most elaborate and specific manifestation, shamanism is a ritual of healing in which a male or female shaman presides. In a more general sense, shamanism is a way of talking about and interpreting problematic events.[2] Shamanic talk, in both ritual and nonritual contexts, tends to deflect tensions inherent in problematic events onto an invisible symbolic terrain in which spirits and shamans contend. As Taussig's (1987) work in Colombia shows, shamanic talk may encode and work through events that stretch back into the history of conquest and colonization, and forward into present relations between indigenous peoples and others. Such is also the case for the Emberá, who lived through the conquest in the Chocó region of Colombia. Many have since migrated to the Darién of Panama, where their shamans work through the consequences of colonization specific to that region and time.

167

In the 1960s and 1970s, the Darién and its inhabitants were targeted by forces of development (e.g. OAS 1978). Most Emberá have already moved their households into concentrated villages, abandoning (at least temporarily) their traditional dispersed settlement pattern. By 1984, Herlihy (1986) found 75 percent of the Emberá living in villages, and a new, formal political system established to argue in the national legislature for government schools and clinics, as well as claims to a semiautonomous Emberá land reserve, or comarca.[3]

As the Emberá become more tightly surrounded by the world outside the forest, more intricately articulated with international networks of culture and economy, shamanism is confronted with contradictory bases of truth from religious, political, and medical angles. But despite this confrontation, or perhaps because of it, shamanism continues to be the touchstone of Emberá identity, sustaining a remarkable degree of independence from the forces of change that have already reshaped much of the society in which it is embedded. At the same time, shamanism is constantly reconsidered in the context of these changes: How will men accepting the new role of village leader deal with the more hidden authority of local shamans? How will the effectiveness of shamanic healing be evaluated when dispersion through space can no longer be part of a cure for illness related to interpersonal conflict? How will children learning about national culture in village classrooms think of shamanic healing? How will shamans focus their practice when the option of Western medicine becomes more available to their patients? Shamans have been resisting the effects of Christian missionization since the conquest, but in the most recent set of changes accompanying development, problems put before shamans have altered in scope and intensity. In recurring incidents, shamans themselves have been identified as problems, as signs of backwardness or ungovernable power.

This essay contains a textual reenactment of a moment of fieldwork. In this moment, a struggle over changing values is articulated by social actors with distinct agendas. It is the day a Catholic priest, working to unite the underclass of all races, comes to the village. Simultaneous with the voices of the villagers singing the priest's song, an elder Emberá man tells me a story from local history. The story contrasts so sharply with the mind-set of the priest that it seems to make concrete the gap in communication and historical experience that cannot but subvert the good intentions of the priest. A shaman figures powerfully and fearfully in the story. Subsequently, a second elder tells me another version of this story. The second version makes clear that there is no unified Emberá point of view towards shamans. In this paper, these alternative versions of local history demonstrate how the future role of shamans is a subject of negotiation in the new politics of village and nation.

Following the ethnography of speaking approach, this essay uses spoken text and descriptions of the context of speaking in the analysis of culture (Hymes 1964; Bauman and Sherzer 1974). In this presentation, however, context intrudes into the texts and expands into history. The context—including priest, ethnographer and an assenting group of Emberá—demands the production of an opposing text. The conjuncture of priest, ethnographer and Emberá is preceded by and calls forth the history of colonization as locally experienced and magically interpreted. It is that history that gives voice to the

Emberá compelled to speak his opposition. As ethnographer, I found myself between dialogues of different codes, one of Western religious politics, the other of Emberá shamanic politics. To simulate the experience I had of jotting down the Emberá story at the same time I was over-hearing the song sung in the priest's seminar, opposing discourse is broken into fragments and juxtaposed. The content and form of discursive fragments, selected, translated and interpreted, are ordered here to highlight difference. Consistent with recent approaches of reflexive anthropology, my knowledge of the Emberá is thus shown to be dependent on the conditions and manner in which it is shared (Jameson 1981; Fabian 1983; Clifford 1986).

ETHNOGRAPHIC CONTEXT

From Dispersed Settlement to Concentrated Villages

Traditionally, the Emberá settle in a dispersed pattern extending up the banks of the rivers that flow out of the mountains between what are now the nations of Colombia and Panama. This pattern is consistent with an ecology of tropical forest subsistence, as well as a history of colonization and conquest calling for tactical evasion. In addition to ecological and historical factors, the dispersed settlement pattern is also consistent with a shamanic mode of interpreting experience. According to this mode, vision of another's action accords power over that action. Shamans are dispersed in the landscape, effectively hidden from strangers without inside information. Indeed, whether one is a shaman or not, it has always been preferable to build one's house at least a river bend apart from neighbors who are not part of your extended household, thereby protecting one's activities from another's sight.

Recruitment into slavery is in the past, and the random violence of strangers evokes more fear than state-sponsored violence characteristic of the conquest. The Emberá now feel safer in the concentrated villages composed of anywhere from 10 to 100 houses. They continue subsistence activities of slash and burn horticulture, supplemented by hunting, fishing, and gathering. Planted fields radiate outward a great distance from villages. As fields close to home become over-used, people carry heavy loads of produce out to rivers on their backs. Increasing volume of agricultural production for market further increases pressures on forest resources (Herlihy 1986). As fish and animal populations decline and Emberá have more cash at their disposal, canned foods are added to the diet. Considering both the concentration of households and the increased production of individual households, the ecological wisdom of village settlement seems questionable.

Instead of the traditional river bend apart, houses are now separated by only a few feet. Open walls let in breezes and light, but put neighboring families within scope of each other's vision: a tense contrast to the privacy of dispersed settlement. But while they have moved their houses close together, the Emberá do not easily relinquish the political and economic autonomy traditionally accorded to households. Market activities are, for the most part, organized independently. Given a choice, male and female household heads usually maintain control over their own resources, resisting regional development schemes that urge them to cooperate and unify. Most decisions affecting family members still take place in the household, even though village and regional political meetings are now held on a regular basis. Family groups in and across households often are associated with particular shamans.

Regional Shifts in Political and Economic Relations

In Colombia, slavery ended by the middle of the nineteenth century (Castrillón 1982). Once free, the blacks of the Chocó settled in the lower reaches of the rivers, pushing Emberá settlements further upriver and hastening migration across the mountains into Darién. With time, the blacks established towns at the mouths of the major rivers in both Chocó and Darién. It is to these towns that the Emberá have brought their produce in trade. They have carried their produce by canoe, have sold it to the black-owned cargo boats to carry to urban markets, and have bought goods in black-owned stores, e.g., cloth for women's skirts, men's pants, kerosene, salt, alcohol, plastic buckets. Thus the blacks have mediated between the Emberá and the outside world, allowing the Emberá to keep their distinctive way of life and, at the same time, participate in trading. In exchange, the blacks have controlled regional politics and economics.

These trading practices continue today, but in the context of dramatic shifts in political and economic relations. Emberá village formation has not been the only plan of regional development. It has been accompanied by the construction of the first highway connecting a Darién town (Yaviza) to Panama City. Agrarian reform has brought *campesinos* (peasants) from land-poor western Panama to settle along the highway and turn the forest into pasture. Polling booths are now distributed in upriver villages and along the highway, splitting regional political power among blacks, Emberá, and *campesinos*. As trucks from the city find their way to Darién, cargo boats are no longer the only, or even the cheapest, mode of transport. Relations between Emberá and black, once fairly stable if unequal, are now, through a multitude of material and social interactions, being contested, adjusted, and renewed. In this field of interethnic contestation, the radical priest who visits the village in which I work attempts to unify all according to economic class.

Boundaries between Everyday Life and Other Worlds

In their homes along the rivers, in villages and dispersed sites, the Emberá recreate homogeneous centers which define and verify the universe of their everyday world. The "Emberá way," the way the Emberá agree to approach the world, is reproduced in form and material, such as style in women's dress (the men's tends towards Western style), ways of speaking, architectural forms, ritual practice, and agricultural methods. In the Emberá way, a new basket is woven by following the pattern of an old one; one of two house shapes are built with experience memorized in youth. As an aesthetic which cuts deep into, as it is formed by, the ground of material practice, the Emberá way constitutes established patterns of survival.

The highly valued center of Emberá life, marked by redundant, familiar patterns, contrasts with town life downriver, which is dominated by *kampuniá* (Emberá for "non-Indian(s)"). Like the animals and spirits in human form that mythic adventure stories tell about, the unfamiliarity of *kampuniá* may signify traces of another world. Being of another culture and another race, *kampuniá* are not fully human in the Emberá sense of the term. And it is possible that what may appear to an Emberá as a *kampuniá* may be an illusion sent by other world forces. The crew of *gringos* (Emberá for "white persons") in the story related to me in the village the day the priest came is just such an illusion. It is on such illusions that shamans focus their practice.

Shamanic Practice

The possibility of acquiring shamanic power is open to all Emberá. Shamans appear to be no different from any other Emberá, i.e., they are men or women who may or may not have children, they work and own land, and may or may not wear traditional dress or body paint. Any man or woman willing to risk magical encounters with a master shaman can learn to heal with song. According to experiences related to the ethnographer Vasco (1985:36) by Emberá in the Colombian Chocó, the process of learning opens one up to animal spirits which then must be confronted and conquered. If the student is successful, then rather than getting sick from this contact with spirits as would an unsuspecting person, one becomes the spirits' owner, turning them into helpers whose extraordinary abilities of sight and movement are bent to tasks motivated by one's intent. In Darién, explanations of shamanism emphasize learning through song. Building up a repertoire of song, or better said, investing *the* song with more and more power, is the condition for gaining control over spirits. As one's encounters with different shamans multiply, the knowledge one acquires opens one's sight. Sight is the power to heal. Sight is also the ability to discern shamans of good heart from those of evil heart and thus allows students to assess danger inherent in entering new relationships with master shamans.

Each shaman builds up his or her own storehouse of power by using song to capture spirits. Just as animals can be let out of a corral, spirits can be let loose and trapped again by someone else. For instance, a shaman who cures may capture the sickness causing spirits sent by another shaman. Thus healing requires spirit helpers and also provides a means to gain control over more spirits. As one acquires spirits, one also assumes responsibility for them. In order to maintain control, a shaman must keep "feeding" spirits by holding "a song" (i.e., healing ritual) periodically. To some extent then, a shaman is dependent on patients who provide financial means to stage a song that is their cure. Without patients, a shaman must either sustain the material cost of alcoholic beverages for feedings, or find the power that is the basis of his or her practice receding.

It is in this way that power and knowledge are sustained by a population of potential patients and circulates from shaman to shaman.[4] Together, all practicing shamans constitute a net-like organization that extends throughout the demographic range of the Emberá population. Any person hooking into the net of shamanic encounters becomes a vehicle of power. By maintaining a personal store of this circulating power, and manipulating it in song, a shaman can either heal or kill. It is the former effect of power that is sought by people with sickness; it is the latter that they seek to reverse.

SOUNDS OF VOICES COEVAL AND DISCORDANT

Enter the Priest

The initiation of capitalist development in a local preindustrial terrain involves a complex set of issues with which a Spanish priest and Emberá engage in distinct and determined ways. The struggle between colonizers and colonized, missionaries and missionized, has been going on since the sixteenth century in this part of the world.[5] The priest arrives in the village with a global vision based on spiritual and economic equality. Originally from Spain, he was sent to Panama by the Catholic church. There he became involved with a politically active, church-related movement started in the late 1960s by a Colombian priest named Hector Gallego. Gallego was working with *campesinos* in western Panama. One night in 1971, a military jeep picked him up at his home. As he left, he said: "If I disappear, don't look for me. Carry on the struggle." He was never seen again (Servicio Paz Y Justicia-Panamá, 1985). To the Emberá, the priest identifies himself only as Catholic. Raising class consciousness, he works toward utopia. But it seems that history has already brought too many Spanish priests with good intentions. They all failed to rectify the Emberá experience of betrayal at the hand of the white man, Spaniard or *gringo*.

This time, when the priest comes up the Chico River from the Catholic church in the town of Yaviza, he brings two women, a nun and an educator to hold a health seminar. As always, his specific purpose is a vehicle for his deeper message; the message is expressed in the song sung between lessons. The Emberá welcome this priest, like others before him, with caution and politeness. They accept his service, within limits. When he is not present, they often question the logic of the Christian God in whose light all are equal, but in whose material world white people have all the money and desk jobs. But they would not say this to his face. The Emberá have come through history distrusting missionaries of religious change and have learned to depend instead on the boundaries they construct between themselves and those of other race and culture. The priest, on the other hand, while also working on the problem of economic inequality, sweeps people of all race and culture within his vision. True, most Emberá are willing to pronounce signs of conversion: what is it to slip their views under wrap, while they join the priest in song? But in the wake of neocolonial doubt and rumor of nuclear holocaust, consider: what Emberá would presume that the priest's form of spiritual knowledge could replace their own?

To examine the discursive dimension of the uncomfortable coexistence of priest and Emberá, I pull a dialogue out of a notebook. Conversation with priest/conversation with Emberá on either side of a line penned down a sequence of pages. The penned split reflects a gap in time (first I talked to one, then the other, then resumed my conversation with the first). The gap results from their avoidance of direct confrontation and their certain juxtaposition. The gap is transformed into an ethnographic event because of my presence. We are contemporaries struggling to understand and represent ourselves to each other: the white priest with worldwide conviction fails to convince; the Emberá man counters with a vision from local memory that is worlds away; the white ethnographer, a more neutral representative of the foreign, is between these others who do not communicate directly.

We appear together in the text that follows. The priest's song becomes a frame from which Emberá memories of magical encounter stand out, bold and esoteric. The voice of the frame carries a message from Western culture that is left at its most fixed and ideological, i.e., the work that it takes to convey the message of unity is not explicated in the text. Out of this frame that is a message reduced to a song, the Emberá text, a detailed description of an encounter between everyday and otherworld, is highlighted. The boundary between the worlds explicated in the Emberá text comes forward luminous and puzzling; it is at this kind of boundary that shamanic acts take place. Between the passages of priestly song and Emberá text running against each other, descriptions and interpretations are provided. In a move to reverse authorial mastery, the voice of the Western observer in the text below, i.e., the ethnography, provides a foundation for the translation of the voice of the Emberá, but does not dominate it. Together, the voices of priest, Emberá, and ethnographer convey a sense that the cultural knowledge we are trading is partial and in a process of becoming.[6]

A MOMENT RECREATED

[Note: This section was originally written as a script for performance and the same format has been retained. The priest's song is in italics. The order of song lines do not reflect the actual order in which they were sung. Valentín's story is written in plain text. Sections that describe the events occurring at the time the story is being told are in square brackets, as are translations and explanations inserted in Valentín's story. Sections of interpretation are in braces. Valentín told me the story in Spanish, and the subsequent declaration in Emberá. The real names of people and villages have been replaced with fictional ones.]

We want to construct communities in peace.
We want to share the same bread, the bread of unity.

[The visiting priest, nun, health educator and two resident *campesina* schoolteachers were leading a full gathering of Emberá in song. They were under the old schoolhouse, on the one cemented area large enough to accommodate long logs arranged in rows and around the outer edge. The rows were full of people, all facing the priest's group standing up front around the desk. Behind the desk stood a blackboard upon which a body was drawn, its parts labeled in both Spanish and Emberá.]

That there be no slave or señore.

So that we may live in equality.
Here there is no class or difference.

[I kept my distance from this official function of the Catholic church, writing up field notes on the porch of the teacher's house facing the river, just on the other side of the little cooperative store. But I could hear the many-voiced song. It was the end of the dry season, in 1985, in a village named here as Palo Blanco, halfway up the Chico River.]

We all have the same right.
We all have the same gospel.
We all have the same father, the same heaven.

[Valentín came up on the porch. (The teachers' house was one of the few built in "Panamanian style" with walls and a staircase instead of notched pole.) An Emberá who called himself an Evangelical, Valentín was also avoiding the Catholic event.]

That there be no class nor difference.
To stop us from sharing the same bread.
Here among us all we will share pain, courage and love.
Here amongst us all we will discover a great seed of the forest.

[Valentín himself was a *curandero*, one who has bought and practiced the curing powers of two or three plants, not a shaman who cures or kills with song. He wanted to sell me the knowledge of the plant that cures snakebite, but I was not sure I wanted to buy it. Earlier that week I had begun working with him and his wife, planting rice on the hillside they had cleared and burned. In exchange he had told me some things. Now he began again intently, as always, telling me about *brujería*.]

We all have the same right.
We all have the same obligations.

[One was a story of a man who was electrocuted by *jai* (Emberá spirits) when he went to check the trap of a small rodent in the forest. Then came the long story, the one that started over 30 years ago and still continues:]

Back when I was a little boy, Easter time, I went with my grandfather on a journey to the Congo River to seek a buried chest of money. We had to cross the great bay, by the island they call Enchantment. The moon was clear. My cousin Bernabe was there. We saw a boat of many colors, luminous, with pure *gringos* on board. It sounded its horn and we, in the canoe, hauling, hauling, trying to catch up to the boat. We wanted to sleep alongside it, but the boat moved out to sea, escaping us. Then we smelled gasoline. Our vision could not stand the fumes and grandfather said: 'Let's go back. This is not a boat. This is a thing of the devil.'

We all have the same father, the same heaven.

[{The attractive boat of *gringos* is an illusion, a deception from otherworld spirits that diverts them from the Easter quest for riches.}]

We made it to the shore. This thing comes from below the earth, from the Chämbërara. It is the familiar of that. The Chämbëra sent a *jai*, a spirit: that is the boat. They offered it to grandfather in challenge. [Valentín had told me previously that his grandfather was a *jaïmbana*, or shaman.]

We want to share the same bread, the bread of unity.

[The song from under the old schoolhouse goes round and round. Valentín, sitting in one of those old wooden schoolhouse chairs, leaning over its small initial inscribed desk:]

As grandfather owned his own *jai* he scolded them, growling, he grabbed and scolded his *jai*, his own spirits, he told his *jai* to protect him and the two boys from harm.

We want to construct communities in peace.

Then he felt something like a fever coming on. 'Let's go back to La Palma [the port nearest the large bay].' Bernabe, his cousin, was only little then; I, a bit older, had to make all the arrangements. In La Palma, I talked to Chaco, black captain of the cargo boat, and asked him to take us along to Yaviza as we had no motor on the canoe back then. [Yaviza is the interior port near the mouth of their home river.] We arrived badly, we arrived badly, we arrived badly. Fever, fever, fever.

[{The black captain makes his money going back and forth from regional market towns to Panama City, buying plantains from the Emberá and selling them to the city market, taking paying passengers along the way. Note how even though the passengers are involved in an other world struggle, they depend on the black man to move across the physical landscape. They are trying to get back home upriver, the grandfather-shaman's remote center of power.}]

Here among us we will share pain, courage, love.

By the time grandfather got back to the village he couldn't speak. We made preparations for a *chicha*, a shamanic ritual. Grandfather showed us how to paint the specific patterns necessary with the black dye called *jagua* [Spanish black dye from *Genipa americana*], how to work the balsa wood, and how to paint the young girls for the *chicha imamá-kiráka* [Emberá like jaguars]. He put the girls in floor-length *parumas* [Spanish wraparound, knee-length skirts worn by Emberá women].

[{The story moves to those actions which effect a direct mediation in otherworld forces. The acts are specific. Their ritual prescription depends on the

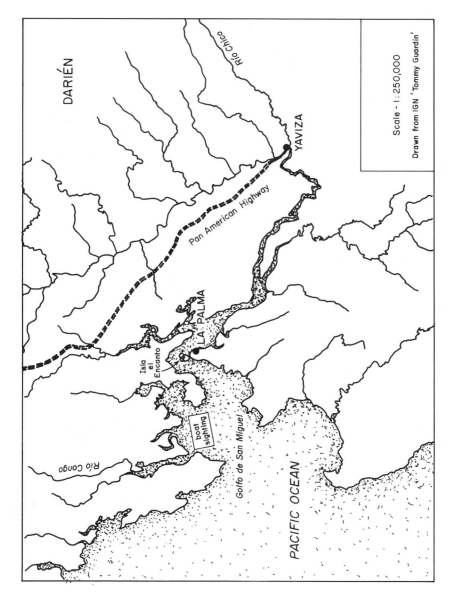

MAP 9.1. MAP OF DARIÉN, PANAMA SHOWING PLACES PAST IN VALENTIN'S AND BERNABE'S MAGICAL JOURNEY WITH THEIR GRANDFATHER.

shaman's capacity to see into the otherworld for the actions and arrangements of objects required. Grandfather/shaman has interpreted the message of the chimerical *gringo* boat as a challenge from beings below the earth called Chämbëras. He is now about to take up that challenge. He might have left the challenge unheeded, healed himself, and gone his way. But he wants to win so that he can become owner of the macabre *gringo* crew. Here Valentín implies lust for power as motivating force.}]

We all have the same right, the same obligations.

Grandfather could see all the crew members of the boat. And he made [a model of] the boat and put the crew in it. The captain with no head or neck, another crew member with no feet. He built a boat with a roof and a plane on top for the *jai* to go back to the other side. These Chämbëraras were prepared.

Here amongst us we will discover a great seed in the forest.

He had the people bring everything necessary: the poles to build the ritual house and the black palm whose yellow fronds are woven to make its walls. One of the two girls was my daughter Veronica. He began to sing: little humming noises. It was the best he could do as his throat was closed up. He was there, he was there. By dawn, his throat opened a little and by the next day he could talk again.

[Figure 9.1 is a picture of grandfather's cure drawn while Valentín was telling me the above story. He drew the decorated *ranchito* with its spirit boat on the shelf above and gourds placed upside down on the shelf below; he asked me to put in the figures, little bench, shaman's leaf drum.]

We all have the same father, the same heaven.

Grandfather brought the boat from Yaviza. By means of his knowledge he made a tide, a current that came from below, like a motor, to get the boat up here. He tied it below the calabash tree, there next to Abibéba's house. The boat is still here.

We want to construct communities in peace.

[It's been years since grandfather died. {Valentín invokes the image of an epidemic of spirit attacks caused by a continuing series of encounters with the *gringo* crew that grandfather drew up to the village and left there. Using this image, Valentín brings the events of 30 years past into the ethnographic present. In this process, his telling becomes a tactical maneuver which addresses current village politics, the implications of which become more apparent through comparison with his cousin Bernabe's version of the story later told to me.} Valentín comments on his own story:]

Grandfather is alive with the Chämbëra. He won't let any *brujo* take the boat away. And the crew have all left for the land. Dzaya can see the boat. [Dzaya

FIGURE 9.1. GRANDFATHER'S CURE

is a local, itinerant shaman.]

[{The presence of otherworld spirits are a mixed blessing, for they can be controlled only by the power of shamans. And in order for the spirits to be used for benefit of the community, the controlling shaman must be not only strong, but good in heart.} Valentín continues:]

One year, two years after this *chicha*, grandfather said, 'This will all be forest around here again, because one by one you will all die. After I die you will all be finished off by the *jai*.' 'Why are you doing this, grandfather?' Valentín asked.

And truth, it fell. My Veronica, the same one who was chosen to be in the *chicha*, went mad. She had one week left and she would have been dead. She already stopped eating. The community met. They all cooperated, each one some money, to bring a shaman who is my grandfather's cousin from the Tuquesa river. They bought rum. Testing, the shaman told them: 'This is the boat, the familiars that my cousin [=Valentín's grandfather] scattered about. My cousin has the Chämbëras, they brought him alive.'

We want to construct communities in peace.

So these [spirit] familiars are walking around loose and when a person sees one they go crazy. Last month Arípo's woman caught it. I cured her with plants. The Nonamá [=Waunan] named Dino who lives in Bongo knows seven plants against the Chämbëraras. The best one is *inaníta*. I want to learn this one. And that Dzaya, grandfather's nephew, performs miracles.

[There is a recess in the health seminar. Valentín's cousin Bernabe climbs up on the porch. Once the other small boy on the Easter journey of long ago, Bernabe is now a village elder, like Valentín. Valentín defers to him, saying: "Here's the man that *really* knows the story." Although Bernabe stays but a moment, Valentín would not resume his telling.]

MYTHIC HISTORY

A Chimerical Gringo Boat and the Origins of Epidemic Madness

Not long after this day, I tape recorded Bernabe's version of the story. It was quite detailed, about two hours long.[7] In regard to the past journey, and the causal connection between grandfather and the epidemic, the two versions basically agreed. To recapitulate: As a result of his encounter with otherworld beings known as the Chämbëra, grandfather used his magical power to bring the *gringo* boat up the Chico River to the present site of Palo Blanco. This took place decades before, when Palo Blanco was a dispersed settlement site, not a village. But according to Emberá, the boat and its crew remain where grandfather left them, and may remain long after the village households scatter their dwellings again. Fear of spirit attacks from the invisible *gringo* crew could trigger household dispersal, regardless of progress toward community development.[8] No one wants to encounter a spirit-thing like this; such an encounter brings on a whirling madness. Madness may lead to death; it may also provoke the shaman's extraordinary sighted song in a nonspecialist. Through the years, a number of spirit attacks have taken place. A spirit from the *gringo* crew caught Valentín's daughter Veronica and sang through her to other villagers in a healing ritual. It caught others too, mostly women and youth. Memory confirms: madness from spirit attacks has reached epidemic proportions (Bernabe counted 21 cases of sickness, see Kane 1986:483).

Linking together as an epidemic the spirit attacks that have been occurring in the village and referring the cause of the epidemic to the past actions of their grandfather/shaman and the journey they took with him, Valentín and Bernabe take responsibility on themselves. They were at the source. Their agreement concerning the origins of present danger indexes the collective nature of the shamanic mode of interpreting experience. Their interpretation of events makes sense to other Emberá. Forced by mutual, mounting concern, the community achieves a rare consensus. Collecting from each some money, they send for a good shaman from another river, one related by kin who knows the same song that grandfather used to capture the spirits in the first place. This shaman tries to recapture the scattered *gringo* crew he left behind. But he could not match grandfather's power and meets with only partial success. The travelling shaman, Dzaya, can still see the boat. For the Emberá of Palo Blanco, continuing confrontation with the spirit crew is a real, but invisible confrontation between community and otherworld forces. In this, the footless *gringo* crew and its headless captain are no more than an illusionary vehicle of the Chämbëra.

A Declaration

Although Valentín would never repeat into the tape recorder the version of the story he told me the day the priest was in the village, eventually he asked me to sit down with him to record this declaration:[9]

Kwéntoda nembɨríya.
I am going to tell a story.

Naënabéma kwéntoda.
A story from olden times.

Idíbema wárrara diánumba atúa-béata.
Today's youth don't know.

Sawábɨrɨ pasa-bëata.
How things have come to pass.

Jäïmbaná trabájora.
The work of *jäïmbaná* [Emberá shaman].

Que jäïmbaná trabájora bíabɨta.
[Know] that the work of *jäïmbaná* is good.

Porque jaira bubera mäübe túwadáda män jaira.
As *jai* [Emberá spirit] exist, so those *jai* are learned.

Curábɨta jäïmbanábara curábɨta.
[They] cure *jäïmbaná* [Emberá shaman] cure.

Jai Chämbërärä puru áwarabíta mäüra é-huá-étrre-bita.
But then, the *jai* of the Chämbëra's village are different, below the earth.

Edaúde män jaíba kakuá áwabɨríde män Chämbëra jaíra ébuda unúwibíta
Sometimes when the bodies of those Chämbëra *jai* want sex, they show themselves clearly.

Pero jän jai Chämbëräbä peaítabíta idzaba jaimbänára bió atúabaíbɨrɨ.
But those Chämbëra *jai* can also kill a *jäïmbaná* who does not know well.

Mänba idzí bí-ë-sentínumebɨríde në-ina óbɨta.
So when he [the *jäïmbaná*] senses evil, he does something.

Män jai jitaíkäréä.
To seize those *jai*.

Edaúde Chämbëräbä bárcoda móstrabíta.
At times the Chämbëra show a boat.

Män jaíba jitá-märéa.
Those *jai*, in order to capture [the *jäïmbaná*].

Idzí jaimbäräba män dobirú jaíta kawabíra.
He the *jäïmbaná* knows that [other] *jai* of the tide.

Atá idzí puértoma idzí bíma jüébita.
He even makes it come up to his own port.

Chi jäïmbaná bíma jüénta bárkoda
The boat comes to where the *jäïmbaná* is.

Chi jambanata sokadrrí-baíbirɨ ke idzí peúda-kärëä.
If the *jäïmbaná* is of evil heart when he dies.

Män jaíra Chämbëränͤ drrúa-bekuaíta.
Those Chämbëra *jai* are left in the land.

Mänbɨrɨ embërära lokía-koíta.
Then Emberá turn *loco* [Spanish/Emberá crazy].

Mäüra baratan zókara-nɨmɨta.
Then there are many there are many.

Män jaíra.
Of those *jai*.

Mänbɨrɨ bɨ́-ë́ ópanɨta idzí kakuá awá-birɨ́ra emberáka unubíta.
Then they do evil, the body has sex like a person/Emberá, [they] make
    themselves be seen.

Tadzía.
By one/we.

Mawá unúbɨrɨde kïrä́ purrugá-dogoíta.
When one sees thus, one's face turns circles.

Mäüra mamabésira chi jäïmbanáda Chämbëräbä etésirá.
And if they remain, the *jäïmbanä́* takes the Chämbëra.

*Mäüra asta beúbɨrɨdeda jumá baritúa jäïmbanába jai kosa-béa mamá män
    púrude bébɨrɨra.*
And so it is until the *jäïmbaná's* death, when all, whichever *jai*, things that
    remain, are there in that village.

Mäüra kɨnɨ́numébɨrɨ, kɨnɨ́nubëíta.
Then they [the people] start to die, continue dying.

Aramamabé jumáraba ürɨ́-nämäréa búyamɨa, ya.
I am going to put down [on tape] until there, so that all can listen, end.

This declaration is based on a logic of magical action drawn from the core
of Emberá culture. In this sense, it is "*puro* Emberá" (pure Emberá).

Valentín spoke slowly into the microphone, considering each phrase. When his declaration was complete he asked me to get an older Emberá neighbor woman to listen and judge the playback. She came from her house nearby and confirmed that Valentín's words were correct. Later I translated from Emberá to Spanish with the help of a young Emberá man, and when that was done, I read it to Valentín. He said it was good, but was annoyed that I paid for assistance in translation and did not pay for his telling.

Interpretation of the Past, Orientation Towards the Future

And so Valentín records his truth so that all could listen. The struggle of significance to him occurs between Emberá and the other-world; the rest of the world is peripheral to or used merely as vehicles in the shamanic struggle. The priest, whose presence brought forth Valentín's story, remains in the background. For the message the priest carries is based on assumptions that erase the history of racial and ethnic inequality that, from the Emberá point of view, cannot be erased. The priest's carefully repeated distinctions that separate him from the pope's pomp and circumstance, and his promise of salvation that is even better because it is material as well as spiritual, remain unheard. Valentín is impressed only by shamanic power; he gets caught up in his telling of aggressive/seductive attacks of spirit-beings who roam the village outskirts. His telling is testimony to the necessity for shamans who can gain control of spirits through song. But confounding this magical system is the inevitable existence of evil-hearted shamans like his grandfather, who widen, instead of close, breaches in the boundary between the worlds. The potential for evil is in every Emberá, and shamanic power, while essential to survival, makes that potential dangerous. As figures of power, shamans can either ameliorate or worsen dangers inherent in otherworld contact. According to Valentín, the only hope is to distinguish good-hearted from evil-hearted shamans, and to destroy the evil ones before they destroy everyone else.

From an ethnographic perspective, however, a problem exists with the form of Valentín's solution, i.e., no single shaman is always perceived in the same light. As individuals, shamans cannot be morally split, for they are both good and evil depending upon the perspective of the person who judges them. They are figures of ambivalence. If one is within the familiar scope of a shaman's protective force, one has a positive relation with that shaman. On the other hand, if one is outside a shaman's protective scope, one may have a negative relation. Furthermore, one's relation to any particular shaman is also influenced by interactions in the social and material world. So, for instance, it is possible that Valentín claims that his grandfather is evil because he always has been a bit outside of grandfather's protective scope. Both he and Bernabe are cousins. Valentín is the son of grandfather's eldest daughter and Terezu, the son of grandfather's youngest daughter. Both Valentín's and Bernabe's mothers married men who came from outside the small settlement, but Valentín's father was Waunan, not Emberá. The Waunan are a sister linguistic group of the Emberá. While some Waunan live closely with Emberá, their linguistic and cultural differences are usually pointed out in discourse. Legally, the *comarca* of the Emberá includes provision for the Waunan as a minority. In any case, it is possible, but not necessarily so, that Valentín did not inherit any of grandfather's extensive plantain orchards because he was half Waunan. Bernabe, in trust for his younger siblings, inherited it all.   Bernabe attributes his wealth to grandfather's affection (Kane 1986:471).

Where it is used to interpret and guide current events, Bernabe's telling of the past diverges from Valentín's (see note 7).   (The fact that they would not present their stories or interpretations to me in front of one another is a clue to the significance of this divergence). Unlike Valentín's interpretation, which places the blame for madness on the evil of grandfather's heart and his misanthropic use of magical power, Bernabe takes the onus off the old man. Bernabe makes the old man, like anyone, a subject of history. He tells how the Evangelical missionaries frightened the old man with hell. They told him he must burn his curing batons, or bury them far away in the forest. The old man knew he would weaken and retrieve them if they were in the forest, so he had them burned. Bernabe was there when the *gringos* stood and poured gasoline on the batons. The other Emberá watching ran from the invisible spirits running wild out of the burning "idol" that was their home and their trap.

Bernabe claims that the epidemic of madness continues to threaten village survival.   Furthermore, he claims that the epidemic is the result of the Evangelicals' well-meaning but nonsighted intrusion into local history. He thus displaces the madness, which indeed may be linked to other causes, back out onto the global field of religious politics where Evangelicals and Catholics contend for souls. (Sometime after the baton burning, Bernabe turned away from the Evangelicals and became a Catholic; Valentín remains an Evangelical and makes no mention of the episode with the missionaries in his telling). And Bernabe might well want to displace the madness out of this community and into the world outside where he, as a result of his large inheritance, has been able to gain some experience.

As elder village head, with experience at politics on the level of *comarca* and nation, Bernabe's perspective on shamans is broader than Valentín's. He envisions new kinds of relationships obtaining between shamans and the social field, expanding links from members of family to include members of village community. In his vision, shamanic authority could be linked up to village, *comarca*, and national levels of government.

Sporadic attempts to incorporate shamans into the new official politics have also been made by men with greater influence than Bernabe on Emberá *comarca* leadership. A shamanic convention has been proposed more than once. But how could those whose practice relies on the benefits of hidden loci in the tropical forest convene without destroying their joint yet dispersed effectiveness? To my knowledge, no convention of shamans has ever taken place.

There are problems with the notion that shamans could be incorporated into the power structure of village and *comarca*. For one, village identity is tenuous, and not coextensive with the practices of shamans. Villages are made of households which may not identify with one another to a great extent. Households in one village may identify with different shamans. Different shamans act independently, in series, or in opposition to one another. While shamans may cooperate with one another in the everyday world, there is no precedent for cooperation between shamans *as* shamans. A second problem is that shamans act in and on the invisible, and it would be impossible to monitor their actions.

In any case, the difference between Bernabe's and Valentín's renditions is not so much in the story that refers to the past, but rather, the difference is one of interpretation, i.e., the meaning that each accords past events in the present. Amidst the recurring visions of those struck mad, the interpretations of Valentín and Bernabe circulate as alternative proposals for community action. The story of grandfather serves a dual purpose for Valentín: it allows him to represent the Emberá mode of interpreting reality in contrast to the Catholic priest's, and at the same time it allows him to put forth his specific point of view regarding the control of evil shamans. Bernabe has another agenda. Recognizing the reality of outside pressures, Bernabe calls for supporting shamans who are needed and are, after all, only human. He wants to figure out a way to include shamans in the process of institutionalization taking place with village formation. By means of this story based on shared experience, the cousins recreate a contestable drama in which grandfather/shaman, chimerical *gringos*, missionary *gringos*, and otherworld Chämbëra act out the bases for determining future possibilities. (Most of this drama is invisible to the priest; it is no wonder that his message of class unity is not given much weight.) In this discursive process, the Emberá adjust their point of view to change, and readjust it to the things that never change.

SHAMANISM RECONSIDERED

This paper takes two steps back to the past, one step to the ethnographic moment, and another to the long-ago journey that was related to me in that moment. In each step, multiple voices approach, describe, and interpret the image of the shaman. Each voice uses the past strategically. Juxtaposed, the voices reflect the contradictory field of cultural contestation in which contemporary shamanism is reproduced. As other aspects of Emberá life become more oriented towards village and *comarca* organization, pressures build to displace, regulate, and redefine shamanism. Emberá shamanic practice today is both vulnerable and powerful. The current running through it is long, deep, and counter to the culture of capitalism. Can shamans preserve their power and autonomy in this historical context?

NOTES

Acknowledgments: My thanks to Lynn Stephen for helping to pluck this paper out of another and Claudia Kane for the illustrations.

1. This paper is based on 1984 to 1985 field work for my dissertation. Research was funded by the Organization of American States and the Institute of Latin American Studies of the University of Texas at Austin. In keeping with precedent set by my dissertation, I continue to use fictive names for people and villages.

2. I draw here on Favret-Saada's (1980) ethnographic analysis of witchcraft in the French Bocage. For background on Emberá shamanism see Torres de Arauz (1962) and Vasco (1985).

3. In general, it seems inappropriate to assume that a unidirectional model of development is applicable to the Emberá case, as they have frequently responded to historical and ecological change by moving their houses. For a comparative case see Rosaldo (1980). The political crises that has been taking place in Panama since 1987 makes it particularly unlikely that Emberá adherence to the village settlement model persists. I would surmise that the process of establishing their *comarca* is also at risk.

4. This discussion draws on Foucault (1980:98) with the caveat that shamanic power is different from the hierarchical and dominating power of which he writes.

5. For a review of Emberá history see Castrillón (1982).

6. See Clifford (1983); Popular Memory Group (1982); Price (1983); Taussig (1986).

7. A transcript and analysis of Bernabe's story can be found in Kane (1986: 424-499). The text is too long to include here.

8. An example of this was told to me by William Harp (personal communication). He worked as an ethnographer in a village that dissolved after a series of two accidental deaths, and then hesitantly reformed after a time.

9. Emberá words are spelled as is Spanish, with the letter /j/ sounding as an English /h/. The double dot (e.g., /ë/) over vowels indicate nasalization. The additional vowel /ɨ/ has a sound between an English /i/ and /u/.

REFERENCES

Bauman, Richard and Sherzer, Joel, editors.
  1974 *Explorations in the Ethnography of Speaking.* Cambridge: Cambridge University Press.
Brodzky, Anne, Daneswich, Rose, and Johnson, Nick, editors.
  1977 *Stones, Bones and Skin: Ritual and Shamanic Art.* Toronto: The Society for Art.
Castrillón, Héctor
  1982 *Choco Indio.* Medellín, Colombia: Ediciones Centro de Pastoral Indígena.
Clifford, James
  1983 "On Ethnographic Authority." *Representations* 1(2):118-146.
  1986 "On Ethnographic Allegory." In *Writing Culture: The Poetics and Politics of Ethnography.* James Clifford and George Marcus, editors, pp. 98-121. Berkeley: University of California Press.
Fabian, Johannes
  1983 *Time and the Other: How Anthropology Makes its Object.* New York: Columbia University Press.
Favret-Saada, Jeane
  1980 *Deadly Words: Witchcraft in the Bocage.* Cambridge: Cambridge University Press.
Foucault, Michel
  1980 *Power/Knowledge: Selected Interviews and Other Writings 1972-1977*, Colin Gordon, ed. New York: Pantheon Books.
Herlihy, Peter
  1986 "A Cultural Geography of the Emberá and Wounan (Chocó) Indians of Darién, Panama, with Emphasis on Recent Village Formation and Economic Diversification." Ph.D. dissertation, Louisiana State University.
Hymes, Dell
  1964 "Introduction: Toward Ethnographies of Communication." In *The Ethnography of Communication*, John Gumperz and Dell Hymes, editors, pp. 1-34. Washington, D.C:American Anthropologist 66, pt. 2.

Organization of American States (OAS)
    1978   "Aspectos Sociales." In *Proyecto de Desarollo Integrado de la Región Oriental de Panamá-Darién*. Washington DC: OAS.
Popular Memory Group
    1982   "Popular Memory: Theory, Politics, Method." In *Making Histories: Studies in History-Writing and Politics*.   Richard Johnson, Gregor McLennan, Bill Schwarz, David Sutton, editors, pp. 205-252. London: Hutchinson Press.
Price, Richard
    1983   *First-Time: The Historical Vision of an Afro-American People*.   Baltimore: Johns Hopkins University Press.
Servicio Paz Y Justicia-Panamá
    1985   "Hector Gallego...a 14 años de su desaparición, vive en la lucha del pueblo!" *Boletín Informativo*, no. 4 Junio. Panama City, Panama.
Taussig, Michael
    1986   "Montage." Paper presented at the 85th Annual Meeting of the American Anthropological Association, December 3-7, Philadelphia.
    1987   *Shamanism, Colonialism and the Wild Man; A Study in Terror and Healing*. Chicago: University of Chicago Press.
Torres de Arauz, Reina
    1962   "El Chamanismo entre los Indios Chocoes." *Hombre y Cultura* 1 (1):17-43.
Vasco, Luis G.
    1985   *Jaibanás: Los Verdaderos Hombres*.   Bogotá, Colombia: Talleres Graficos Banco Popular.

CHAPTER TEN

Martyrs and Virgins: Popular Religion in Mexico and Nicaragua

Michael James Higgins
University of Northern Colorado

PROLOGUE

The Virgin of Juquila

The Virgin of Juquila is my guardian and protector. She can give you the things you need if you demonstrate your faith. Rosa, my oldest daughter, went on the pilgrimage to the Virgin last year and asked for more chickens to help feed the household. Now look at all the chickens we have! I go every year on the pilgrimage to her shrine and keep an altar to her in the house. I have the image of her on my altar. It is in gold and lace. I keep fresh flowers and candles on the altar all the time. Each year, when I visit the shrine of Juquila in the mountains, I ask for the protection and well-being of my whole family.

My strong devotion to the Virgin comes from the death of my children. When my oldest daughter died (some twenty years ago), I promised the Virgin that I would be her devoted follower. However, this was not strong enough, for later she took my oldest son. I was going crazy. I could not understand why she had taken my son when I had been so faithful. I told her that if she would help me through this and stop these feelings of craziness, I would never question her ways and work harder on my devotion to her. Since then, times have been hard, but she has been our protector. I must maintain my faith.

María Eleana de Sosa
Resident of the Colonia Linda Vista
Oaxaca, Mexico

The Martyrdom of William Díaz Romero

William Díaz Romero was a very fine young man. He was a school teacher. During the struggle against Somoza, like many of the youth in the barrio [neighborhood], he was part of the

Sandinista Front. He was a messenger and provided information and news between various safe houses in the area, like the ones in our houses. He also participated in many of the clandestine activities with other Sandinista youth.

Early in the morning of June 24, 1979, the Somoza national guard stormed his house and he was taken in his underwear from the house and was never seen again. After the triumph (July 19, 1979), his mother began searching for him. In one of the Red Cross hospitals, she encountered one of William's friends. This young man was in critical condition from the torturing he had received from the national guard. He told her that William had been tortured for several days before he died. He thought that his body had been taken to the lake outside of the city, where many tortured bodies had been left by the national guard. William's friend told William's mother that he had been brave to the end and had not given the national guard any information. She searched the area around the lake, but was not able to find William's body.

William was a brave young man. He knew the location of the safe houses in the barrio, but he gave no information. His courage was a symbol to us of what revolutionary struggle meant. Now each year we celebrate his martyrdom here in the barrio. This celebration always begins with a mass said in his honor. We place his photo on the altar alongside that of Jesus Christ.

Ruth Arena and Mabel Curtis
Neighbors in the Barrio William Díaz Romero
Managua, Nicaragua

INTRODUCTION

María Eleana de Sosa is a woman in her mid-50s who resides in an urban poor community, Colonia Linda Vista, in the city of Oaxaca, Mexico. Her comments are representative of many in the popular classes of Mexico who are devoted followers of guardian virgins and saints. Though beliefs in guardian saints and virgins are seen in the formal theology of Catholicism, the views expressed by María Eleana de Sosa are part of a complex set of beliefs and activities found in the religion shared by Mexico's popular classes.

Ruth Arena and Mabel Curtis are in their mid-40s and have lived in the Barrio William Díaz Romero for more than 20 years. Their narrative on the martyrdom of the young William Díaz Romero is expressive of how the popular classes of Nicaragua feel towards those who "fell" during the struggle against Somoza. The deaths of many were ennobled through the process of martyrdom.

These people's beliefs in a guardian virgin and in martyrdom are part of the general Catholic heritage in Latin America, but these beliefs have particular ethnographic features that are derived from the social and historical contexts of contemporary Mexico and Nicaragua. This paper will provide an ethnographic comparison between religious concepts and activities found among urban popular classes in Oaxaca, Mexico and Managua, Nicaragua. The ethnographic information is based upon my long-term research in the urban community of Colonia Linda Vista in Oaxaca and in the urban *barrio* (neighborhood) of William Díaz Romero in Managua, Nicaragua.

The ethnographic focus in the case of the city of Oaxaca will be on the activities of ritual co-parenting and on the cult of the Virgin of Juquila. In the case of Managua, it will be on popular religious fiestas and the processes of social martyrdom. This paper emphasizes the way these popular religious concepts and activities are constructed in the everyday lives of social actors. It will be argued that these concepts and activities represent aspects of cultural production among the popular urban classes in Mexico and Nicaragua. Further, it will be argued that these cultural activities provide these actors with concrete means of reading and altering the hegemonic terrain of their respective social contexts.

To develop this argument, I will first define what is meant by popular religion and popular classes in reference to contemporary Mexico and Nicaragua. I will then explain what I mean by "cultural production" and "hegemonic terrain" and the relationship of these concepts to popular religion and classes. After this explanation, I will proceed with the ethnographic comparison of the two communities of Linda Vista in Oaxaca and William Díaz Romero in Managua.

POPULAR RELIGION AND POPULAR CLASSES

The popular religious concepts and actions on which this paper will focus will be those that are "carried on within the framework of institutionalized religion which offer a critique of that framework and of larger political and economic inequities" (Stephen and Dow, *intra*). As stated above, the activities of the cult following of the Virgin of Juquila in Mexico and the process of martyrdom in Nicaragua are not actions outside the Catholic tradition, but cultural expressions of how the popular classes within that tradition use these symbols and activities.

Who are the Popular Classes?

Throughout Latin America, the terms popular classes or popular cultures have been used to describe the complex social composition of this region (C. Gonzalez 1986). European and United States discourses of class composition and class struggle have not been able to capture accurately the texture or context of social action in Latin America. The reality of indigenous populations, peasants, urban poor, urban workers, informal economic actors, politically radical or reactionary middle income actors, petty producers and merchants, and elite power groups have not fit into models of social stratification or workers' revolutions (Harris and Vilas 1986). Since the early writings of Mariatequi, Latin writers have been attempting to construct a discourse that could capture these various realities (C. Gonzalez 1986). Popular classes and cultures, then, represent the various groups within this social composition and their relation to each other. In the simplest terms, they represent all those groups outside the internal power structure of the elite. In Gramiscan terms, popular culture represents the war of positions among the various social actors within the hegemonic terrain of their social and political context (Bobbio 1977). In terms of this paper, popular culture refers to how the urban popular classes of Oaxaca and Managua position themselves in complex hegemonic terrain through their cultural production of popular religious concepts and actions.

CULTURAL PRODUCTION AND HEGEMONIC TERRAIN

What is meant by cultural production and hegemonic terrain? An answer to that question requires a summary of Stefano Varese's arguments on these processes and an explanation of how these concepts relate to the ethnography of urban popular classes and their religious concepts and actions.

Varese has long argued for an hegemonic understanding of indigenous cultures. He maintains that the oppression of indigenous peoples and other popular sectors in the Americas comes not only from national ruling elites, but also from transnational capitalism and the ways it effects people's experiences and self-definitions. In Latin America, the neocolonial and colonial bourgeoisie failed to create an airtight nation state and class hegemony which would allow them total ideological and cultural control over people. Transnational capitalism has also succeeded in imposing some ideological control over people through enforced homogenized consumption. Varese proposes that the current gap or hegemonic terrain between the agendas of national elites and transnational consumer capitalism creates spaces for counterhegemonic activities on the part of marginalized peoples (1988:64-65). These are margins of autonomy which become the terrain for actions of cultural resistance. This terrain is located on the fringes and boundaries of social interaction, not in formal modes of institutional power. It is found in people's everyday lives.

Varese sees the construction of popular hegemony (counterhegemonic actions) as a pluralistic enterprise involving all the subordinate groups within the social context. This difficult task involves "demystifying one's own history and culture...and knowing how to appropriate and transform the culture of the subjugator" (1988:69). If we look closely at the religious activities of the urban popular classes in Oaxaca and Managua, we can see examples of popular counterhegemonic activities such as those described by Varese.

ETHNOGRAPHIC COMPARISONS

In order to understand the hegemonic terrain of María Eleana de Sosa, Ruth Arena, and Mabel Curtis, I need to provide background information on their respective communities. This also involves a brief presentation of the economic, political, and social context of the nation states of Mexico and Nicaragua.

Oaxaca, Mexico

María Eleana de Sosa lives in the Colonia Linda Vista on the northern side of the city of Oaxaca. The Colonia Linda Vista is representative of the urban communities composed of sectors of the popular classes. In Linda Vista, there are school teachers, small merchants, working class, urban poor, and some marginal households. The population of the community is about 3,000 and began as a squatter settlement some 30 years ago. Over 60 percent of the urban population of Oaxaca lives in communities like Linda Vista. The Colonia

Linda Vista is neither the poorest nor the richest of such communities in Oaxaca. It is located in the northern foothills of the city and looks somewhat picturesque, with houses spread along the side of the hill. In its 30 years, it has attained all the basic city services and has attained legal status as a formal neighborhood in the city. Although the residents of this community represent different sectors of the popular classes of Mexico, they have shared the common factor of distance from primary sources of political and social power. Most of the residents tend to be cynically critical of current Mexican political and social conditions. Though some have expressed interest and hope in such developments as "Frente Democratico" (a national political opposition during summer 1988), this community has never been very politically active beyond its own community interest (Higgins 1974, 1983, 1987). This is in contrast to other urban popular communities in the city (such as Colonia Emilio Zapata) and other areas in the state (such as Juchitán) (Higgins 1986).

The city of Oaxaca has a population of over a quarter of a million. In the late 1960s, the population of the city was just over 70,000. This urban growth has taken place in communities such as Linda Vista (Murphy and Stepick 1990). Though Oaxaca is the largest city in southwestern Mexico, it is still a provincial town controlled by local merchants and a political elite. While the city is often the site of turbulent political activities and campaigns, its basic power structure remains conservative and local. The PRI (Party of the Institutionalized Revolution, the dominant political party in Mexico) is still the primary political and social power base for the city. Outside the city, in the rural areas of the Sierra and in the coastal cities of the Isthmus, strong opposition movements exist and have been able at times to attain political power at the local level (Barabas and Bartolome 1986).

The state of Oaxaca has a population of over three million. The majority of that population resides in the rural areas of the state. There is a high degree of ethnic diversity in the state, with the major groups being the Zapotecs, Mixtecs, and Mixes. Overall, the state is underdeveloped and the majority of rural peoples live in very harsh poverty. Currently, the state and city governments of Oaxaca are controlled by the progressive sectors of the PRI. The current governor of the state and the mayor of the city are committed to new forms of economic and social development for the state, however, their plans are hemmed in by competing national priorities (Higgins 1986).

These national priorities are the economy and the national political process. As is well known, the Mexican economy has been in a crisis for the last eight years. A combination of high interest loans and falling oil prices has left the Mexican economy on the doorstep of bankruptcy. The central government's overall position has been one of attempting to pay on their debts, to control production, and to reduce or eliminate subsidies on basic goods and services to the general public. These actions have taken place in the context of high inflation and reduction in earning power for many Mexicans. The PRI's power and longevity has been maintained through a somewhat stable economic context, at least for middle and upper income sectors. This economic failure has encouraged many to seek other political solutions, as witnessed by the opposition movement to the PRI (Reding 1988).

The depth and strength of this new political opposition in Mexico is an example of the politics of popular sectors in Mexico. Though these current political and social movements seem to be centered in the capital and the northern sections of the country, this political "earthquake" is being felt throughout the whole country. The quality and extent of these changes will depend on how the economy fares. There is a new sense of political hope and activism developing in Mexico, especially within the popular classes. However, many, like María Eleana de Sosa, remain skeptical and believe that the Virgin of Juquila is still a stronger guardian for their futures than the hope of the "Partido Revolucionario Democratico," (political opposition party formed out of the Frente Democratico). (Higgins 1988b).

Managua, Nicaragua

Ruth Arena and Mabel Curtis live in Barrio William Díaz Romero, an established *barrio* roughly in the center of the city of Managua. It is composed of some 30 blocks and has a population of 4,000. This is a mixed population that provides a panoramic look at the popular sectors of Nicaragua and its revolutionary society. The *barrio* is occupied by middle class, working class, small merchants, and marginal groups. There are some 150 small businesses that operate in the *barrio*, along with two small factories (Coen 1988). This is a politically active *barrio*. It has a strong local political structure for community development. The *barrio* committee (CDS, Committee for the Defense of the Revolution) is currently organizing a housing project for 42 families in the *barrio*, developing a community store, and community center (Coen and Higgins 1987). This political activism came from being in the capital and experiencing the social and political realities of the Nicaraguan Revolution.[1]

On June 19, 1979, the Sandinista National Liberation Front entered Managua as the triumphal revolutionary forces against the Somoza dictatorship. Thus began a bold experiment in social change. The goal of this revolution was, and still is, to explore how to construct a popular revolution. This is a process that includes traditional civil political actions, a mixed economy, nonalignment, ethnic and regional autonomy, the construction of social services, and the development and participation of mass organizations in the overall political process (Ortega 1988). These mass organizations involve women's groups, workers, ethnic groups, peasants, youth, local *barrio* groups, and religious activists (Cabezas 1988).[2]

Managua has been transformed from the backwater capital of a poor nation to the revolutionary center of a still very poor country seeking multiple paths to self-determination. This, however, has not made Managua a cosmopolitan center. Like Oaxaca, it is still in many ways a provincial city which has become the center of attention because of the social and political change in the country. Its current population is near a million and many of these people reside in squatter settlements. In these new communities, there are groups organized to attain basic city services such as water, roads, electricity, etc. Managua was never rebuilt after the earthquake of 1972; therefore, the city seems to have no structure beyond the random scattering of various neighborhoods and commercial centers. Further, because of the war and the economic crisis, Managuan needs are not given priority over those of the countryside (Morles, Ardaya, and Espinoza 1987). Currently, communities like the Barrio William Díaz Romero are encouraged to seek their own solutions to their own problems and not to look to the national government as the problem solver (Cabezas 1988).

The rationale for this continued form of experimentation in problem solving, as in Mexico, comes from the problems of economic crisis and national political processes. Unlike Mexico, many of Nicaragua's problems have been grounded in the war against American imperialism which the government has been forced to fight for the last seven years (Higgins 1988a). Just as that war seemed to be winding down, the country was hit by the horror of Hurricane Joan (Envio 1988c). Nicaragua's economic crisis comes from attempting to build a popular revolution with no support from international monetary agencies and while fighting an unwanted war. Further, this revolution has attempted to keep the political process open and flexible (Envio, 1988a). This has been possible because of the willingness of people like the residents of Barrio William Díaz Romero to continue to work and struggle for their hopes and concerns. The drama of this commitment to the future can be seen in many of the local social activities of the people of Nicaragua (Ruckwarger 1987) and, most dramatically, in their fusion of revolutionary spirit with the spirit of religious concepts and actions (Lancaster 1988). People such as Ruth Arena and Mabel Curtis do not see themselves outside these processes of change. They see themselves as participants in a struggle that will require that fewer of their children become martyrs in the war and which will instead allow them to experience the joy of constructing a new society (Coen and Higgins 1988).

POPULAR RELIGION IN OAXACA

In Mexico, a central component of popular religion is *compadrazgo*–the institution of ritual co-parenthood. Its basic structure comes from the Catholic church and involves the co-parenting or sponsorship of children. Adults serve as the co-father or co-mother for other people's children. The co-parenting obligations correspond to the Catholic rites of passage, baptism, confirmation, communion, marriage, and funerals at death. The formal system involves a special relationship between the sponsored child and the co-parent, with baptism being the most important aspect. Further, the co-parent should not be an actual relative of the child. One should also have a different sponsor for each child's rites of passage (Higgins 1974).

In the popular Mesoamerican context, however, the structure is altered. First, in both the rural and urban areas of Mexico, the *compadrazgo* system's primary focus is not on the relationship between the co-parent and the godchild, but between the parents and the sponsors–that is, the *compadres*. In both the rural and urban context, the *compadrazgo* system becomes a mode of alliance construction. The nature of the alliance can be economic, political, familial, or personal. To illustrate these types of alliances, I will draw upon my own experiences in this system, which are urban examples (Higgins 1974 and 1983).

Among the urban poor, *compadrazgo* relationships are often constructed to develop economic alliance. In urban poor communities such as Linda Vista in the city of Oaxaca, residents look for co-parents who are economically better off than themselves. This involves asking such persons as bosses, merchants, school teachers, low-level government officials, or visiting anthropologists. Here one can see an interesting blend of formal and popular concerns. The urban poor attempt to find nonrelatives for these obligations and to find different *compadres* for every child or for the rites of passage of each child. As this is not always possible, family members may accept the obligations or co-parents may sponsor several children from the same family.

The attempt to abide by the formal rules is not theological, but pragmatic. The urban poor use *compadre/comadre* relations for economic purposes. If one accepts the role of *padrino* for baptism of a child, and one is economically better off than the requesting persons, one then accepts the responsibility of economically assisting the family in general, and the child in particular. If the family is having an economic crisis, they can, without shame, call upon the *comadre/compadre* for help. At any important rite of the child (entering school, medical concerns, etc.) that co-parent will be called upon to help. Thus, from the point of view of the urban poor, one would want a nonrelative in that position for the following reasons (1) most of one's relatives are in the same economic situation; thus, they would be of no economic advantage; and (2) a nonrelative in a higher economic position gives one greater access to new networks; that is, the *comadre/compadre* becomes a means to increase one's social network which is referred to as *personalismo* (Higgins 1983).

These types of economic relations are quite asymmetrical between the co-parents. María Eleana de Sosa is skilled in constructing these kinds of co-parent relations. She has raised seven children to adulthood. She has been widowed for the last decade, but even when her husband was alive she always worked. Most often, this involved doing small scale catering. She would prepare various fiesta meals for middle class families in the city. From these commercial relations, she would seek co-parents for her children. She would freely seek out aid from these co-parents in times of need. There was a formal presentation of civility between her and her co-parents, but it was asymmetrical. For example, these middle class co-parents would attend María Eleana's fiestas as guests; whereas when María Eleana went to one of their social events, she went as a volunteer domestic worker (Higgins 1983).

For the urban poor, *compadrazgo* illustrates the counterhegemonic role of popular religion for these actors. Independent of the Catholic theological structure, the urban poor use *compadrazgo* systems as forms of insurance against economic hardship, as the means to increase alliances of several types, and as a means to protect friendships. Like Mexicans in other social strata, they use *compadrazgo* as a form of *personalismo*. This form of *personalismo* gives the urban poor the *palanca* (pull or influence) to cross class lines or solidify internal relations within their own class group.

Virgin of Juquila

In Mexico, the practices of popular religion are not always centered around church attendance or direct participation in church-sponsored activities. The church is seen as a site where particular activities take place, such as baptism, marriage, or special masses. The church provides shelter for images of important virgins or saints. The focus of household worship is virgins and saints, not respect for the church or the priest. This can be illustrated by looking at the participation of María Eleana de Sosa in the cult of the Virgin of Juquila.

Doña María Eleana de Sosa is a very impressive person. She has lived in the Colonia Linda Vista for over 25 years. Her husband passed away ten years ago. She has lost two of her adult children, suffered through numerous stillbirths, and has raised seven children to adulthood. She has worked most of her life and continues to do so now. She is a woman of profound intelligence, strength, and integrity. She is also argumentative, abrasive, and self-righteous at times. She integrates the complexity of her life through a strong belief in the Virgin of Juquila.

Centuries ago, in the central highlands of Oaxaca near the town of Juquila, the Virgin made her appearance and promised to help those who committed their faith to her. The Virgin offered to provide help for the most faithful, regardless of their concerns or backgrounds. The rewards were to be for the faithful. María Eleana's faith in the Virgin of Juquila involves both her cultural and personal history. She grew up on the pacific coast of Oaxaca. The *mestizo* population of this region shares the concept of animal spirit companions found among the indigenous populations on the coast. The belief in miracles and divine intervention in one's personal life is a given in this cultural formation.

In terms of personal history, her belief in the Virgin is intimately connected to the deaths of her two adult children. She had one daughter out of wedlock before her first marriage. This daughter died while giving birth. This death convinced María Eleana that she needed to reaffirm her faith in the Virgin for the protection of her other children. This involved the maintenance of a household altar for the Virgin and a pilgrimage to the shrine of the Virgin in the central highlands of Oaxaca. Several years later, her eldest son was killed in a truck accident while driving for a tanker company. María Eleana believed that he had procured the job through the aid of the Virgin. The death of her oldest son traumatized María Eleana. She felt betrayed and could not understand why the Virgin had not protected her son. She felt that she was going crazy and losing control of her life. She finally decided that the only relief from her suffering would come from the Virgin. She told the Virgin that if she could quiet her suffering and stop the feelings of craziness, she would stop questioning why she had lost her son and daughter and accept that the Virgin had her reasons. María Eleana feels confident that she and the Virgin have reached an accord. María Eleana continues her yearly pilgrimage to the shrine of the Virgin of Juquila and keeps candles constantly burning on the home altar. She has been the *madrina* for many people making their first pilgrimages to the shrine of the Virgin. She also gives *limpios* (ritual cleanings of the soul) in front of the house altar for those seeking the aid of the Virgin. Though she does not question why the Virgin took her children, she does allow herself infrequent outbreaks of sorrow and pain when she thinks of her departed children.

María Eleana's beliefs and the rituals she performs that are associated with the Virgin of Juquila are shared by many in Oaxaca. The majority of followers of the Virgin are working class, urban poor, and rural peoples. The house altars to the Virgin are simple structures. Generally, they are shelves that sit high up on the wall. On the shelf will be vases of flowers, images of the Virgin, remembrances from chapels and the shrine of the Virgin, and various candles. It is the duty of the faithful to maintain the altar and keep the candles lit as a demonstration of faith in the authority of the Virgin.

Crucial to demonstrating one's faith to the Virgin is the annual pilgrimage to her shrine in the central highlands of Oaxaca. Currently, there are bus services within an hour of the shrine. Several years ago, the pilgrimage involved at least a three day walk. This pilgrimage draws thousands to the shrine. As happens in other pilgrimages, many of the faithful walk the final distance to the shrine on their knees. One brings offerings and pledges of renewed faith to the Virgin. There are masses given during the day in the small church in the pueblo of Juquila. The faithful camp in the courtyard of the church or in other parts of the town.

The way people interact with the Virgin illustrates how popular religion operates for rural and urban poor people. The cult worship of the Virgin is predominantly practiced by these social groups. They do not come with theological concerns or seeking the cleansing of their sinful souls. They come to get direct help from the Virgin in their everyday lives. They come to ask for health, jobs, money, new household items, or to have their chickens lay more eggs. Outside, in the courtyard, people make small stone altars to the Virgin. They will place some kind of representation of the Virgin on the altar and a representation of what they desire from the Virgin. If the household needs a new stove or refrigerator, then they will place a plastic replica of it on the shrine. When María Eleana sought the help of the Virgin to get the truck driving job for her son (who was killed in the accident), she placed a small plastic truck on the altar. After constructing one's altar, one goes inside the church to touch the altar and shrine to the Virgin.

Those who participate in the cult of the Virgin expect concrete results from their devotion, not some kind of theological grace. I have often referred to this interaction as a form of cosmic *palanca* (Higgins 1983). The social dynamics of Mexico are built on personal connections and the kind of pull or authority one has with the people one knows. The middle and upper classes have more contacts or pull and authority and use them to their own benefit. For persons in the popular classes, like María Eleana de Sosa, this cosmic *palanca* provides a means to confront this hegemonic terrain of social influence.

POPULAR RELIGION IN NICARAGUA

Among the urban popular classes in Managua, popular religion involves the blending of theological and popular concerns. This can be illustrated by looking at the fiesta of Santo Domingo and the celebration of the Martyr of the Barrio William Díaz Romero.

The Fiesta of Santo Domingo

The fiesta of Santo Domingo begins on August first and lasts throughout the week. The history of this fiesta goes back to the turn of the century and its organization is associated with a famed homeopathic curer of that time (Lancaster 1988). This is an important difference from Mexico, where such popular fiestas tend to have an indigenous base. The fiesta of Santo Domingo begins with the arrival of the image of the Saint in the city from its village residence. The image of Santo Domingo is taken to the church of Santo Domingo near the center of town. The actual fiesta of Santo Domingo is on August fifth and, at the end of the week, the Saint is returned to its village location. During the week that the Saint is in the city, there are numerous folkloric events taking place in the church courtyard.

What makes the fiestas of Santo Domingo interesting is the large following they have and the style and structure of the procession that brings the Saint into the city. This is a major summer event for the residents of Managua. It is a constant source of conversation for weeks before the event.

Mabel Curtis and her family attended the procession of Santo Domingo this year. Noel Curtis works at a soft-drink plant and Mabel Curtis is a school teacher. Their five children range in age from six to fifteen years of age. Both Noel and Mabel support the Sandinistas. On the day of the procession, they walked several blocks to the bus stop and, with the luck of the day, caught a bus that was not full. They went toward the main avenue (near the city market) where the Saint is to pass. Noel, Mabel, and the children began to search for the best place to sit and watch the procession. Several blocks down the street, they found a small bluff where they joined numerous others who had already selected their seating. There were several thousand people in and on the street. The procession was still several hours away and many people were walking towards the procession to join it. From a village some 20 kilometers outside of Managua, more than 20,000 had been marching since late the night before. This procession brings the Saint into the city, places him on a large float in the shape of a boat, and then proceeds to the church.

The street scene was quite similar to religious fiestas in Mexico. There seem to be as many vendors as spectators. People were there more for the carnival quality of the event rather than the religious experience. Most of the people in the street and those watching seemed to be working class or rural people. Noel and Mabel's children were running about buying candy and playing various children's games. They were joined by several members of Noel's family who lived nearby.

Similar to other religious processions involving saints or virgins in Mexico and Central America, many people participated in order to repay favors granted to them by the saint or virgin. Requests to Santo Domingo reflect the same kind of pragmatic appeals made to the Virgin of Juquila. However, the expressions of faithfulness are quite different than in Oaxaca. In Managua, those who have to show their faithfulness to the Saint do this with two types of costumes—either as a black native American or as what appears to be a Plains Native American costume with nose plugs.

The black native American costume is the following: whether adult or child, the person is dressed in a small skirt and wears numerous necklaces; the entire body is blackened with something referred to as burned oil. This custom creates a second novel item, the attempt to spread oil on those watching the procession. Young children and adolescents will cover their hands with this burnt oil and then attempt to spread it on the faces of those watching the procession or those walking toward it. Most of these attempts are treated humorously and are seen as part of the event. The costumes of those dressed like Plains Native Americans involve the following: large headdresses of feathers, leggings, nose plugs, numerous necklaces, vests of feathers, and bows and arrows.

At about two in the afternoon, the procession passed by where the Curtises were sitting. There seemed to be some 40,000 people in the streets. At least a third of the people in the procession seemed to be in the costumes described above. Many people in the procession were riding horses. Many were carrying *calindas* (large paper-mâché heads of cows, pigs, and other domestic animals which are carried in the procession). There are also paper-mâché *calindas* of very large women and the devil, in the form of *torros*. There were also numerous people lighting sky rockets. In the middle of the procession, came the Saint himself. He is carried on a large platform with many flowers and candles by some ten or twelve people. The Saint sits inside a glass vessel. Its overall size cannot be more than ten inches in height.

The *palanca* of Santo Domingo seems to be similar to that of the Virgin of Juquila. He has the power to concretely help people with their material concerns. However, unlike the Virgin of Juquila, he does not demand an obedient following. He encourages his faithful to express their devotion in outlandish costumes (like the painting of the body with burned oil) or through rituals which reverse the common social order (the domination of the devil and large women *calindas* in the procession). Santo Domingo's *palanca* involves reminding the popular classes that the hegemony of the accepted social order is contestable (Lancaster 1988).

The Barrio's Celebration

Ruth Arena was a member of this year's planning commission for the *barrio's* celebration of the martyrdom of William Díaz Romero. This celebration is on June 27, the day of Romero's death. Ruth Arena has been quite active in the politics of the *barrio*. As a single mother, she has raised her five children to adulthood. For the last year, she has been coordinator for the health programs in the *barrio*. This position also involves being part of the general committee of the *barrio* (CDS). From this committee, Ruth and several others were chosen to plan this year's celebration. The martyrdom of William Díaz Romero is a concrete reality for Ruth. All of her children participated in the insurrection and, from her view, by the grace of God they all survived. Others were not as lucky as Ruth's children. Over 40,000 "fell" during the insurrection (Massey 1987). Throughout Nicaragua, one finds schools, parks, factories, streets, and communities that are named after the thousands that died to build the new Nicaragua. William Díaz Romero was not the only martyr in the *barrio*. Many other families lost loved ones. The horror of his death and his resistance to the national guard so moved the people of the *barrio* that they chose him as their symbol of hope and struggle for the future.

Ruth and her commission had to plan the full day of events for the celebration. That involved inviting the priest who would offer the mass to begin the celebration. The commission was also responsible for inviting the honored guests for the celebration. These always included the mother of William Díaz Romero and Señora. Saavedra, the mother of the president of Nicaragua, Daniel Ortega. Señora Saavedra lives near the barrio and has many friends who live there. The commission also planned the speeches (which included Ruth's report on the health programs she had organized during the year), entertainment, and refreshments for those who attended.

Early on the morning of June 27, Ruth's committee begins cleaning the area around the house of William Díaz Romero for several blocks in each direction. This involves sweeping the sidewalks and streets, putting up banners, and whitewashing the curbs. While these activities are going on, other committees are preparing the refreshments, putting up chairs, and completing other chores.

The celebration begins about one in the afternoon in front of the house of William Díaz Romero where an altar has been erected. The altar contains various floral arrangements. Located on the altar are images of Jesus Christ and a photo of William Díaz Romero. The event begins with a mass. The priest gives a mass on the virtues of social change and commitment to salvation for all. The mass is followed by a short talk by the mother of William Díaz Romero on the importance of her son's death as an example of the type of strength that had built the popular revolution and that is now needed to defend it. This is followed by speeches by different members of the *barrio* on the importance of the day. Next follows modern dancing by groups of young males and females. This is followed by a Salvadoran singing group. Afterwards, awards of merit are presented to people who have worked hard on health or education projects in the *barrio*. During this time, refreshments were served to those in attendance (about 200). This is followed by a surprise: a teenage drum and bugle corps come marching down the street and play for more than half-an-hour.

In this celebration, elements of the community's symbols of cooperation, formal and popular religious symbols, and the revolution are blended together. There is no sense of being morbid or morose. Sorrow is felt for the family of Díaz Romero as well as for others in the *barrio* who lost loved ones in the struggle against the dictatorship. There is also a joy in community involvement. The martyred youth of the *barrio*, like William Díaz Romero, did not die to build some abstract new society. They died to begin that process in their own community. This also creates a form of *personalismo,* not the *personalismo* of social and economic networks, but a network of involvement in the history of one's own community. This is a *personalismo* that emotionally and politically connects the spirits of this struggle (those who have fallen) to those who continue the struggle. The martyrs of the *barrio* become the daughters and sons of the whole community (Coen and Higgins 1988).

The activities of events such as the procession of Santo Domingo and the celebration of the martyrdom of William Díaz Romero are expressions of a general politicization of popular religious action through the discourse of theology of liberation (Lancaster 1988). The theology of liberation involves transforming popular religious concepts into strategies of political action. The fiesta of Santo Domingo can be seen as a construction by the masses of their own theological statement about society (Lancaster 1988). The martyrdom of William Díaz Romero is the politicization of this process into people's everyday lives (Dalton 1987). In Linda Vista and William Díaz Romero, people use their popular religious concepts and beliefs as cultural means to understand and act upon the hegemonic terrain of their everyday lives.

CONCLUSION

In both of these communities (Colonia Linda Vista, Oaxaca and William Díaz Romero, Managua), social actors are blending their religious concepts and actions (*compadrazgo* networks and guardian Virgins and popular fiestas and martyrdoms) with strategies of social action (*personalismo* and *palanca*) into cultural statements in order to understand and alter their respective hegemonic terrains. They are not using their popular religious concepts and actions as strategies for the attainment of salvation or purity. They have personalized these concepts and actions into concrete strategies for dealing with their particular social context or hegemonic terrain. What are the particulars of these hegemonic terrains? Do these readings of this terrain represent important aspects of cultural production among the popular classes of Mexico and Nicaragua?

To answer these questions, I will develop an interpretive analysis of the ethnographic data that I have presented (Clifford 1988). Given the constraints of space, these comments will be a summary and will be general in tone. Further, they invite comparative analysis with other ethnographic material on urban popular classes.

What constitutes the hegemonic terrain of Mexico and Nicaragua? Mexico is a complex and contradictory postmodern nation state. Its population has moved beyond 80 million. It has a large industrial infrastructure, yet the majority of the population lives in economically marginal conditions. It is a country that uses the history and traditions of its indigenous population as the ideological cornerstone for national identity while many of these groups still wait for the revolution to pass through their villages. It is a country that is now more urban than rural and has built impressive social services (education, health, and urban housing), yet finds the urban mass the most dissatisfied and alienated from these accomplishments. Though current political developments give indication of possible changes within this terrain, it is still one that the majority of popular classes perceive as distant and nonresponsive to their everyday concerns (Higgins 1987; Murphy and Stepick 1990; and Reding 1988).

Nicaragua is also a complex and contradictory country. It is attempting to construct a popular revolution in the context of war and economic crisis. It seeks and explores new means of social action and justice amidst runaway inflation and with a public treasury that is empty. It encourages all sectors of society to seek new and novel methods of problem solving while its governmental agencies often exist in bureaucratic inertia. The government seeks new means to integrate the popular sectors of society into the political and economic process while attempting to provide a context for the private sector and the accumulation of international currency for development programs. While attempting to build a political structure that is durable and functional to the needs of the total nation, it explores possibilities of regional and ethnic autonomy. Though the ruling Sandinistas often speak with a knowing voice of power, they remain open to new directions and to the admission of past and current mistakes. In terms of such honesty, they have the support of the majority of the popular sectors in Nicaragua. The government and the Sandinistas are perceived as being concerned and responsive to the needs of the majority of Nicaraguans (Envio 1988b).

The hegemonic terrain of Mexico is perceived by the popular sectors of Mexico as unresponsive to their everyday concerns; whereas, in Nicaragua the terrain is perceived as responsive to such concerns. However, the actors in both contexts construct similar responses to their differing social terrains. In both communities, people seek local solutions for their local problems, the difference being that, in Colonia Linda Vista, solutions to one's problems are based within the family or household while, in the Barrio William Díaz Romero, solutions are sought at the community level. María Eleana de Sosa constructs her *compadrazgo* networks as a means to increase her household resource base for problem solving. When expenditures are beyond the means of the household or an emergency arises, it is the *compadrazgo* network that will be used. If problems are more general or involve forces beyond the control of her *compadrazgo* network, then the *palanca* that she has with the Virgin of Juquila is used. María Eleana de Sosa does not work from a class or community base, but connects her household to other concrete and cosmic networks of *personalismo* and *palanca*. Like others in the *colonia*, she and her household have united for common concerns (such as attaining water for the *colonia*), but they do not see such actions as anything more than ad hoc. Like other members of this community, she is neither politically naive nor uninformed. Instead, she is skeptical that political networks would function any better than those she constructs.

In Barrio William Díaz Romero in Managua, the residents use *personalismo* and *palanca* to build a community responsive to their common concerns. In the constructing of their community and naming that community after William Díaz Romero, these residents personalize the revolution in relation to their own concerns. Their commitment to the revolution is not on some abstract level, but on a level of the suffering of the Díaz Romero family and their own personal loss in the struggle to build a new Nicaragua. For Ruth Arena, this process of social martyrdom is not abstract, but something very real, for her son Roberto died two years ago in a swimming accident. He was quite active in working in the *barrio* and in the popular revolution. His death was mourned by the whole *barrio* and he was seen as an exemplary youth for his militant work for others and for his own family.

The fact that the tragedies and triumphs are personal for the people in the *barrio* can be seen in the way they interact with social and political networks outside the *barrio*. Their involvement in the revolution as well as the martyrdom of their youth gives them *palanca* to deal with the powers that be. They feel that if they need the help of regional or national leaders, then they just go to that person or a relative of that person for help or involvement in their concerns. If they cannot see President Ortega on issues, then they will ask his mother to help them. They do not go to bureaucratic offices for help with their housing projects or health campaigns. They request that officials of such agencies come to the *barrio* to explain and resolve problems there. The martyrdom of their youth and their continued involvement in the revolution give these people the means to demand through their own personal networks within and outside the community that others listen to their concerns and demands. For the residents of Barrio William Díaz Romero, Santo Domingo's encouragement to contest the social order is concretely acted upon (Coen and Higgins 1988).

In terms of relating these local strategies to national concerns, two obvious themes emerge. First, in the case of Mexico, if the political opposition wishes to attract people of communities such as Linda Vista, then along with their political concepts and actions, they must also demonstrate to people like María Eleana de Sosa the value of community solidarity as a means to meet her everyday concerns. Second, in the case of Nicaragua, Sandinista leaders of the revolution must maintain the openness and concreteness of the revolutionary process so that people do not begin to feel distanced from such processes and will begin to seek individual or household solutions to their problems. It would also seem evident that, for the popular sectors of Mexico and Nicaragua, religious concepts and actions are not otherworldly, but are concretely a part of their definition of their own social context and their everyday concerns.

Varese stated that hegemony building involves the "development of concrete social consciousness and its application" (1988:67). In the context of Linda Vista, we can see such action in the way people use their popular religious concepts and actions as means of counterhegemonic action against the powers that be in Mexico. In the case of William Díaz Romero, we can see the direct participation of these people in the construction of new popular hegemony. That is, we can see these processes if we acknowledge that urban popular classes are also cultural actors and that their cultural productions are part of the hegemonic terrain that we need to understand as anthropologists and as social actors in this collective postmodern world in which we all reside.

Like all discourse in this postmodern world, the religious concepts and actions of the popular classes in Oaxaca and Managua are overdetermined (Laclau and Mouffe 1985). The complexities of cultural production and hegemony building are not only contained within this domain, but this domain cannot be excluded. Since the failure of Lewis's concept of the "culture of poverty" to capture the full complexity of urban popular classes, there have been few attempts to interpret urban popular classes from a cultural perspective (Higgins 1986). We need to return to such concerns. Hopefully, by looking at religious concepts and actions, we can begin to explore these cultural domains again. María Eleana de Sosa offers us a concrete suggestion in this pursuit when she demands to know, "Why do we have to pay for all the things in the world that God gave us free?"

NOTES

Acknowledgements.   I wish to thank Tanya Coen, Marsha Moore-Jazayeri, Marc Ringel, and Lynn Stephen for advice and criticism in the writing of this paper.   I have been doing fieldwork in the city of Oaxaca since 1968.   My fieldwork in Managua began the summer of 1986.   Further work was done during the summer of 1987 and the spring and summer of 1988. The work in Managua was done in collaboration with Tanya Coen.   Research in Nicaragua has been funded by the University of Northern Colorado Research and Publication Committee.
1. This chapter was completed during 1989, while the Sandinistas were still in power.
2. On February 25, 1990, the United Nicaraguan Opposition Front (UNO) defeated the Sandinista government at the polls.   While this is a victory for the Contra war and for United States foreign policy, the Sandinistas remain the largest and best organized political force within Nicaragua.   The twin underpinnings of class politics and liberation theology which formed the basis of the Sandinista revolution will continue to be an important part of Nicaraguan political life, as reflected in this chapter.

REFERENCES

Barabas, Alicia and Miguel Bartolome , editors.
    1986   *Etnicidad y pluralismo Cultural: La Dinamica Etnica En Oaxaca.*   Mexico D.F.: INAH.
Bobbio, Norberto
    1977   *Gramsci y la Concepcion de la Sociedad Civil.*   Barcelona: Editorial Avance.
Cabezas, Omar
    1988   "No Se Debe Mandar: Memos a Las Masas."   Managua, Nicaragua: Barricada, June 22.
Clifford, James
    1988   *The Predicament of Culture: Twentieth-Century Ethnography, Literature and Art.*   Cambridge, Mass.: Harvard University Press.
Coen, Tanya
    1988   "Images of Urban Household Organization in a Barrio in Managua, Nicaragua." Paper presented at the Rocky Mountain Association of Latin American Studies, April 17, Fort Collins, Colorado.
Coen, Tanya and Michael Higgins
    1987   Field notes, Summer. Managua, Nicaragua.
    1988   Field notes, Spring and Summer. Managua, Nicaragua.
Dalton, Roque
    1987   *Miguel Marmol.*   New York: Curbstone Press.
Envio, E.
    1988a "The New Economic Package."   *Instituto Historico Centroamericano* 7(86):14-42.
    1988b "Sandinistas Surviving in a Percentage Game."   *Instituto Historico Centroamericano* 7(79):10-23.
    1988c "In the Hurricane's Wake."   *Instituto Historico Centroamericano* 7(89):2-8.
Gonzalez Casanova, Pablo
    1986   *El Poder al Pueblo.*   Mexico D.F.: Oceano.
Harris, R. and Carlo Vilas
    1986   *La Revolucion en Nicaragua.*   Mexico D.F.: Ediciones Era.
Higgins, Michael
    1974   *Somos Gente Humilde.*   Mexico D.F.: INI.
    1983   *Somos Tocayos.*   Lanham: University Press of America.

1986   "Quienes Son Los Migrantes Al Teatro Urbano del Valle de Oaxaca." In *Etnicidad y pluralismo Cultural: La Dinamica Etnica en Oaxaca*. Barabas, Alicia and Miguel Bartolome , editors, pp.404-421. Mexico, D.F.: INAH.

n.d.   "Portraits of Urban Poor Women in Oaxaca." In *Mujeres de Oaxaca*. Margarita Dalton and Guadalupe Musalem, editors. In press.

1988a   "Oigame, Oigame! The Sounds of Popular Decision Making in Nicaragua." Paper presented at the 84th Annual Meeting of the American Anthropological Association, November 16-20, Phoenix.

1988b   Field notes, Summer. Oaxaca and Mexico D.F.

Laclau, E. and C. Mouffe

1985   *Hegemony and Socialist Strategy*. London: Verso Books.

Lancaster, Nelson

1988   *Thanks to God and the Revolution: Popular Religion and Class Consciousness in the New Nicaragua*. New York: Columbia University Press.

Massey, Doreen

1987   *Nicaragua*. Philadelphia: Open University Press.

Morales, N., R. Ardaya, and B. Espinoza

1987   "Asentamientos Espontaneso No Son Causa de la Crisis Urbana." *Boletio Socio-Economico* 2:7-14. Managua, Nicaragua.

Murphy, Arthur and Alex Stepick

1990   *Adaptation and Inequality: Political Economy and Cultural Ecology in a Secondary Mexican City*. Boulder: Westview Press.

Ortega, Daniel S.

1988   "Nadie Hizo Tanto por los Ninos." *Barricada*, August 7.

Reding, Andrew

1988   "Favorite Son." *Mother Jones* 12(9):35-45, November.

Ruckwarger, Gary

1987   *People in Power*. South Hadley: Bergin and Garvey.

Varese, Stefano

1988   "Multiethnicity and Hegemonic Construction: Indian Plans and Future." In *Ethnicities and Nations: Processes of Interethnic Relations in Latin America, Southeast Asia, and the Pacific*. Remo Guidieri, Francesco Pellizzi, and Stanley J. Tambiah, editors, pp.57-77. Austin: University of Texas Press.

Part V.
Conclusions

CHAPTER ELEVEN

The Dynamics of Religion in Middle American Communities

James Dow
Oakland University

&

Lynn Stephen
Northeastern University

INTRODUCTION

The preceding chapters have provided new information on the integration of religion and politics in Middle American communities. This chapter will discuss various viewpoints on the subject in light of this and other new knowledge. The ethnographies in this volume present a rich reality of symbolic expression, mingling Catholic and folk elements that, although exotic to some outsiders, are meaningful in the social and political life of a people living fully in the modern world.

The religions of Middle America are vitally important in the social and political lives of Mexican and Central American people. Religion and politics in Middle America are related to the roles of ecclesiastical organizations in society and to the ways in which local populations develop religions to serve their own purposes. The ecclesiastical organizations today are represented by a variety of sects, some of which are now far removed from the Catholic church, such as in Guatemala where "born-again" evangelical Protestantism has been linked to state pacification programs.

An earlier generation of anthropologists described a rich complex of ritual and belief in Middle American communities, and thereby painted a picture of peasant people whose religion detached them from the modern world and steeped their lives in moral relationships with supernatural forces (Parsons 1936; Redfield and Villa 1934). This earlier generation was followed by one that tended to study political and economic relationships and painted a picture of religion being determined by political, demographic, and economic pressures (Cámara 1952; Cancian 1965; Wasserstrom 1983). The image of the Mesoamerican peasant thus changed from a moral, religious one to a political, secular one. The secularization process implied by this shift in philosophical perspective, however, has not been a real cultural process. The cases described here suggest that contrary to theories that predict the increasing worldwide secularization of society, religion remains a major force at the popular level in Middle America.

The cases also underline the importance of the ideological as well as the material dimensions of religion and religious institutions in Middle American politics. The work of several contemporary theorists in the arena of religion, such as Assad (1983), Commaroff and Commaroff (1986), and Axtell (1985), highlights the necessity of examining the political economy of religion in conjunction with its cultural and ideological dimensions.

A thorough examination of religion in Middle America must examine the ways in which popular religious forms and institutions interact with (1) capitalist development and emerging class relations; (2) state intervention in local political systems, state collaboration and support with missionary groups, and, in the case of Nicaragua, formal state support for liberation theology; and (3) struggles for local political and economic autonomy often tied to an assertion of independent ethnic identity.

POPULAR RELIGION, ECONOMIC DEVELOPMENT, AND CHANGING CLASS RELATIONS

Capitalism and the exploitation of lower classes has a long history in Middle America (Wolf 1959). Harris' (1964:25-43) suggestion that religion is primarily a means for capitalist exploitation of indigenous peoples finds little support in the new data. Often, religious institutions continue to be repositories of cultural resistance to exploitation. Although classic civil-religious hierarchies can resist the intrusion of state political power, other religious forms develop in harmony with new forms of capitalistic wealth and with new economic classes. Sometimes, local religious institutions can maintain apparent community solidarity in conjunction with emerging class stratification.

Some chapters of this book support the idea that fiesta systems can modify capitalist development by maintaining redistributive activities and reciprocal labor exchanges. The ideological influence of religion in Mesoamerican peasant communities stems from the way in which redistributive activities carried out in conjunction with fiesta sponsorship can justify differences in wealth. The continued existence of redistributive economic activities and reciprocal labor exchanges provides an ideological framework in which household wealth can be legitimatized by contributing part of it to a community celebration. As new sources of capitalist wealth are created, religious systems can shift to accommodate them, legitimating their existence within a religious framework. As such, the continued existence of fiesta sponsorship can in turn modify the impact of capitalist development by maintaining redistributive activities and reciprocal labor exchanges. In some cases, popular religion can continue to offer the benefits of the redistribution of wealth, the generation of prestige motivated surpluses, the development of a politics of consensus, and the creation of a community identity.

These chapters suggest that the relationships between popular religion, capitalist development, and class relations are not unidirectional. Popular religious forms can be used either to consolidate specific class interests within a community or to unify a population across class lines. Factional loyalty, either ethnically or class-based, can be expressed in religious terms at the local level. Religious institutions and events may be employed to consolidate class interests within a community or, in the case of liberation theology in Nicaragua in the early 1980s, used to unify the poor to support a revolution against a corrupt regime and foreign class interests. In liberation theology, class politics is at the root of dichotomies drawn between rich and poor and is the basis for asserting the rights of the poor. The political processes changing religious institutions in Middle America are more complex than simple secularization caused by increasing government influence in people's lives.

The religious response to new wealth is related to the economic base of a community. Communities such as marketing centers, farming villages, and villages specializing in handicraft production respond differently. Varying class relations develop from the different sequences in which new capitalistic formations appear in the communities. The links to external institutions may also vary. In many cases, community religion maintains a balance, allowing links to the outside, but at the same time, keeping internal politics from being completely co-opted. The current religious response to the emergence of new class relations in conjunction with capitalist development is varied in the cases included here. Both Binford and Cancian document in their chapters a recent decline in the public sponsorship of saint's ceremonies. This does not, however, represent a secularization of society. Binford shows that ceremonies organized along class lines are giving new wealthy middle classes a way to express an identity in what was previously a community of subsistence farmers. Although the *cargo* system is declining as the central social institution in Zinacantan, Cancian notes that additional *cargo* systems are developing in the outlying hamlets of the municipio.

Capitalistic wealth accumulation does not necessarily result in the disappearance of traditional forms of religion. Earle documents the resurgence of *cargo* sponsorship in an area of rural economic development. After engaging in considerable experimentation with new religions, some emigrant Chamula have recently returned to their old pattern of *cargo* sponsorship. Stephen notes that life cycle ceremonies have grown into large semi-public events with similar form and content to *mayordomías* as *mayordomías* declined and wealth differences have increased.

Our general conclusions regarding the relationships between popular religion, capitalist development, and class relations are that :

(1) Factional loyalty, either ethnically or class-based can be expressed in religious terms at the local level. Religious institutions and events may be employed to consolidate class interests within a community or, in the case of liberation theology in Nicaragua, used to unify the poor.

(2) Local religious institutions can coexist with capitalistic economic growth and new capitalistic class formations. However, in such situations, religious institutions often change form.

(3) Traditional religious forms are popular and will be revitalized when they meet the needs of local groups.

The cases suggest several general conclusions regarding the evolution of religious *cargo* systems and fiesta sponsorship:

(1) Ceremonial systems of either the civil-religious type or the fiesta type can rationalize wealth differences and promote a significant level of community solidarity through maintaining redistributive economic activities and political leadership legitimatized through ritual sponsorship.

(2) People can cease to participate in religious *cargo* systems when authority derived from economic class status is perceived to be legitimate in its own right.

(3) Public ritual ceremonies can be linked to life cycle ceremonies in the context of emerging class differentiation. Elements of former community-wide ceremonies can be incorporated into life cycle ceremonies, thereby changing the meaning of public and private.

THE ROLE OF THE STATE

Although the state is often an agent of economic change and has supported the development of new capitalistic classes in different parts of Middle America, it has played a particularly direct role in the politics of popular religion. The historical analyses included in this volume highlight the importance of state intervention in shaping popular religious institutions. Chance suggests that the local political power generated by religious hierarchies declined in the wake of the Mexican Revolution. He suggests that civil hierarchies are uncoupled from religious hierarchies when there is an expression of state institutions at the local level. Stephen indicates that during the Calles administration in the 1920s, the Mexican government launched an apparent attack on the power of village elders. Many civil-religious systems of government survived this period, but the increasing connection of rural communities to seats of state and national power eroded the links between the civil and religious institutions at the local level. Cancian pegs the turning point in popularity of the Zinacantan central civil-religious hierarchy at 1966. In Mexico, as the state was increasingly centralized and community political and economic institutions were brought under state control (Hamilton 1982), civil-religious hierarchies lost some of their political importance.

The manner in which the power of the state manifests itself can have an effect on the religious-political response. When the state is not responsive, or antagonistic to local needs, religious institutions can articulate local political sentiment. The absence of state authority does not always mean strong popular religion.   Earle suggests that *cargo* systems wither as state institutions remain distant and allow local civil authority to respond to local rather than external needs.

This picture is further complicated by the possibility of *cacique* politics, raising the level of violence. According to Greenberg,*Caciques* can represent either the mestizo patronage domain or peasant interests, as did Emiliano in Yaitepec. No matter which side of this struggle they emerge on, *caciques* bring more violence and signal an inability of superior government to resolve conflicts at the local level.

In Panama, government support for both Protestant and Catholic missions, as described by Howe, allowed the missions to operate in Kuna territory. While the missions never had the effect desired by either the missionaries or the Panamanian state, state intervention was critical in their original occurrence. In Nicaragua, as discussed by Higgins, the Sandinista government actively supported liberation theology during the 1980s, using it to promote important revolutionary martyrs. This intervention was just as important as the state's censuring of Catholic officials who were critical of state policy and were not aligned with liberation theologians.

Our general conclusions regarding the relationship of the state to popular religion are:

(1) In Mexico, post revolutionary anticlerical policy and integration of the municipio system of governance with the state and federal political structures were major forces in some areas in reshaping civil-religious hierarchies.

(2) Popular religious symbols can unite people at the national level when they are actively supported and promoted by the state and accurately represent the sentiments of a majority of the population.

(3) Popular religious symbols can unite people at the community or ethnic group level against state interests when people are economically exploited and denied access to adequate political representation in state institutions, and these symbols can be an ideological basis of political action in the popular interest.

RELIGION AND AUTONOMY

Religious institutions in Middle America have an internal dynamic which is often reflected in the role they take on in local struggles for political and economic autonomy. Popular religion can affect political action through what Greenberg calls the politics of consensus. He points out how the informal system of authority based on religious *cargo* sponsorship allowed the community of Yaitepec to unite for a successful protest over a *ladino* land invasion in a context of growing *ladino* and Chatino class polarization due to commercialization of coffee production. The political power bestowed on elders through their sponsorship of *mayordomías* was backed up by community consensus. In Sandinista Nicaragua, state-sanctioned religious martyrdom provided a politics of consensus for neighborhood oriented political and civic action as described by Higgins. Among the Emberá of Panama, as described by Kane, shamanism provides a medium of consensus by which outside religions and individuals are judged against the experience of the Emberá. Earle attributes new religious forms to a need to articulate ethnic solidarity in the face of external threats.

The potential political impact of popular religion is related in part to the way in which popular religious institutions are linked to wider social organization. Dow (1974:110-114) describes the organizing potential of popular religion in terms of the structure of religious corporate groups. Such groups draw together a community of worshipers under the leadership of a subgroup of individuals who represent the entire group to supernatural entities. *Mayordomías, cofradías,* villages under civil-religious authority, oratory groups, and the networks of kin and *compadres* described by Stephen for Teotitlán del Valle in this volume are examples of religious corporate groups. In such groups there is a potential for local level political organization and networking. While entire groups may or may not coalesce around a particular political question or party, the existence of such religious groups can be vital for the growth of grass-roots opposition movements, as in the case of the COCEI (Isthmus Coalition of Workers, Peasants, and Students) in Juchitán. These cases highlighting the relationship between formal corporate religious groups and political organization also suggest the importance of new forms of corporate religious groups in peasant social movements.

New forms of corporate religious groups such as those composed of catechists in Chiapas and Guatemala have been critical in the formation of independent peasant unions. Harvey (1988) describes the leading role of catechists in the formation of the Frontera Comalapa in Chiapas and peasant organizations in the municipalities of Independencia, la Trinitaria, and Chicomuselo (Marie-Odole 1987). Rigoberta Menchu's description of catechists involvement in the creation of the CUC (Comité de Unidad Campesina), one of Guatemala's largest and most successful peasant unions in the 1980s, provides additional evidence of the important link between popular religion and peasant opposition movements (Burgos-Debray 1984). The organizational potential of religious corporate groups is one reason that religion has a dynamic role to play in Middle American political systems.

The following observations can be made on the capacity of religious institutions to serve as a basis for organizing autonomous groups at the grass-roots level:

(1) Traditional religious forms such as religious *cargo* systems can be revitalized when they meet the needs of local groups in situations where there is a unified perception of an outside threat to collective resources, as in land invasions or encroachments.

(2) Religious ideas promoted by missionaries are selectively adopted and modified by peasant populations, sometimes providing a basis for social movements. While this trend has been discussed here only in terms of social movements of the poor, religious ideas can be used just as easily by peasants for the promotion of free enterprise and conservative political causes.

(3) Under regimes which have little or no tolerance for opposition activity, the apparent morality of a progressive church can provide a protected arena for the formation of social movements of the poor. Religion in the form of liberation theology gains support by combining an ideal which says

everyone should have an equal share of available wealth with the idea of equality between human beings advanced by Christian religions.

CONCLUSIONS

The cases presented in this volume underscore the importance of examining local popular religion in relation to the political and economic systems to which they respond. Popular religions are by definition separate from the formal Catholic and Protestant churches in Middle America and are dynamically linked to local and national level political and economic systems. In our examination of popular religion in Mexico and Central America we have seen that local religious forms respond to the national institutions of the state and to the forces of capitalist development, the details of which vary across region and with the economic base of particular communities. While popular religious forms can encourage existing inequalities, the chapters included here emphasize the potential which popular religious institutions have to support social movements and give form to ethnically and class-based assertions of autonomy.

The cases in this book highlight the importance of religion as a source of political legitimacy. As long as local communities do not become mere patronage extensions of the state, one can expect religion to offer paths to political legitimacy, although these paths will not always resemble those of the past. The analyses presented here display the ways in which popular religious forms and ideology are reworked and adapted to meet changing political and economic situations. In the volatile political landscape of Mexico and Central America, popular religious forms and institutions will continue to play a vital role in the political and economic struggles which characterize the region.

REFERENCES

Assad, Talal
   1983   "Anthropological conceptions of religion: reflections of Geertz." *Man* 18 (2):237-259.
Axtell, James
   1985   *The Invasion Within: The Contest of Cultures in Colonial North America.* New York: Oxford University Press.
Burgos-Debray, Elisabeth, editor.
   1984   *I, Rigoberta Menchu: An Indian Woman in Guatemala.* London: Verso.
Cámara, Fernando
   1952   "Religious and Political Organization." In *Heritage of Conquest.* Sol Tax, editor, pp. 142-175. Glencoe, IL: The Free Press.
Cancian, Frank
   1965   *Economics and Prestige in a Mayan Community.* Stanford: Stanford University Press.
Comaroff, Jean and John Comaroff
   1986   "Christianity and Colonialism in South Africa." *American Ethnologist* 13(1):1-22.
Dow, James
   1974   *Santos y Supervivencias: Funciones de la religión en una comunidad Otomí, México.* Mexico City: Instituto Nacional Indigenista y Secretaría Educación Pública.

Hamilton, Nora
    1982   *The Limits of State Autonomy: Post-Revolutionary Mexico.* Princeton: Princeton
        University Press.
Harris, Marvin
    1964   *Patterns of Race in the Americas.* New York: W. W. Norton.
Harvey, Neil
    1988   "Personal Networks and Strategic Choices in the Formation of an Independent
        Peasant Organization: The O.C.E.Z of Chiapas, Mexico." *Bulletin of Latin
        American Research* 7 (2):299-312.
Marie-Odole, Marion
    1987   "Pueblos de Chiapas: Una Democracia a la Defensa." *Revista de Sociología
        Méxicana* 4 (4):37-73.
Parsons, Elsie C.
    1936   *Mitla, Town of the Souls.* Chicago: University of Chicago Press.
Redfield, Robert and Alfonso Villa Rojas
    1962   *Chan Kom: A Mayan Village.* Chicago: University of Chicago Press.
Wasserstrom, Robert
    1983   *Class and Society in Central Chiapas.*   Berkeley: University of California Press.
Wolf, Eric
    1959   *Sons of the Shaking Earth.* Chicago: University of Chicago Press.

NOTES ON CONTRIBUTORS

Leigh Binford is Assistant Professor of Anthropology at the University of Connecticut. He has studied the economics of brickmakers in the Valley of Oaxaca, Mexico and the role of the state in economic development and class formation in the Isthmus region of Mexico. His latest field research with the Isthmus peasants is on the impact of the Mexican national economic crisis on their lives. He has just completed a book on capitalism in rural Mexico with coauthor Scott Cook.

Frank Cancian is Professor of Anthropology at the University of California-Irvine. He received a doctorate in anthropology from Harvard University in 1963. His interests include economic anthropology, social stratification, peasants, Mexico, and photography. He has done fieldwork with the White Mountain Apache (1955), Italian peasants (1956-57), and Mayan Indians (1960-62, 1964, 1965, 1966-67, 1971, 1981, 1982, and 1983). His major publications include the following books: *The Innovator's Situation* (Stanford U. Press, 1979); *Change and Uncertainty in a Peasant Economy* (Stanford U. Press, 1972); *Economics and Prestige in a Maya Community* (Stanford U. Press, 1965); and *Another Place: Photographs of a Maya Community* (Scrimshaw Press, 1974).

John K. Chance is Associate Professor of Anthropology at Arizona State University and received his Ph.D. from the University of Illinois at Urbana-Champaign in 1974. His research focuses on Mexican ethnohistory, particularly in the state of Oaxaca. He is the author of *Race and Class in Colonial Oaxaca* (Stanford University Press, 1978) and (with Douglas Butterworth) *Latin American Urbanization* (Cambridge University Press, 1981). Among his many other publications are "On the Mexican Mestizo" (*Latin American Research Review*, 1979) and (with William B. Taylor) "Cofradias and Cargos: An Historical Perspective on the Mesoamerican Civil-Religious Hierarchy" (*American Ethnologist,* 1985). He is currently working on a book dealing with colonial Spanish-Indian relations in the Sierra Zapotec of northern Oaxaca.

James Dow is Professor of Anthropology at Oakland University. He received a doctorate in anthropology from Brandeis University in 1973. His interests include peasant economics, religion, and mathematical and computer methods. He has done extensive field work with the Otomí people of the Sierra Norte de Puebla in Mexico. His publications include *The Shaman's Touch: Otomí Indian Symbolic Healing* (University of Utah Press, 1986); *Peasant Livelihood* (Co-edited with Rhoda Halperin, St. Martin's Press, 1977);

The Otomí of the Northern Sierra de Puebla (MSU Latin American Studies Center, 1975); and *Santos y Supervivencias: Funciones de la religión en una comunidad Otomí, México* (Instituto Nacional Indigenista, 1974).

Duncan M. Earle began his research on the social and cultural life of the Mayas of Highland Guatemala in Chiapas, Mexico in 1974. Since that time he has worked with international and local development agencies and has carried out research on shamanism and other religious aspects of Maya world view. In 1979 he followed Tzotzil-speaking colonists into the Chiapas rain forests to examine the transformation of their social, cultural, and economic lives in new surroundings, and examined their relations with the home community of San Juan Chamula, as well as the history of the interface between political power and religious affiliation. He is currently Assistant Professor of Anthropology at Texas A & M University.

James B. Greenberg received his Ph. D. in anthropology from the University of Michigan in 1973. He is head of the boarderlands section of the Bureau of Applied Research in Anthropology at the University of Arizona. Aside from his work on border issues, he has done extensive fieldwork in Oaxaca, Mexico among the Chatinos. He has published three books: *Santiago's Sword: Chatino Peasant Religion and Economics* (University of California Press, 1981), *Religión y Economía de los Chatinos* (Instituto Nacional Indigenista, 1987), and *Blood Ties: Life and Rural Violence in Mexico* (University of Arizona Press, 1989).

Michael James Higgins received a Ph. D. in anthropology from the University of Illinois in 1974. He is Professor of Anthropology and Chair of the Department of Anthropology, Black Studies, and Women's Studies at the University of Northern Colorado. He is currently working on an urban ethnographic project in Managua, Nicaragua. His previous work has been with the urban poor in the city of Oaxaca. He is the author of *Somos Gente Humilde: Ethnography of an Urban Poor Community*, and *Somos Tocayos*, and has produced ethnographic videos on Oaxaca and Managua. He now coordinates a sister barrio project between Greeley, Colorado and Managua, Nicaragua

James Howe educated at Harvard, Oxford, and the University of Pennsylvania, has carried out research in Paraguay and Panama. Author of *The Kuna Gathering*, and papers on ritual, myth, politics, and ethnohistory, he is currently preparing an edition of the missionary memoirs of Father Leonardo Gassó and is writing a book on the Kuna Revolution of 1925. He is currently Professor of Anthropology at the Massachusetts Institute of Technology.

Stephanie Kane received a Master's degree in tropical ecology in 1981 and a doctorate degree in social anthropology in 1986 from the University of Texas at Austin. She has done extensive ethnographic work with the Emberá (Chocó). She has recently conducted fieldwork on women at risk for AIDS and is going to Belize in 1990 with a Fullbright Hayes post doctoral grant.

Lynn Stephen is currently an assistant professor of anthropology at Northeastern University. Her research concerns class formation and gender roles in relation to economic development, ethnicity, and the forms that political participation takes in indigenous communities in Mexico. She has recently completed a book, *Weaving Changes: Class and Ethnicity in the Lives of Zapotec Women* (University of Texas Press, 1991) which examines the changing roles of Zapotec women in local ritual, economic and political institutions and compares their emerging political participation with that of other peasant women in Mexico. She was a post doctoral fellow at the Center for U.S.-Mexican Studies in San Diego during 1989. During 1990 and 1991 she will begin a comparative project looking at women's participation in popular peasant movements in Mexico, Brazil, and Chile.